King of Thieves

King of Thieves

Adam Shand

ALLEN&UNWIN

First published in 2010

Allen & Unwin
83 Alexander Street
Crows Nest NSW 2065
Australia
Phone: (61 2) 8425 0100
Fax: (61 2) 9906 2218
Email: info@allenandunwin.com
Web: www.allenandunwin.com

Cataloguing-in-Publication details are available
from the National Library of Australia
www.librariesaustralia.nla.gov.au

ISBN 978 1 74237 147 4

Set in 12/14.5pt Adobe Garamond by Midland Typesetters, Australia
Printed and bound in Australia by Griffin Press

10 9 8 7 6 5 4 3 2 1

Mixed Sources

Product group from well-managed
forests, and other controlled sources
www.fsc.org Cert no. SGS-COC-005088
© 1996 Forest Stewardship Council

FSC

The paper in this book is FSC certified.
FSC promotes environmentally responsible,
socially beneficial and economically viable
management of the world's forests.

For my children Noliwe and Jack.
And for those who live in the moment.

22 June 1990. New Bond Street, London W1

The long journey had returned the King to where his legend had begun. Lost to authorities in transit, the master thief was back in London. He should have been in a jail cell in Australia, but events had taken a different turn.

The next few minutes would write the final chapter of his story, he thought.

For now, he was free, walking through the most expensive shopping precinct in the world. En route to the biggest job of his career he felt no fear, just a calm and clear resolve. There was no plan in his mind, only the outcome he desired. The 'how' was already in his pocket, a flat piece of lead, the size of a key.

What mattered now was to move with the flow without hesitation and to react instinctively to the slightest change. It was a state of mind beyond confidence. It was an acute awareness of everything and everyone around him, even of the energy moving unseen between people. It was an aerial view of the scene. The thief would contrive a moment when he could simply disappear.

After 40 years and countless hundreds of jobs, the King was still hoisting to survive—just as he had when he learnt the trade in Sydney. He had never had a bank account or a mortgage, much less owned a home. He lived from a suitcase, hotel to hotel across the globe. Always travelling—always working, gambling, drinking and philandering in an endless cycle.

There was no trace of an Australian accent anymore. You would have sworn he was English, a proper gent in his hound's-tooth jacket. He carried no papers. The well-used passport stored in a bank safe deposit box identified him as James Duffield, 60, a native of North London. But that James Duffield had never left the country. He had never been beyond Southend-on-Sea, in fact. 'Jimmy Duff' was a regular drinker at the Crowndale, a pub in Chalk Farm once notorious as HQ for the best thieves in London and much else besides. The man strolling down Bond Street this grey summer morning was of a different cut. He exuded world-liness, he was a globetrotter, perfectly dressed and groomed.

He had left Australia as the Duke in 1962, but now, by virtue of his style and record, he liked to be known as the King. Few would argue.

There was a courtly sway from the hips in his walk, reminiscent of the Bond Street loungers of the seventeenth century, the foppish wasters who paraded themselves like gentlemen around Mayfair. A lounger was derided as 'a man with two suits' back then and that aptly described the King 300 years later. At 60 he wasn't up for running. Beneath the floppy hair and tailored clothes, he was gaunt and thin, hollowed out by cancer, but in remission he would have his moment, one last hurrah in Mayfair. He was the last of the Kangaroo Gang—the King with his small band of subjects.

Most of the Aussies had been cleaned out by the cops or gone into the drug business years before. Many were dead, some of the best of them. In the mid 1960s the Kangaroo Gang had been 60-strong, a network of mercenaries working for five master thieves, elusive, ever changing, a parade of career criminals in their prime. Add to that a bevy of young Australian women seeing the world for the first time. Most of them would return to Australia to lead honest productive lives, but for a short, fabulous time they would enjoy an experience straight out of the movies.

Perhaps it was the age or it was something special in these men and women that gave them such confidence. For a dozen years, they had run amok across the globe stealing jewels, furs and any luxury item they could lay their light fingers on. Their success and how it was achieved seems unbelievable, mythical almost. They had stolen more than a hundred million pounds worth of treasure in broad daylight. There was no violence, never a firearm was drawn or even carried. They had never so much as broken a window during a job. It was hard to believe, but the King had been there from the beginning and had seen it all.

Now, of the master thieves, only he, Arthur William Delaney, remained. With him today were the remnants of the Kangaroo Gang. 'Petite Philippe', a disinherited French count, walked beside him flashing his Gallic charm at women passers-by. The others were coming at the target from various directions. It would not pay to approach in one group. There were a couple of Australians still; John 'Bimbo' James and 'the Colonel' had been with Arthur since the 1970s. Some ring-ins took the raiding party's total complement to ten, enough to control the scene.

Arthur took his time strolling down New Bond Street. He glanced at his reflection in the windows of the fine stores: Cartier, Dior, Watches of

Switzerland, Piaget, Chopard, Van Cleef & Arpels, Yves St Laurent, Gucci, Tiffany and Graff Diamonds. He had robbed them all over the years, if not here, somewhere around the world. Many of the old names were long gone, but there were new brands to replace them, beautiful new treats to mesmerise and captivate. It had always puzzled Arthur why anyone would waste time on ancient ruins, musty art galleries and museums when there were sights like these to enjoy.

The street had changed for sure. They hadn't seen him coming in those early days. They hadn't imagined a thief like Arthur could exist. But in 1990, Mayfair was ready for him, or so the Bond Street Association believed. At every door a burly shop detective stood watch, scanning the street for anything sinister. The former policemen and ex-soldiers kept in contact through their earpieces, relaying observations up and down the street. Any suspicious characters would be noted and tracked before they got halfway down the narrow one-way street. But the thieves were in fact a secondary concern that day.

The West End was on high alert as the Irish Republican Army had stepped up its campaign of London bombings in support of self-rule in Northern Ireland. A month earlier, the IRA had detonated a bomb under a mini-bus at Wembley, killing a soldier and injuring another. A month later, the Irish bombers would strike the London Stock Exchange two and a half miles away, blowing a ten-foot hole in the wall. In 1993, after a string of IRA attacks, authorities would create the 'Ring of Steel', a network of street-based surveillance cameras around the financial district and the West End which would change life in London forever.

In 1990, you could still walk the streets of London without being filmed every few steps as you are today. You could still manipulate reality, if you understood a few simple laws of perception. In a busy street, it's the person standing still that gets noticed. A piece of wood standing in a fast flowing stream creates an eddy before it that draws the eye. Everything else passes unseen. The amateur thief on Bond Street who stops and hesitates before entering a store has failed before he begins.

In his demeanour, he has communicated his anxiety, a sense of impending doom. The more he is noticed by security the more fear he exudes. The professional thief can use this to his advantage. Standing sentry on a fine jewellery house where the prices (not to mention the toffy staff) exclude 99 per cent of the population is a boring, tedious job. After a while the flow of people must indeed seem like a river, the eddy around the stationary object is a welcome relief to the eye. The diversion allows the thieves to pass right by.

As he crossed Conduit Street, where New Bond becomes Old Bond, Delaney could see his destination. This day had been coming since 1962. For all that time he had dreamt of knocking over this store. Asprey was not just an institution but a statement of English achievement.

Since 1781, Asprey had offered 'articles of exclusive design and high quality, whether for personal adornment or personal accompaniment, to endow with richness and beauty the tables and homes of people of refinement and discernment'. It had begun as four separate shops connected by a central courtyard. It had been consolidated into one and enclosed by a single roof. Now it sat there brooding and substantial on the corner of Old Bond and Grafton streets, a parade of archways framing gleaming windows, a mirror for passers-by to judge their unworthiness.

Looking up, a royal coat of arms: 'By Appointment to H.M. The Queen, Goldsmiths, Silversmiths & Jewellers' reinforced the message. When the Duke of York, Prince Andrew, had married Lady Sarah Ferguson in 1986, the wedding gift list had been posted at Asprey. One of the Rolling Stones had spent £30 000 on an engagement ring here. There were no cheap souvenirs to pull in tourists like Harrods had been forced to offer over at Knightsbridge. A box of Christmas crackers cost £500. Other Australians had pulled off jobs at Asprey, but nothing on the scale that Arthur intended. In 1985, another Australian had slipped a sterling silver elephant worth £7000 into his pocket as he left Asprey, but he got nabbed later. He told police the commissionaire Tom Farra had told him to have a nice day. He replied that he already had. He got seven years' jail and was deported for his trouble, never to return. Everyone said the Kangaroo Gang was now defeated, its modus operandi a quaint reminder of a bygone era.

Arthur and Petite Philippe approached the double semi-circular doors of Asprey. Only the uniformed figure of the commissionaire stood between them and the rich interior. Farra had seen these men before; in the weeks prior, they had been in several times. He had been greeting people like this his entire career at Asprey—well-dressed, classy, relaxed people. He could smell a phoney but as Asprey had described its customers in 1851, Arthur and Philippe were obviously 'people of refinement and discernment'. Farra stepped to one side and the double doors glided open. A warm rich aroma of fine leather and cologne enveloped them immediately. If rich had a smell this was it. A few years earlier writer Christopher Long had imagined himself a thief standing on the same celebrated spot:

> [Stretching] into the distance, is one of the most sensational sights to be seen in London. Gleaming, glittering, enticing and beguiling is a vast expanse of unique craftsmanship in gold, silver, leather, porcelain, glass, brass, precious stones and rich mahogany.
>
> To the right is modern silver, jewellery, watches and the innumerable small, exquisite items that range from money-clips to bejewelled shirt-studs; from cuff-links to the first item on my shopping list—a £15,000 gold wristwatch with a perpetual calendar—so rare that Asprey's only have two or three for sale each year.
>
> Beyond that is the exotic and self-explanatory Gold Room leading on to displays of birds and beasts in gem-encrusted precious metals that are the unique products of Asprey's own workshops three floors above.
>
> Standing at the doorway and looking straight ahead is the sumptuous staircase which leads to the raised 'Boat House', still containing a huge array of luggage and travel goods which hark back to Asprey's origins. Beyond that are the antique silver, glass and furniture . . .

They passed under the gaze of a dozen cameras as they approached the staircase leading to the mezzanine level where the most rare and valuable diamond jewellery was displayed. A shop assistant approached them.

'Good morning, gentlemen. Welcome to Asprey. May I help you?' she asked.

'No thank you, madam,' said Arthur. 'Just browsing. We'll help ourselves,' he continued, with a wink.

As they climbed the stairs, Arthur began softly singing a song from 1968: 'Just help yourself . . .'

The scholar and the thief 1

'I was a scholar,' said the Raven, adjusting his fine silk tie in the mirror.

'I went to seven schools by the time I was eight years old. My family were carnival people. I grew up around showgrounds and on the road. But I determined very early that if I had any hope in this life, it would come from education. I could learn to be anything I wanted to be,' he said.

He was bathed in the diamond blue light of a men's bathroom, empty but for us. He was a small trim bald man with lively eyes. At 85, in a $6000 Briony suit, he could have been the retired chairman of a bank. But outside, in Sydney's finest Chinese restaurant, a flouncy 35-year-old blonde was waiting with a table of lobster, crabs and champagne. His life had been better than any banker's.

'But before you can become what you learn, you must first learn to speak,' he said precisely. 'I was always top of my class until I gained entry to a selective primary school. There I met a boy who would later become a

1

Supreme Court judge and he took first place, with me always second. His diction was beautiful. He never showed his back teeth when he spoke.' Not like the 'side-valvers' the Raven knew, the knockabouts and thieves who spoke from the corner of their mouths on racetracks and in pubs to shield their conversations. 'So every night I would stand in front of the mirror and practise speaking the way that boy did.'

And now every other year he travelled to Royal Ascot where he was a guest in the Queen's enclosure, he said, his eyes twinkling. 'In top hat and morning suit,' he said, proudly addressing the mirror.

The Raven never became a Supreme Court judge though he rubbed shoulders with many in his life. He had made his living on the racetrack as a tipster and consort of trainers, bookies and touts. He ran the best organised two-up schools New South Wales had ever seen. Places where barristers and politicians mingled with crooks. He was discreet in all things, counsel and quartermaster to powerful forces in Sydney's under-world of the 1960s and '70s. Short of violence and murder, there was no blue with a cop that couldn't be solved with a quiet word and bribe. And it was to the Raven everyone always turned.

But Arthur William Delaney was getting too hot.

'I said to Arthur, "You are going to have to get away from here for a while. As a thief, you have outgrown the opportunities around you. On the other hand, in regard to the matters of adultery and reckless behaviour, you are still very much a little boy. It's only a matter of time before you get a long stretch in jail or a bullet from a jealous husband." I told him England was the answer—a new frontier for a thief as capable as him. And if anyone could have success there, it was Arthur. There is no limit to what you can achieve, if people think you are one of them,' said the Raven.

He broke into a gleeful smile that exposed his gleaming back teeth.

'Arthur, can you tell me who you believe to be the greatest thief in history?' the Raven asked rhetorically. They were in Andre's nightclub, Sydney. The year was 1962.

Arthur wasn't much for history. He knew some great thieves, men like 'Wee Jimmy' Lloyd, Georgie G, Jack 'the Fibber' Warren or Billy 'the General' Hill. They were 'hoisters' that he admired greatly. They were all stealth and charm. They were never violent and so clever that shopkeepers didn't know they had been hit till much later. Walking calmly away from a job, as opposed to running with a gaggle of store detectives on your hammer, was a mark of success for the professional hoister.

But to the question of who was the greatest on earth, he had no answer. Unlike the Raven, Arthur hadn't taken to school at all growing up in Newcastle, north of Sydney. His parents, solid working-class types, had pushed him through the front gate at school and he had simply run out the back one. And besides, the world was full of thieves and he hadn't begun to explore what it offered. His attention drifted to a buxom cigarette girl passing by.

'It was Queen Elizabeth I,' exclaimed the Raven, not waiting for Arthur's answer. 'She sent her privateers, Francis Drake and John Hawkins, to plunder the treasure ships of King Philip II of Spain as they travelled back from South America to Europe in the sixteenth century,' he said. Arthur's ears pricked up at the mention of treasure. 'And when they got home with the booty, she whacked it up with them, half each,' he cried. 'Then she knighted them for their good work. Imagine that, she knighted those thieves,' the Raven continued.

She spoke six languages, was a master in the art of rhetoric, she wrote her own poetry and inspired the Elizabethan Renaissance that gave us Shakespeare, Jonson and Marlowe. And the Raven was right, thieves had paid for it. King Philip had put a price on her head, the robber queen of England, the rogue state. He had sent the Armada to square up with Elizabeth, but the mighty flotilla had been devastated by weather and her admiral Drake's superior tactical nous, honed in his years as a pirate of the Caribbean.

'So when you go there, show them no mercy. Those great buildings and pleasant avenues you will see were built with the proceeds of crime. For all the airs and graces, they are no better than you,' said the Raven. 'Behind every great empire, there is always a crime,' he added.

He handed Arthur a wad of notes totalling £1000, the fare for two on a three-month world cruise ending at London's Southampton Docks. He and his offsider Kevin Conway could have made the journey in just four weeks through the Suez Canal on one of the many converted troop ships plying the British migrant trade at that time. But Arthur, despite his modest means, was already accustomed to luxury. He was not made for the crowded lower decks, huge open spaces without cabins crammed with triple-decker bunks. Not for him the communal toilets reeking of vomit and White King bleach. His natural environment was the first class deck, where he would enjoy shuffle board and quoits in the sunshine with the finest people aboard. With their fares paid, Arthur and Kevin could use the three-month voyage to prime their pockets by sneaking into the cabins of their first class chums. Or in port stopovers, they could try their hoisting skills in such exotic locations as Singapore, Penang, Bombay, Aden, Port Said, Naples and Lisbon. For a pair of thieves, this sea cruise was a working holiday, an introduction to the cultures and opportunities they would find in England and on the Continent.

At 32, Arthur Delaney was one of Sydney's best hoisters, but the pickings were slim. There wasn't the wealth in Sydney and Melbourne to fulfil his ambitions. You could knock over all the best retailers in a day's work back then. It wouldn't be long before the shop detectives and the police became very familiar with you. From there, working as a shoplifter got expensive. If they couldn't catch you on the job, the cops just waited for you at home with their hands out. If you didn't buy them dinner, you got nicked. Or worse, informers would shop you and other police would turn up to relieve you of your hard-earned graft. Pretty soon, you were working for cops.

The Raven could see Arthur's dilemma. Arthur was 'a shirts and sheets man' in Sydney, cutting a swathe through the department stores, but he had only a modest fortune and a lot of jail to look forward to. You had to move up into the next league to make the serious money in Australia back then. The 'tank men' (safecutters) and the 'gunnies' (armed robbers) ruled the roost. But those professions required a man to possess a streak of violence. Without it, you were vulnerable to the other crooks, who would relieve you of your hard-earned. You needed a touch of psychopath in you to survive that life. And Arthur was no psychopath, just a run of the mill sociopath, a thief through and through. He was a naughty boy, the Raven liked to say. Like most criminal activities, thieving is a vocation, a specialised trade even. A tank man cannot be a hoister, no more than a dip (pickpocket) can be a gunnie or a bust man (burglar). There were few true all-rounders like Arthur's great mate the Fibber, but we will speak of him later. Most villains had a single skill they spent a lifetime perfecting.

As a teenager, his father had made him work on the roads with him, but he just ran away. He dreamt of being a jockey, so he stole a horse and rode to Sydney, only to be apprehended upon his arrival. A stint at a boys' home followed. His family disowned him, so he disowned them and set about surviving on the streets of Sydney by the early 1950s. In 1952, he was sentenced to two years' jail with hard labour for robbing the manager's office at a Sydney cinema. This stint was as close to employment as Arthur ever came. He let his light fingers do the work for him.

Now he was the finished article. He was immaculately dressed in suit and tie (stolen of course), with his floppy brown hair side-parted and plastered down with Brylcreem, smoothed to a high sheen. He was always scrubbed clean till he squeaked, clean-shaven and aromatic with expensive lotions and colognes. The only clue to his origins was the tattoos on his forearms he concealed beneath perfectly pressed shirt sleeves. His fingernails were neatly manicured and lacquered. He might have been a male model or a matinee idol, but for those eyes. He had the shiftiest eyes the Raven had ever seen, forever darting here and there, looking for opportunities for enrichment or escape. But for the piercing blue, they were the eyes of a fox and he had the long snout to match, perhaps a little bent from poking it where he shouldn't have. He had slender quick fingers that could open a showcase or the catch of a woman's brassiere with equal ease.

He was mischief personified with a soft cloying voice that drew people to him. You couldn't trust him, but you couldn't help liking him. Who else would shout the bar at Sydney's Rex hotel with his last dollar but Arthur? How many villains in 1962 would park a big American convertible outside the Rex in seedy Kings Cross and drink French champagne with three beautiful girls? Who else but Arthur would lose the convertible later that night playing cards? He couldn't tell an ace from a king but it never stopped him gambling.

In this small criminal realm he was already royalty. The Duke, they called him. There were better thieves than Arthur, but there were none with more dash. So what is this dash? The French call it 'élan', to the English it was 'bottle', the Americans crassly called it 'balls'. But dash, as Australians knew it in the 1950s, was a very special, fleeting thing. It was the confidence of a young country that had been spared the worst ravages of war, now gaining a sense of identity.

The Aussie spirit had been tested during the First and Second World Wars and had survived, even in defeat, from Gallipoli and the Western Front to Tobruk and the Kokoda Track. Dash was the myth of Australia's laconic optimism, the irrepressible belief that all would turn out for the best, if you had the courage to have a go. Dash was thinking like a millionaire when your pocket was empty. Whatever shortage you faced, the world was a place of abundance. There was unlimited money, you just had to go and get it. How you got it would reveal itself.

The Raven didn't expect to see his £1000 again. Many of the bunk-ups he had given blokes over the years had never been repaid but he was a generous man. It would almost be worth the price to see what Arthur Delaney made of his opportunity.

A few months later, a Qantas steward who flew the Kangaroo route on the 707s came to see the Raven. He had a parcel from Arthur. Inside was one of the most beautiful things that the Raven had ever seen. The Vacheron Constantin Patrimony Extra-Plate was among the finest watches in the world, and would later be regarded as a design classic of the twentieth century. Created in 1955 to commemorate the Swiss maker's centenary, the ultra thin 18-carat gold timepiece was purity, simplicity and perfection. No thicker than a shilling, the aesthetic was understated and almost anticlimactic, but there was no mistaking its monumental refinement and elegance. Just putting it on made you feel special; stealing it must have been intoxicating. The Kangaroos were loose in Mayfair, nothing would be safe, he thought.

Each morning, the fine jewellers of Bond Street and Knightsbridge must lay out their precious wares for the day's trading. Today, as you watch from the street, hands in white gloves appear through the heavy velvet curtains bearing magnificent treasures. Working from photographs, the staff fit the glittering rings, necklaces and other baubles into their blocks, each a carefully conceived display. Just a sheet of security glass separates the jewels from the bustling street, but this is unavoidable. A jewellery store is like a bank that must put its money in the window to persuade people these little coloured things indeed have value. Despite the obvious security issues, there is no other way.

Diamonds are not rare, there are enough hidden away in vaults or still in the ground to give every woman in the world a sparkling stone on her finger. The value is not in the super-compressed carbon structures of the diamond but in the longing and desire they create, the myth of value. A man watches his beautiful woman stop at a jeweller's window and linger. Mesmerised by what she sees, the woman exudes the most perfect unguarded sensual energy he has ever felt. The stone becomes infused with the same energy, fluid, bright and crisp, as flawless as an ice castle. He'll do anything to win it now. The 'squarehead' returns to work calculating the years of wages it will take to afford it. The thief is thinking of the quickest way to possess it. The jewellery stores know they are vulnerable: hang around the front window and they will say you are acting sinister and chase you off. But go inside and greet them warmly and they will smile and offer you a cup of tea.

When Arthur and Kevin Conway got to Mayfair, they could not believe the wealth they saw. For every nice store in Sydney, there were five or ten there. You could rob one every day and not run out of jobs for five years. And the diamonds were like none they had ever seen. It was the tail end of the big diamond era, a time when the De Beers Company had persuaded the world that the size of a diamond corresponded to the strength and ardour of a man's love. In 1962, stores all along Old and New Bond streets were offering great glittering rocks; trays of three- to five-carat rings were not unusual sitting right there in the window. As Arthur stood before the window of Asprey, the finest jeweller in the finest retail precinct in the world, he murmured softly, 'How long has this been going on?'

It had been a tough introduction to London. Arthur and Kevin had thoroughly enjoyed the voyage, the other passengers had unwittingly subsidised their fine dining and drinking. It was amazing how many left their cabins unlocked. They had picked up some spending money while in port too, but of course Arthur had lost it all at the card table. By the time they got to London, they were skint, so they spent the first couple of nights in an all-night cinema in Soho and even one in a doorway huddled together. Lucky it was summer, or they might not have survived that first fortnight. Arthur spent the time observing everything. There was no time for sightseeing at Buckingham Palace or posing in front of Big Ben for photographs, it was Mayfair that Arthur was interested in. He watched the comings and goings of the staff in the fine stores like Bensons of Bond Street and Antrobus, which had supplied the engagement ring when in 1947 Philip Mountbatten had proposed to the future Queen Elizabeth. He quickly worked out that the security was almost entirely focused on the street.

A shop detective would be posted on the door to watch for suspicious characters on the street. Once inside, only the shop assistants stood between you and the prize. This was because the favourite method of English villains of the day had been 'the blag'. A gang of blaggers would run up and smash the shop windows with bricks or pick-axe handles and simply reef the jewellery off the displays and run. It was crude, dangerous and often ended in violence against staff. Certainly, it wasn't Arthur's modus operandi.

On 8 August 1963 mailbags stuffed with used bank notes totalling £2 million were stolen from a train just south of Leighton Buzzard. Arthur applauded the thieves' ingenuity but for one detail. The Great Train Robbers had belted the driver Jack Mills with an iron bar. He died a year later. To Arthur, violence showed poor planning and desperation. In a world of abundance, there was no need for desperation. Some might have called Arthur a coward; his friends knew better. There was part of him that needed to be liked by the people he robbed. Moreover, he wasn't robbing the staff, but the rich, often absent, owners of the stores. Insurance would cover the losses. Terrorising staff showed weak character and would get you nicked on the double. Arthur was a gentleman thief. Guile and wit were his weapons of choice.

The Vacheron Constantin heist introduced Bond Street retailers to a new style of robbery. Kevin and Arthur had entered the small jewellery store independently. They had waited until one of the shop assistants had gone to lunch, leaving just a single assistant in the store with another couple of staff out back in the workshop. Arthur came in first, an overcoat slung over his arm, posing as a wealthy businessman looking for a present for his wife. He chatted for a while as the pretty young assistant brought out various items, unlocking showcases with a bunch of keys. He noted that the assistant hung the keys to the showcases on a hook behind the counter. 'The collection is lovely,' he cooed. 'But do you mind if I browse? I'll know what I want when I see it,' he said, looking her up and down approvingly. 'Feel free,' she said, blushing.

Enter Kevin. Loud and chatty, he dragged the hapless assistant all around the store, peppering her with questions about the fine detail of their wares. Kevin 'the head puller' was doing his job to perfection. With the assistant's back turned Arthur scooted under the counter and grabbed the keys off the hook.

He had got back to the front window, unlocked it and returned the keys before the assistant had turned around. Now Kevin asked to see the showcase in the other corner of the shop. As Kevin launched into more questions, Arthur was savouring the moment, the lull between getting set for the hoist and the actual 'take'. It's just a few seconds to scan every potential threat, to ensure the escape route is clear. The best takes can feel the beat of a room, the rhythms and the mood of everyone there. It's called timing. Just before the adrenalin took over and the hoisting began, he waited to see if Kevin dropped a particular word into his patter. 'Tommy' was the signal that everything was off. Something as innocuous as 'My uncle Tommy would love this' would tell Arthur to get out fast, something was wrong. But on this occasion Tommy was nowhere around.

The speed of Arthur's hands was something to behold, people said. In a blur he scooped up more than a dozen Vacheron Constantins which disappeared into the half lining of his overcoat. On Arthur's signal, a little cough, Kevin made his excuses and left the store. Arthur lingered, talking to the shop assistant, enjoying the delicious feeling of adrenalin coursing through him. In his overcoat he had £60 000 worth of Swiss watches and he was flirting with the shop assistant. He could have seduced her right there. He had tuned her to a fine pitch, she was malleable and compliant. But first he had to off-load her watches to organise food and lodgings. Maybe next time he would take everything, every showcase and her too.

Finally, Arthur walked out into the weak sunshine on New Bond Street and the world seemed to be beckoning.

2
A nation of shoplifters

In the early 1800s, as the Emperor of the French prepared for his vainglorious attempt to overrun Europe in the Napoleonic Wars, he was disparaging of England's preparedness for war. '*L'Angleterre est un nation de boutiquiers* [England is a nation of shopkeepers],' Napoleon sniffed.

In the sixteenth century, Elizabeth's pirates had transformed London into the trading capital of the world as merchants fenced the spoils of Drake, Hawkins and a legion of privateers—tons of gold, spices, textiles and millions of slaves. The English then turned their attention to India, Africa, the Pacific, Australia and much of Asia. Great trading houses like the East India Company and the British-South Africa Company were created to bring the booty home from the colonies.

The new pirates wore suits and traded beads and mirrors with tribesmen for fabulous wealth and territory. In 1898, Queen Victoria handed Cecil Rhodes an entire country, Rhodesia, and its people as they created the world diamond monopoly, De Beers. Each fine store in Mayfair became a fence for Africa's stolen diamonds. 'Merchant and pirate were for a long period one and the same person,' wrote the nineteenth century philosopher Friedrich Nietzsche. 'Even today mercantile morality is really nothing but a refinement of piratical morality.'

The Industrial Revolution had turbo-charged England's economy, opening global markets for the textiles, iron and manufactured goods, meanwhile creating ever increasing demand for consumer goods at home. Enter the archetypal British shopkeeper.

Long before the department store and the shopping mall transformed retailing, England was dominated by small independent stores, often family owned. Every high street bustled with local commerce, independent grocers, bakers, butchers, tailors and, in more upmarket areas, jewellers and watchmakers. In 1776 economist Adam Smith, writing in his *Wealth of Nations*, was ambivalent about the prospects of such a nation of shopkeepers: 'To found a great empire for the sole purpose of raising up a people of customers may at first sight appear a project fit only for a nation of shopkeepers. It is, however, a project altogether unfit for a nation of shopkeepers; but extremely fit for a nation whose government is influenced by shopkeepers.'

By 1962, when Arthur and Kevin first hit Bond Street, England was in danger of becoming a nation of shoplifters, or at least one divided into those who paid and those who realised they didn't have to. And there was evidence that Adam Smith's national government 'influenced by shopkeepers' had become soft on hoisters. In the eighteenth century, the English had hung them high. A typical week at the Old Bailey Sessions made grisly reading for those in the trade. On 19 December 1713, it was reported that of 23 persons condemned to hang, five had been shoplifters, and another seven were housebreakers or burglars. The message was clear: if there was thieving to be done it would be the state's privilege to license it.

Of the 162 000 convicts transported to Australia between 1788 and 1868, the overwhelming majority were thieves. Simple larceny, or robbery, brought a thief transportation for seven years. Compound larceny—stealing goods worth more than a shilling (about $50 in today's money)—would still earn the offender an 'air dance' on the scaffold, death by hanging. But by the 1960s the attitude to shop stealing had softened remarkably. It was viewed more as a psychological condition than a crime. In 1969, the Secretary of State for the Home Department, Mr Elystan Morgan, was asked in the House of Commons if he believed the penalties for shoplifting in England and Wales were a sufficient deterrent. He replied that in the years 1966, 1967 and 1968 the average fine imposed by courts in England and Wales for stealing from shops and stalls was a paltry £9. The maximum fine a magistrate could impose was £400. There was no limit to the fine from a judge, if due to the value of the goods, the case went to a higher court. Upon the discretion of the court, imprisonment may also be ordered, he said.

Conservative Party member for Crosby, Graham Page, then asked whether the government was aware that convictions for larceny from shops had doubled in the years 1960 to 1967. Was he further aware of the grave concern of retailers about the loss occasioned thereby? Did he not think that an average fine of £9 when the maximum fine was £400 indicated that the courts were treating the matter a little lightly? The Home Secretary said he was aware of the problem, but the rate of increase was not disproportionate to the increase in crime generally. There was no reason to consider amending the statute. It was not for the Executive to interfere in such a matter, he said.

There had in fact been a push in the Commons to further relax the enforcement measures against shoplifting. In 1967, Mr Kenneth Lewis MP had introduced a bill that would have limited the right of store managers to question customers 'without limit or caution, in private'. He accused stores of placing too much temptation in shoppers' way. Do shops have a moral responsibility to the shoppers they tempt? he asked.

There was precious little understanding of the profile of a shoplifter despite evidence of a boom in hoisting around the world in the years after World War II. *Businessweek* magazine reported in 1952 that shoplifting in American stores had risen 25–50 per cent in the previous year. This was due to three factors: the growth of 'self-service selling'; the rising cost of living; and 'the peculiar psychological temper of our times'. Remarkably, living in peace had become boring. 'Some observers feel the reason is a general break down of morale after the War. Life has suddenly become humdrum, the pilfering breaks the monotony. Women culprits complain they have marital troubles, need distraction.'

In England, it was the same. During the war, people needed 'a fiddle or two' just to survive, so there was a rather sympathetic attitude to hoisting. But in the 1950s, when the shortages of basic commodities had eased, the hoisting continued, even intensified. Having discovered how easy it was to steal, people now couldn't help themselves. Or indeed could not *stop* helping themselves. There was a thrill, a shot of adrenalin, that came with theft that made it worth the risk.

Shoplifting was no longer a crime of necessity, but a pastime for middle-class folk with nothing else to do. One of the few academic studies on the subject was carried out in 1947 by Dr Alex Arieff of Northwestern University. He studied 338 cases referred to Chicago's Municipal Psychiatric Institution in 1941–46 and found that many offenders were 'of social and political consequence and high intelligence'. But 77 per cent had a 'definite mental, emotional or physical disorder'. There were four classes of shoplifter: the professional, the general delinquent for whom shoplifting was part of a defective personality; kleptomaniacs; and 'normal people who stole on impulse while emotionally disturbed'.

In his study group, 313 were female and only 25 male. More than half had no prior convictions. Arieff found that the age groups most heavily represented were 17–20 years 'where desire outstrips ability to buy' and 36–50 who were 'chiefly women, [in] a period of increased tension' caused, in many cases, 'by the onset and development of the menopause'. So in 1962 the shop detectives weren't looking for jewel thieves like Arthur and Kevin, dressed head to toe in stolen Savile Row threads. They were after anxious middle-class women suffering hot flushes and a loss of libido stealing silk stockings, or their own staff, who were the champion pilferers of the age.

In 1955, of $250 million in losses in US stores, only 17 per cent was attributed to shoplifters. In 1958 business writer EB Weiss wrote that 'store employees of all ranks outsteal the shopper to such an extent as to put the shopper out of the running completely as a factor in stock shortages'. Moreover, most stores were prepared to live with this so-called 'shrinkage' which accounted for (and still does) around one per cent of retail turnover.

In May 1967, London's *Sunday Telegraph* newspaper reported that 'unofficially all shops admit to a problem of pilferage . . . But publicly an astonishing number of stores are reluctant to discuss it. The manufacturer of a convex mirror which hundreds of stores use to deter theft said: Our biggest problem is getting retailers to admit they have pilferage. Some say *their* type of customer wouldn't pilfer.' Even as the shoplifting wave gathered pace in the mid 1960s, few shops were taking it seriously. The security chief of one retail chain admitted he had only twelve detectives to cover 540 stores. And they had hired detectives whom they believed could spot the kind of thieves they were chasing.

The security chief at supermarket chain Tesco told the *Sunday Telegraph* 'my detectives are mostly ordinary housewives [who] go round with butterflies in their stomachs'. There was some attempt at stealth. At Christmas, some retailers hired private agents and dressed them as Santa Claus to patrol their stores. But mostly, there was a tacit acceptance of shoplifting as a cost of business. Many retailers, especially the upmarket merchants of Mayfair and Knightsbridge, would never admit to the press they had been robbed. Police reports would be filed only in order to claim on insurance; beyond that, cooperation was minimal. To prosecute shoplifters would only generate bad publicity, demonstrating how easy it was to rob them. And besides, rising profits disguised the effects of shrinkage.

In 1960 the House of Fraser with its Knightsbridge flagship Harrods, a bellwether for the luxury goods market, reported a near 50 per cent increase in sales. Turnover of £32.4 million in 1958 had reached £99.4 million by 1967. It was a time of plenty for the hoister and hosts alike. There were a few public campaigns to deter shoplifters. They tried to make the customer realise it was their money being stolen. Or make thieves realise the era of 'scold them release them' was over. Signs saying 'Shoplifting is a crime punishable by law' were pasted up all over shops. Employees were urged to speak to every customer as they entered because 'the shoplifter hates to be noticed'.

They had never met a shoplifter like Arthur Delaney. The method that he pioneered relied on *being* noticed. He and his accomplices *wanted* to be the centre of attention, at least until it was time for the take. The distraction method or team-handed thieving relied on simple principles executed with the utmost confidence. But it was virtually unheard of till the Duke and his courtiers began to practise it in earnest in London. Was it because the English villains lacked the courage to pull it off? Arthur didn't think so. There was no shortage of bravery amongst the English. They had survived 57 consecutive nights of bombing during Hitler's Blitz and still won the war on their reserves of courage. As Arthur roamed around London he could still see reminders of those days. The Barbican area of east London was in ruins in 1963. Across London there were gaps in the rows of white Victorian terraces like missing teeth, the legacy of the bombardment.

The reasons were to be found much deeper in the class system and the English psyche. The English upper classes, steeped in their own history of merchant piracy, could spot another phoney a mile away. English society was coded with all kinds of traps for the arriviste, from the intricate protocols of cutlery and crockery at the dinner table to the telltales of English grammar and diction. English thieves knew their place. And that was through the window, the blag, the frontal assault, the smash and grab. It didn't matter if you dropped your haitches while swinging an axe handle.

Surely, they would do what we're doing if they could, Arthur thought. But they didn't and just as well. Arthur and Kevin had begun to gather more associates, some random Australians met in bars or the occasional local man or woman they could trust enough to get the job done. With a team of three or four, they could have a man outside watching the window and street. Another could provide 'a smother' as Arthur emptied the window showcase.

And this method would keep them below the radar for as long as possible. There would always be days when things went wrong, but a £9 fine held no terrors for the Kangaroos. If they pleaded guilty, the bobbies wouldn't even take their fingerprints. They could give the magistrate a false name and go on their way. And if a copper began to get too interested, they would just slip him 'a monkey' (500 quid) and he would soon drop off. It was remarkable that life for the hoister was so comfortable. It was like England had sent all its worst to Australia and promptly forgotten how clever they were. Now they were coming back strong, sun-bronzed and confident with an extra 200 years of learning and a ton of freshly minted dash. Once news of this lurk got around Sydney and Melbourne, thought Arthur, every decent tea-leaf (thief), dip and take would be heading for the docks. And some evil, desperate men would come too. He resolved to enjoy every moment of this while he could.

Arthur had not confined himself to England in his first international foray. As he gained confidence and a network of associates, the Continent had beckoned. It was just a two-hour ferry ride from Dover to the French port of Calais. From there the rest of Western Europe was at his mercy. He would often just drive from country to country, looking for opportunities. To a city boy like Arthur, the vast expanses of Australia had been uninviting. Beyond the towns, there was just the outback, a mind-numbing emptiness. But here in Europe, the traveller was constantly rewarded with new sights and civilisations. There was a depth and breadth of wealth that seemed to nourish Arthur's soul. In those first years, he crisscrossed the continent, ticking off the great cities—Rome, Paris, Brussels, Madrid, Lisbon, Basel, Frankfurt, Athens and Copenhagen. Then there were the countless smaller towns and cities. He never spent a moment in any art gallery or a museum, never climbed any cathedral steps or wandered an ancient chateau.

All the sights he was interested in were to be found in shops. And if English jewellers had been unprepared for Arthur, the Europeans seemed completely unaware. In provincial towns and cities especially, he would find venerable family-owned jewellery houses that had virtually no security. Where the English might have interior cabinet doors to protect the displays in the front window, the French and Swiss shops would have only a heavy velvet curtain. Too much security could spoil the elegant ambience of a fine jewellery store. These were small intimate boutiques where the little chubby proprietor would be all over him, but Arthur would find a way.

If there were no jewellery stores on offer, he would turn his attention to general providores or merchants. On a Monday morning, many shop-keepers still had the takings from the weekend in a cash drawer. It was easy to buy a small item with a big note and discover where they kept the takings and the keys. Or a simple piece of deduction would assist. The most worn and well-used drawer behind the cabinet invariably held the cash. A quick distraction and Arthur would replenish his pocket.

And then there would be celebration, the best food and finest wines and spirits. New friends and lovers would be acquired, toasts drunk late into the night to the sheer pleasure of living. If some gendarmes were in the bar, he would send them a bottle of the finest champagne, a tribute to the wonderful and charitable order they maintained, seemingly for Arthur's benefit and enjoyment. And Arthur would spend every last sou in search of a good time. In Monaco's Monte Carlo Casino, he discovered roulette and baccarat. Any funds left over were spent on first class hotel rooms and expensive gifts (when he couldn't steal them). It seemed like he could go on forever, darting back and forth to London between jobs.

It was the giant can-opener gag that finally sent the Fibber to England in 1965. Patrick William Warren, as he was known to Australian authorities, had a long and varied rap sheet, starting with a conviction for riding on the foot board of a Sydney tram in 1938 when he was 15. Jack, as he was known amongst knockabouts, had shown a natural aptitude for almost every kind of theft, except those requiring the use of violence or firearms. He had picked pockets, cut safes, broken into homes, stolen from shops, hijacked vans and pulled every kind of confidence trick there was. In the 1940s and '50s he had been arrested dozens of times for illicitly playing two-up, Australia's national gambling game. And the way he played it, the mugs never had a chance. By the 1960s, the Fibber was sweet with police right up and down Australia's eastern seaboard, but the can opener was something even the most bent copper could not straighten.

The cigarette trade had been a lucrative business for Sydney villains, with a little help from New South Wales police. The hijacking of delivery vans as they moved around the suburbs was a common occurrence. Armed robbery had been deemed the most efficient method, despite the risks. The vans were securely locked repelling most attempts at forced entry that could be mounted on a public street. So with a little knowledge, acquired from police, it was an easy go to intercept a van and stick a gun in the driver's face. The van could then be driven away to be pulled apart in private for the precious cargo.

But sticking a gun in a worker's face offended the Fibber's sensibility as a professional crook. It was only money after all. It was nothing to be taken so seriously. In fact, there was nothing in life, beyond the inevitable facts of sickness and death, to be taken seriously. The heads who took themselves too seriously seemed to end up with extra holes and the Fibber's oversize melon was not made for that. He would disarm his critics with wit and outrageous good humour. He was generous and kind-hearted because, as the song goes, he had started with nothing and still had most of it left. Just as in Arthur's world of abundance, there was always a go. You just had to think your way through it. Firepower was never the answer while brain power remained.

If only there was another way to get into the vans, without troubling the driver. One morning, while opening a can of beans at home, he hit on the answer. The doors of the van were heavy gauge steel, but the sides were only standard aluminium sheet metal. It was really a question of scale. You made a can opener big enough and it would slice through the metal just as easily as a small one opened his can of beans.

Needless to say, the giant can opener he had made was a huge success. Now the Fibber could strike at will. The delivery man would return from lunch to find his van had been peeled open like a sardine tin. Passers-by might see the team dressed in overalls using the imposing implement that looked strikingly like a can opener and think nothing of it. Surely no-one would do such a brazen thing in broad daylight?

No-one but the Fibber. The corrupt elements of New South Wales police that ran the tobacco trade were not happy with his ingenuity. It cut them out of the process and they vowed to put him out of business. They had him charged, but the Fibber got bail and with a false passport in hand he boarded a plane for Heathrow.

Arthur was there to greet him. The Fibber was amazed at how cultured Arthur had become in three years away; already there was just the trace of an Australian accent left. 'I wondered how long it would take you to get here, old chap,' said Arthur.

The Fibber was already 42 when he stepped on English soil, with his son Barry, a roly-poly 18-year-old, in tow. He was medium height but broad across the chest, with soft brown eyes that rolled, teased and implored. He always wore an easy, lopsided smile. It was said that he had the number '1' tattooed on his penis just to remind his many female conquests with whom they were dealing. A specially tailored grey flecked hairpiece tended to wander around his big shiny head, but his appearance could change in an instant. Hoisting had taught him the value of disguise. If pursued, there were few men quicker to the corner. Once there, Jack would whip out his false teeth, slip off his toupee and blend into the crowd. 'If I can make it to the corner, I'm somebody else, a different person,' he used to say.

But sometimes the corner was a vain, distant hope. Three hours off the plane from Sydney and the Fibber was feeling the cold. Arthur suggested a trip to Harrods where all good thieves went to be outfitted. Fibber had chosen a beautiful cashmere overcoat in the menswear department and was about to roll it up and be off with it when he noticed a mild mannered little lady shopper paying rather too much attention to him. 'Hey, Arthur, I reckon we're off here. She's a shop jack,' he whispered to Arthur.

But Arthur, the London veteran, told Jack it was all sweet. 'Don't worry, Jack, she's just changing a tenner,' he said.

The Fibber's instinct, however, had been right. The 'lady shopper' *was* a store jack and she was quietly telling the shop assistant to push the panic button under the counter to summon up reinforcements. Soon a group of burly security guards was striding towards them.

'Well, if it's any consolation, you were right,' said Arthur. 'But now just GO TOMMY!' he yelled.

Fibber made a dash for the door but, deep in the store and jet lagged from the flight, he couldn't outrun the posse in hot pursuit. Soon he was in the back of a police car wedged between two bobbies on his way to the lock-up. It was hardly an auspicious beginning, but the Fibber had not earned his nickname for nothing. By the time they had arrived at Chelsea police station, Fibber had broken the whole thing down. His new friends waved him goodbye and trousered the £150 he had given them. His pocket was empty now, but it was reassuring to know police here were just the same as at home. This was a place he could do business, he told Arthur when he returned.

They went back to Harrods the next day and stole another overcoat. And over the next few days Arthur took Fibber on a hoister's tour of London, sharing his knowledge and introducing his Aussie mate around. Arthur trusted no-one completely, but Fibber came closest. And besides, having got him nicked on the first day, he deserved a bunk-up or two.

They had known each other since the mid 1950s when the Fibber was still a waterside worker in Melbourne. The wharves were the best location for a thief back in those days. They literally brought the stuff right to you. Getting it off the dock was a minor detail, with a payment to the police-man on the gate. Off-loading the goods could take you up to Sydney and beyond. The Fibber soon became known in some of the best crime circles. His love of fine dining and beautiful women made it inevitable that he and Arthur would team up.

But he had begun as a worker on Gang 83 on Melbourne's waterfront. Every morning, up to 8000 men would gather at the pick-up centres in West Melbourne looking for a day's work unloading the ships. There were no full-time positions for wharfies then. You only had work while there was a ship in port. But you stayed in your gangs, and 'did your best' the rest of the time.

At 8 am, the stevedores' agents would front the mob and call out the jobs for the day. On a typical morning they might need 30 or 40 gangs, each of 17 men. Billy Longley was the boss of Gang 83 and a man of growing stature around the docks. Later he became known as the Texan, after Rory Calhoun's character in the 1958 TV western series of the same name. In the sixties, Longley didn't wear Calhoun's cowboy hat, but a sensible stetson. However, he did carry the Texan's Colt .45. It was a more emphatic style statement. Longley called it Matilda for the Colt's ability to set men's feet a-dancing.

They were an unusual pair, the thief and the gunnie, but it was a highly successful partnership. The thief might abhor guns but he knows their value in a tight spot. Knowing Longley, with Matilda in his belt, was there for back-up gave the Fibber an extra shot of confidence. And because Billy knew the Fibber had more dash and smarts than any other thief, Matilda would rarely be required to intervene. He could just stand back quietly in his tailored one-button suit and hat watching Fibber, the artiste, at work. They were together most days through the fifties, either at the docks or pursuing some freelance opportunities.

Travelling jewellers were a specialty. Fibber and Billy would watch the depots where the private unmarked cars would come and go delivering stock to jewellery stores. Then they would follow them on their rounds. Eventually the jeweller would stop for lunch, parking his Holden van on the street. Jack always carried the tools of the trade, a coathanger, claw hammer and a ball of tin foil the size of a marble. Placed between the contact points of the Holden, the silver foil was as good as a key, if you didn't mind the occasional shock. Fibber would reach under the dash and, *vroom*, they would just drive away.

Or it could be spontaneous. They might be sitting in a suburban café and see a sedan pull up. A man takes a sample case into the jeweller's across the street. They swoop and drive away. Fibber was like that. Everything was a potential go. Walking down the street he might see a well-dressed man loading parcels into his parked car. Fibber might have earned £50 000 the day before, but he couldn't help stealing a briefcase if he could. The sneak thief has to keep his hand in at all times.

One afternoon in 1960 they drove off with £6000 worth of jewellery. They were back at the Fibber's place, a flat above a butcher shop in Carlton, when ABC radio broadcast news of the daring heist. A reporter was interviewing the indignant jeweller.

Reporter: Were you upset?

Jeweller: *Was* I *upset*?! You're asking me if I was *UPSET*?

Reporter: Yes.

Jeweller: I'll *SAY* I was upset!

Fibber was rolling on the floor in laughter, his hairpiece down over his eyes. '*Was* I *upset*?' he roared. 'I'll *say* I was upset!' It became a catchphrase as the partnership flourished. The Fibber's good humour made it a pleasure to go to work, and work it was, from dawn to dusk, until the last store closed.

If things were slow, Fibber would joke that they would never starve. He bet Billy 'a thousand pounds to a burnt match' he could go into any city street and bite £400 in a day from passers-by. No thieving or conning, just from a sob story, delivered from the bottom of Fibber's broken heart. When they looked into his big brown eyes, heard his soft beseeching words, they would just hand it over. But never fear, Billy, if all else failed, he would say, the bloke next door would pay him 50 pence a week for the ravenous Barry to sit in his backyard and eat the fruit off his trees.

Or his advice to the soon-to-be-wed Billy on the subtleties of oral sex: 'From the navel to the sewer, son, but you'll nut left at the brown dot or you'll end up with an old tomato seed.' In the argot of the knockabout, to nut left or right was to avert your gaze from the evil eye of a cop or rival—this was an evil eye of another hue.

Unlike most of his mates, the Fibber was no gambler. He might have had ten quid for the place on Daddy Long Legs because he liked the horse's name, but that was it. Of course, he was a ferocious two-up player, but the way he played it wasn't gambling, it was a sure thing.

Two-up was the weekly earner at Flemington Racecourse. Just as correct weight was called on the last race, the run out of punters would begin—the winners, the losers, the diseased gamblers and desperates who couldn't walk past. The Fibber and Billy would set up the ring in the car park and 60 men would gather for a fast and furious game that lasted little more than an hour. The racetrack policeman would be squared away to turn a blind eye and the fun would begin. The Fibber used to say that whether 'he's baked, boiled, poached or fried, a mug is a mug and he is to be treated as such'. There was to be no sympathy for a punter who came and did his dough. Nobody had forced him to play and if he couldn't tumble that he was being took, then more fool him.

Two-up is a simple game—nothing more than tossing two pennies from a flat stick, called a bat, paddle or kip, depending on what part of Australia you are from. Players around the ring bet against each other either two heads or two tails. If a head and a tail come down, the spinner must toss again. To start the game, the coins must always face tails-up, which are marked with white crosses. So, with the pennies always starting tails-up, how do you cheat using a double-headed coin? It was a secret that only a handful knew and only a couple got away with it for any length of time. And the Fibber was the master. He would turn up to a game with his double-headed 'kings and queens'—new pennies with the head of Queen Elizabeth, or older ones with King George VI's noggin—stashed in his pocket. They were works of art—pennies were sliced in half and the head sides soldered together so perfectly the edge was indistinguishable, the weight perfect.

Beyond that, I will invite the reader to speculate as to how the toss was fixed. There are still some old lags earning from the technique even to this day, and far be it from me to stand between a man and a dishonest dollar. Let's just say, only a highly dextrous, confident operator could hope to master these dark arts. If he got it wrong and three (or even four) pennies flew in the air on the toss, there would be no escaping the circle of angry mugs.

So the professional played the double-header sparingly, with finesse, to gently control the game. Or he might impose a run of heads, then drop in the real coin when the right mug bit, putting a wad on tails. The idea was to play them, make a spectacle and build up the tension. Give a mug a lucky break and then slaughter him. If anyone accused Fibber of cheating he would howl and grimace at the insult, he would throw off his shoes and shirt in mock protest. Where am I hiding the double-header, my friend? he would wail. It was an iron-clad rule that no-one handled the coins at a game other than the operators. And if it got out of hand, there was always Billy Longley holding Matilda in reserve. It never came to that. Fibber was unbeatable. Billy never knew how Fibber cheated at two-up; he never asked. As long as it worked, he didn't care.

But inevitably the differences began to tell. Billy was moving with the union heavyweights like Freddy 'The Frog' Harrison, who was a hard, ruthless character, the kind of man who could stop conversation in a crowded pub when he entered. He dressed like a Saturday matinee mobster in a trench coat and trilby hat. But beyond the get-up, he was truly the real deal and he terrified the daylights out of Fibber. Once he and Billy had been at Harrison's house and the host had left the room without a word, most likely just to go to the toilet. But the prior conversation had been tense and unpleasant.

The Frog didn't think much of hoisters like the Fibber. Now the Fibber had become so agitated, he could hardly sit still. 'Has he gone to get his gun?' he asked Billy, anxiously. Guns animated the most cruel and capricious side of man, he said. 'Best to stay clear of them and gunnies too! Present company excepted, Bill,' he would say.

When Harrison was murdered by an erstwhile associate in 1958, the Fibber seemed somewhat relieved. He rushed into the pub where Billy was drinking to tell him of the murder on South Wharf. 'The Frog's given up drinking and smoking,' he said.

For some obscure reason, Fibber once asked Billy for the loan of a gun and Billy obliged. He visited Fibber soon after and was surprised to find the fully loaded .38 hanging on a hook on the back door amongst the raincoats and shopping bags. If Billy wasn't carrying his Colt .45, Matilda would be stored lovingly, meticulously cleaned, oiled and wrapped in cloth. A gunnie, like Billy, regarded his gun as part and parcel of his being and personality. To Fibber, a gun was like a plastic mac—you only wore it when the weather demanded nothing less.

Fibber could see how a heavy reputation became a hairshirt for people like Billy. People expected a level of gravitas and dignity that was entirely unnecessary for the thief. The thief was a survivor, an opportunist, a court jester amongst the proud and belligerent knights. The gunnie had to maintain the image lest his power drain away. The thief's power was subtle and sneaky, or it could be mocking even.

One evening Fibber and Billy stopped in at a shop on their way to a party to buy a packet of cigarettes. Billy handed over his money and the shop assistant turned and reached up for Billy's favourite Craven A brand on a top shelf. Fibber was in a mood for mischief so, quick as a flash, he grabbed a large jar of boiled lollies sitting on the counter and whipped it under the overcoat he had folded over his arm. The space between a thief's armpit and elbow is called his 'notchie'. With an overcoat in place, Fibber could have 'notchied' three of those jars, but this hoist was not for profit, just pure devilment.

Billy was astounded and horrified. He stared at Fibber, his eyes standing out on stalks. Fibber just smiled and clacked his false teeth at Billy. When the shop assistant turned back, Billy's studied sangfroid had fallen away entirely. He was such a bundle of nerves he nearly dropped his change. He didn't know whether to run or turn this into a full-scale robbery. Imagine explaining that to his many followers and hero-worshippers—Billy Longley, a veteran of multiple trips to the Supreme Court for mayhem and murder, gets nicked for hoisting a jar of boiled lollies. The indignity of it, thought Billy. A hard-won reputation would be down the toilet in seconds.

When they got outside, Billy exploded. 'Jack, don't you ever do that to me again. I'll bloody put one through you next time, you bastard!'

But Fibber was laughing fit to bust a rib, tears rolling down his cheeks. 'Your face, your face, if only you could have seen your face,' said Fibber, doubling over.

Pretty soon Billy, in spite of himself, was laughing too. It was hard to stay mad at Fibber. In any case, Billy would have had to shoot him to stop the guffawing.

There were dark times head; Fibber and Billy knew it. A battle for control of the Melbourne wharves was looming that would claim 40 lives; trust between men was disappearing. Relationships were being scrutinised as never before. It was not a time when a thief would prosper. The immediate future belonged to the gunnies.

One evening Billy and Fibber were drinking with a notorious gunman known as the Irishman. Fibber ventured an opinion and the Irishman looked at him with seething contempt. 'What the fuck would you know? You're nothing but a low bloody hoister,' he said, pulling out his gun ostentatiously. Billy had seen Fibber shiver and quake with fear and he knew their time together was limited.

Fibber for his part wasn't going to cop a bullet for the sake of ego. He intended to survive this war by having nothing to do with it. He fully intended to outlive these clowns and sock away some lucre too. And to do that, he had to keep everyone sweet.

One night Billy and Fibber were pulled up on the highway by police. In the car boot was a range of housebreaking implements. If they were discovered, they were looking at five years' jail. Billy was preparing his normal defence, stony obdurate silence, but Fibber had other ideas. 'Leave this to me,' he said, jumping out of the car and bounding over to the coppers.

In the rear view mirror, Billy watched Fibber in earnest conversation with the police. Billy sat glum, resigned to his fate. At least it wasn't a jar of boiled lollies, he thought. But then the mood changed, the trio were laughing and smiling, the Fibber cavorting about like he was in a pantomime. Eventually, he came back to the car. 'That's all sweet,' he said. Billy was relieved, but on another level Fibber's performance disturbed him. You had to be sweet with a copper or two to survive as a knockabout, but the Fibber seemed to be *howlingly* sweet with these coppers. In fact, cops all up and down the coast seemed to have had a love affair going with Fibber. In the murderous days ahead, people would easily get the wrong impression of a bloke that was so sweet with coppers. It might get you killed.

Their relationship was never the same again after that moment. The Fibber drifted off to Sydney in the early 1960s and Billy heard from him only sporadically after that. Once Jack had come down to Melbourne with Arthur, before the Duke had gone to England. For a lark, they had tried to teach Billy how to be a hoister, but he couldn't take to it.

'There's not an ounce of thief in you, is there?' the Fibber chuckled after Billy had botched an easy take in a city shop.

'You're 100 per cent gunnie, just as we are 100 per cent thieves,' Arthur chimed in.

Still, Billy did alright for a gunnie. There was enough thief in him to back up a five tonne truck to the docks each week and drive away with a tray full of stolen goods. But they were right—the thief and the gunnie were two different species of crook—and it was time for the parting of the ways. The can-opener incident in Sydney was of course the clincher for the Fibber. As the bullets began to fly in Melbourne, Fibber was far away.

A contact sent me a long-forgotten black and white picture from the summer of 1966. A happy group of friends is whooping it up in a booth in the Mayfair Club, a London nightclub. They are all sipping at a pineapple rum punch in a big bowl in the middle of the table through long straws. On the extreme right is the Fibber, a glass of fine wine in his hand—he has the straw up his nose.

On the left is Arthur Delaney, resplendent in a pinstripe suit, his hair slicked back to a dazzling sheen. He looks into the camera in mock surprise, like a fox caught in the spotlight. Alongside him is a pretty young blonde, Paddy Burridge, with a freshly set bob and sporting a three-carat diamond ring on her wedding finger, a matching pendant and earrings. Just in front of her, on the table, is a fancy ring box and some discarded wrapping paper. From Arthur's expression, it's unlikely that he could have produced a receipt for Paddy's jewels.

Nestled next to Paddy in the booth is Barry, the Fibber's son. On his left, a gorgeous former Playboy bunny, Sue Powlesand, looks wistfully into the lens, big rock on her wedding finger too. Sue was the Fibber's girlfriend back then, but the engagement ring was just for show. She would move on from the Fibber to marry sixties pop idol Normie Rowe in 1971; newspaper reports of the wedding referred to Sue as 'a former receptionist'. She and Normie had a son together, Adam, who died tragically at age eight in a road accident. It ruined their marriage and Sue herself died young of cancer.

It struck me that everyone in this picture, except for Paddy, had died since. There was sickness, death and a good dose of misery ahead of all of them, but for now they were having a ball.

The Mayfair had a tropical décor with grass matting on the walls and an island lagoon in the centre creating a Tahitian feel. Every half-hour, 'thunder' rumbled and 'clouds' gathered and the patrons would thrill to the spectacle of a tropical downpour into the lagoon.

Back in Australia, Billy Longley would soon stand trial for the attempted murder of some rivals in a South Melbourne pub. He later beat that, but he could never beat his nature. There were hard cold years of porridge ahead for Billy. If he had swallowed his doubts and followed Fibber to London, he might have been sipping on that rum punch too. But as mortal beings, he reflected, we don't get to choose our destiny.

3
Monopoly money

Australians are among the world's most numerous travellers. Australians do not rush into a host country for a few days and leave with vague impressions . . . They stay for weeks, and even months, spending at a reasonable rate, and even earning more money to spend, getting to know the people, their customs and their languages, and in general making themselves far more liked personally . . .

Sydney Morning Herald, 13 August 1962

J ust about everything the Kid knew about London he had learnt off the Monopoly board. And like all kids who ever played the classic board game, it was the properties on the green and neighbouring blue squares that he coveted.

On the corner of the cheaper yellow squares, a frowning bobby could send you direct to jail. But if you got past him, you were into the green and blue. The first one there could buy Regent and Oxford streets for

£300 or Bond Street for £320. If you rolled a small number next you might get a crack at Park Lane for £350 or the prized Mayfair for £400. There were risks. Between the high priced real estate, Chance could send you straight to jail or, two squares further on, that sparkling diamond ring would cost you £100 in super tax. But if the dice fell his way, a player could collect his £200 salary for passing Go! and, with a couple of greens and blues in his portfolio, be well on the way to victory.

But when the Kid arrived in July 1966, he was surprised to find that Bond Street didn't actually exist. He turned from bustling Oxford Street into New Bond Street and at Conduit Street, it just turned into Old Bond Street. Bond Street was nothing more than a Tube station on Oxford Circus. There had been so many surprises since he and his mate, 'Baby Bruce', had boarded the SS *Castel Felice* in Sydney five weeks earlier. Bruce had turned 21 as the ship passed through the Suez Canal.

Who would have thought they would have teamed up on board with a Catholic priest? Father Francis had been a revelation in the Egyptian stopover of Port Said. They were in a jewellery store and the Kid had got his hands on a 15-carat chunk of alexandrite from a showcase. He turned to Father Francis, looked at him, then without a word dropped the semi-precious stone into the priest's pocket. Father Francis just turned and walked out of the store. No-one would interrupt the serene progress of a priest even if his cassock was bulging with stolen goods. Alexandrite is regarded as a good omen and so it was for their relationship. Father Francis later performed the Kid's marriage ceremony, baptised his children and even buried his son.

Like Arthur, the Kid's departure from Sydney had not been entirely his own decision. They were young but the Kid and Baby Bruce were already among Sydney's most prolific dips. They had learnt to pick pockets on the racecourse, where a number of the Kangaroo Gang got their start. The allied arts of dipping and hoisting rely on the principles of magic and illusion. A successful illusionist will always say the big movement covers the small one. The extravagant flourish of cape or the top hat hides the nimble movement at the centre of the illusion. And so it is with the dips.

A drunk stumbles headlong into a successful punter as he moves through a crowded betting ring, his winnings tucked into the pocket of his waistcoat. He is so preoccupied with giving this cloth-eared fool a dressing down, he thinks of nothing else. Only later does he realise that the fool is him. He has been positioned, gulled and taken. The team has watched the happy punter move from the rails to the payment window as soon as correct weight has been posted. They have watched the mark put the wad in the pocket on the right hand side of his waistcoat. This means the drunk, the 'push-up man', must approach from the left. When they collide, the indignant punter automatically turns his head, neck and shoulders to the left. He raises his hands to stop the drunk from toppling over onto him. As he pushes him away, his weight now going left, the right pocket of his waistcoat opens up like a smiling face. The take, walking past unseen on the right, has only to brush against him, dip the wad of notes with two fingers and disappear into the crowd.

The Kid had honed his skills so finely he was terrorising Randwick and Rose Hill racecourses each week. He had to be good; his asthma did not allow the Kid to make fast getaways. But he had begun to dip some pockets that he shouldn't have—policemen, judges, a politician or two. The kindly Joe Taylor, the nightclub owner who ran Sydney back then, had a soft spot for the Kid, but business was business. The Kid was breaking the rules and he would have to go away for a while, Taylor told him. A sea voyage to England was the go, a marvellous chance to see the world. And look at the success Duke Delaney was having on the hoist, said Taylor. Or he could stick to what he knew. The 1966 World Cup finals were to be staged in England that summer and the supporters of 16 nations would be descending for the tournament with pockets full of money ripe for the picking. Only a mug could miss out. Joe Taylor said they could fill their pockets in London for six months and then return as if nothing had happened. New South Wales police would have moved on by then, he said. He would see to that. At 20, Baby Bruce was also fast making a bad name for himself in Sydney and linked up with the Kid for the trip.

The Kid had been born in Melbourne but had moved to Sydney a couple of years earlier. He had come north for the 1963 Golden Slipper won by the equal favourite, South Australian wonder colt Pago Pago. And that was the extent of his travels. To that point, his longest boat ride had been the River Caves ride at Luna Park. As Taylor had suggested, he planned to be away six months. He ended up staying for nearly four years. His mate Baby Bruce stayed off and on for 40 years. The London of the Monopoly board had only been a taste of the riches here. Why hadn't there been a Savile Row with its sumptuous men's outfitters or a Knightsbridge with its luxury department stores like Harrods? Hatton Gardens with its thriving jewellery trade deserved a mention, and surely

Marylebone, the home of department store Selfridges, deserved more than a reference to its railway station.

But of course, no-one had told him that West Indians and Pakistanis would speak like fair dinkum Cockneys. Nothing in the River Caves, not even the Eskimo village, had prepared him for the cold and the rain either. Likewise, the Monopoly board hadn't shown the maze of narrow Georgian streets and the bustling shopping districts that made London a city for thieves par excellence. And below ground there were riches on offer too. The Tube with its 270 stations and 400 kilometres of track was another world—'King Solomon's Mines' to the 'bottle men', picking the pockets of the tourists day and night.

Baby Bruce and the Kid parted company soon after their arrival. Bruce went underground while the Kid with his asthma worked the surface. They found lodgings with other Australian thieves and went to work almost immediately. While Baby Bruce worked on his own, 'the General', Billy Hill, had suggested the Kid look up the Fibber and soon they became a team.

When I spoke to him, 43 years later, the Kid had filled out a little—his hair had thinned, but the spark in his blue eyes fairly blazed when he spoke of those early days. There was a little arthritis creeping into his long slender fingers, but they retained a dexterity that was simply amazing. He was demonstrating his magic, showing off even. He still did kids' parties occasionally—private shows for the children of his mates. He would steal the watch off your arm, and then ask the time to enjoy the shock on your face when you realised it was gone.

As he spoke, he reached under the table into a bag and pulled out photo albums and an ancient bowler hat. He dusted the hat off lovingly. 'The first day on the job with Fibber, we went to Harrods with Arthur Delaney. Arthur was looking immaculate in his suit and tie. He told me, "Kid, in this business you have to look the part." Fibber grabbed a bowler hat off the shelf and jammed it on my head. "There you go," he said. "Now you're ready." But Arthur said, "Not quite." He reached over and tilted the hat a little and said: "Now you're a proper gentleman." And we just walked straight out of Harrods,' he said, chuckling at the memory.

He drummed his fingers on the crown of the old hat and then turned it over to show the label. The gold lettering was a little faded from decades of Brylcreem and hair tonic, and the lining was coming away, but you could still read the label clearly—*Harrods of London*. 'From then on it was like a job, we were at it every day,' said the Kid.

He held up the photo album for the waitress to see: 'Hey, take a look at me when I was young,' he demanded. He flipped to a shot of a smiling young man standing in the foyer of the White House hotel in Regents Park, decked out in a three-piece Savile Row suit with a rolled-up umbrella tucked under his arm and his faithful bowler hat at a jaunty angle on his head, as prescribed by Arthur. As he showed us the picture, the Kid jammed that self-same hat down on his head—he looked like Alfred Hitchcock now.

'That was me!' he exclaimed. A look of wonder spread over the middle-aged waitress's face—she travelled and had no doubt enjoyed quite a life, but the people in these pictures were simply having a ball. There were the Kid and Baby Bruce on the deck of the SS *Castel Felice* bound for London in 1965, the Kid riding a camel in the shadow of the pyramids in Egypt, at the races in Paris, gliding down Venice's Grand Canal in a gondola, standing by a convertible in the Californian sun. And in every shot they were just beaming and laughing. There were groups of smartly dressed people crammed into the booths of night-clubs and restaurants sipping exotic drinks through long straws, bowling down the streets in London, high on the hoist. If there was ever a distil-lation of the Swinging Sixties, then this was it. They were living from moment to moment.

The waitress lingered on a shot from 1969. The Kid was presenting his girlfriend with a 21-carat diamond ring he had recently stolen. It was in a hotel room in Paris and he was just about to leave her to return home to Australia. He had just snapped open the ring box to reveal the ring and, like a starburst, the stone's light had smacked her right in the face. Her eyes were wide and glistening. Her expression seemed to ask: could there be any greater, more dangerous, evocation of love than a stolen 21-carat diamond?

How the Kid and his mate, 'Humour', had come by it made it seem even more delicious. As a joke, the jeweller had put the monster rock in the window on a shelf above the latest novelty craze, pet rocks. The showcase was right in the corner of the shop by the door. The Kid had come in wearing a ten-gallon stetson, chewing on a big Cuban cigar. Puffing clouds of smoke into the shop assistant's face, he had asked to see the pet rocks.

'So what's this one's name?' he asked in a loud American accent. 'Ricky, eh? Have you got a Bruno? Well ain't that swell!' As he went through this inane routine, the shop assistant didn't notice that Humour was now standing in the doorway outside the shop.

'Hey, sweetheart, I want that one right down there at the bottom—Peter, I think his name is. Yeah, he's a real beaut,' he said. The jeweller must have thought him a fool to be paying £70 for a rock but, as she bent down, she was about to be taken for £15 000. Humour's long arm snaked in behind the Kid's block and plucked the 21-carat diamond. He had never even set foot in the store.

But the stone itself seemed dull and lifeless in the photo—it was the light in their eyes that spoke of the spirit of the time. It was a spirit of abundance, of endless youth, of being rich with love like a millionaire, so much to share. And they had taken their share many times over. There was still a gleam of mischief in the Kid even today, though times had been hard. In the 1970s, drugs had begun to corrupt everything and everyone. In the 1960s, crime had for the most part been a thrill, but now it was about money and power. He knew the world had changed the night in Sydney when he was ordered to rob Arthur. It was 1980 and he was running a baccarat game and the King was winning too big, so the boss told the Kid to take him down. Arthur would never have known, but he couldn't do it and there was nearly a big fight over it. Back in London, it felt like they had belonged to something, they looked after each other—their success was shared. Now it was every man for himself. It hollowed out a bloke, living like that.

Many of the old hoisters had gone into drugs and the meanness of that trade had worked its way into them. Friends had murdered friends, or given them up to the cops for a bag of money. But in the great days of the hoist, they had all been mates.

In those early days in London, Arthur had always kept his own counsel. If you weren't working with him or celebrating his success, you didn't see much of him. There would be nights like that gathering at the Mayfair Club in the old photo, when Arthur would be the life of the party, shouting everyone champagne (except the Kid, who never drank) and spreading love and goodwill to all people. Then he would just disappear. After a few weeks, he would reappear with a job in mind.

One day he took the Kid and one or two others to Knightsbridge where he planned to hit Mappin & Webb, a renowned silversmith and jeweller. The Kid was supposed to provide a 'smother' while Arthur ducked down behind the counter to grab the keys and then open the showcase. It was the Girard-Perregaux Gyromatic watches that Arthur was after, beautiful Swiss gold timepieces with an excellent resale value. The Kid would block Arthur from view and hold his overcoat behind his back for Arthur to load up. There was £60 000 worth for the taking if they were good enough. But Arthur was uncharacteristically nervous. The heads in the watch department had all been pulled (distracted) but a particular shop assistant from another counter seemed to be staring at them.

Arthur was all for pulling the pin and trying another day, but the Kid had done his homework. He had done that shop over three or four times before and seen that shop assistant. 'He always stares like that. He's bored out of his mind and he's probably short-sighted too.'

Still Arthur remained edgy. 'Look, Duke, I'll prove it you,' said the Kid, handing him the overcoat.

Before Arthur could argue, the Kid ducked behind the counter and looked up at Arthur from all fours. 'He's still looking, isn't he?' said the Kid. Arthur agreed he was, but that he hadn't made any move to stop them.

Arthur's confidence returned immediately. 'Righto, Kid, let's have 'em then,' he said, turning to face the assistant with his back to the counter, pretending to read a catalogue. He had draped his overcoat inside-out over the back of the counter so the Kid could drop the gleaming watches into the half lining.

When they got outside, Arthur was ecstatic. He was high as a kite, like he had taken some kind of narcotic. 'My boy, you are *good*! You are *very* good,' he said over and over, chuckling and slapping the Kid on the back.

The Kid could see why hoisters became so addicted to their trade. He was floating on air when they came out of Mappin & Webb with those watches. Dipping back home was a thrill but nothing like this, when you could earn £60 000 in just a few minutes.

Anyhow dipping was a closed shop in London, controlled by the police. There were five 'bottle firms' (pickpocketing teams) in London and weekly they all paid their dues to Scotland Yard. And not to some uniformed walloper. The money went right to the top, into the pocket of Flying Squad boss Commander Don Neesham. Baby Bruce had discovered early on that dipping on the Underground was an exclusive business, a cartel between a few master thieves and their police handlers. He had been collared in a crowded carriage not by a bobby, but another dip. He had been frogmarched out of the station to a park where he was introduced to a senior detective from Scotland Yard and later a well-dressed 60-year-old man named Alfie Elborn.

In London dipping was not a free-for-all, said Mr Elborn, as he liked to be called. A thief could not simply come and go as he pleased. Here you worked for Alfie Elborn or you didn't work at all, he said, gesturing to the detective. And there were rules and regulations to this game. Firstly, you could dip the tourists only, no locals. If a 'mark' didn't have a camera hanging round its neck it was not to be touched. Too many complaints from Londoners and Scotland Yard would become interested.

And you would meet the standards that Mr Elborn set for his men and women, or you didn't work. Each morning before a shift on the rush hour trains, Elborn would line up the troops and inspect them like a sergeant major on parade. Shoes would be shined to a mirror finish, suits pressed and shirts freshly laundered. He would then check to see that each dip's fingernails were immaculately clean and manicured. If they didn't pass muster, they were sent home. Baby Bruce had joined Elborn's team, and worked solidly. The only time off came in 1971 when Evonne Goolagong beat Margaret Court at Wimbledon. Alfie had put £15 000 on Court to beat Goolagong for her fourth singles title and when she lost Alfie blamed Australians in general and Baby Bruce in particular. 'You can't bloody trust fucking Australians,' he moaned and thundered. He suspended Baby Bruce for four days on a general suspicion of Australian foul play.

Alfie was a twentieth century version of Fagin, Charles Dickens' master thief from *Oliver Twist*. A thief, a pickpocket and a fence, he was a mercurial character and one of Britain's most assiduous corrupters of police. He was responsible for the collection of 'licence' money for Neesham from all of London's five bottle firms. Once Alfie had gotten over Evonne Goolagong's treachery, he assigned Baby Bruce the task of picking up the money, nearly £5000, each week. Soon Baby Bruce was attending the rugby tests at Twickenham with Neesham. ('You keep your fucking hands in your pockets, son,' he would tell him). The corruption was just as regimented and entrenched in London as it had been in New South Wales. Alfie had been a street thief when Neesham was walking the beat in uniform.

They had been helping each other for years. The Flying Squad included a couple of dip squads working the trains but they focused on the renegades who hadn't joined the 'licensed teams'.

Having escaped the claustrophobic corruption of New South Wales, the Kid had not gone halfway across the world to work for coppers. As a hoister, the risks were greater, but at least every day you made your own destiny. The World Cup had proved to be an over-rated opportunity too. For that fortnight London had been lousy with thieves and pickpockets from everywhere, all trying their best. Someone had even stolen the trophy from a display at an exhibition in the build-up to the tournament. A nationwide hunt ended when a dog named Pickles had sniffed out the trophy, wrapped in newspaper and hidden under a hedge in the Beulah Hill district of south-east London. To make matters worse, England won the Cup—so most of the revelling crowds in the streets were Poms, off limits to the dips.

There were better, easier pickings away from the football crowd. And so began the Massacre on Bond Street.

4
The Massacre on Bond Street

Each morning Baby Bruce would disappear underground into King Solomon's Mines while the Fibber and the Kid would meet up and go to work. It was a job that required a serious and professional approach, said Fibber. The Kid was barely 20 and still slight, but dressed to the nines in a stolen cashmere overcoat with velvet collar, Savile Row suit and an Eton tie, he looked fit for the peerage.

As he spent more time in Knightsbridge and Mayfair, the Kid began to understand the store detective's dilemma. The 'store jacks' might have suspected him, but they took a big risk when approaching him. If they got it wrong and the suspected shoplifter was indeed a valued customer, they knew the management wouldn't back them up. The detectives were a necessary evil, but the other staff and management rarely warmed to them. They were like the rat catchers in the king's palace, valued only when the rats were running amok. Many stores found it distasteful to even admit they employed store security, which reflected on the quality of their customers.

Mayfair Club, London, 1966. The King of Thieves in his court. From left: Arthur Delaney, girlfriend Paddy Burridge, the Fibber's son Barry Warren, Playboy bunny Sue Powles and and Jack 'the Fibber' Warren. Note the sparkling stones Paddy is wearing; they were all stolen.

The General ready for work. In Australia, Billy Hill had been a petty thief but, in London, he could pass as a gentleman while indulging his compulsive thieving. Underrated by many of the Kangaroo Gang, he died a wealthy man.

Arthur with yet another woman in late-1960s London. His lust for other men's women earned him a bullet in the back in Sydney in 1969. Even that didn't slow him down for very long.

On tour during the 1970s: a weekend in Paris with Arthur (left) could end weeks later anywhere on the continent. With the French Count Petite Philippe and other European speakers on the team, this Newcastle boy became the 'World's Raffles'.

Detective Constable Jimmy 'Smudger' Smith of New Scotland Yard's C11 Squad. C11's covert photographers stemmed the Kangaroo crime wave by compiling the first profile of the gang in the *Police Gazette*'s Australian Index in 1968. Like many police, Smith had a grudging admiration for the hoisters.

Alexis and Arthur fishing in Cornwall in 1979. While posing as a respectable couple in England, the Delaneys were the scourge of Europe.

Living with Arthur, the world's greatest rogue, wasn't easy but Alexis gave as good as she got. Never one for grudges, Arthur apologised for his transgressions with diamonds.

Arthur spent much of the 1980s in European and British jails. But having survived that and throat cancer, The King was determined to enjoy his crowning moment in Mayfair. A ghost was returning to Bond Street.

Arthur and Alexis in Sydney, 1990. All Alexis ever wanted was a home to call her own. The King of Thieves didn't need a castle but promised to change his ways for the love of his life.

Tommy Wraith at his last birthday party in 1983. He got away with Grace O'Connor's murder in London, 1973, but got his right whack from another female in the end.

Identification photos from the 'Australian Index' published as a supplement to the *Police Gazette*

Arthur Delaney was featured in the first 'Australian Index' of the *Police Gazette* of December 1967 at number 6, detailing his criminal history and appearance even down to his tattoos. But, by 1975, he had strangely disappeared off the *Gazette*'s 'hoisters' parade'. He did jail time and numerous jobs in the 1980s under various new identities.

Grace 'The Case' O'Connor was the best female take of her generation, a figure beloved by the Kangaroo Gang, but her dubious taste in men proved her undoing.

Georgie G: the handsome dashing thief had a dark past back in Australia but in London gained the admiration of cops and robbers alike. He took the hoisters from department stores to banks.

William 'Wee Jimmy' Lloyd was the most prolific of the master hoisters working in London. He lacked the flamboyance of Arthur Delaney but had more police on the payroll in England and Australia than anyone.

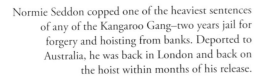

Normie Seddon copped one of the heaviest sentences of any of the Kangaroo Gang–two years jail for forgery and hoisting from banks. Deported to Australia, he was back in London and back on the hoist within months of his release.

Morris 'Morry the Head' Spurling: one of England's most prolific international thieves, Spurling admired and copied the techniques of the Australians. A trusted member of the gang, the Aussies would have made him rich but for his ferocious gambling habit.

David William 'Glasses' Barry was one of a handful of trusted English confederates to the Kangaroo Gang; a fence for stolen goods, confidante and drinking buddy to the Kangaroo Gang. The *Police Gazette* revealed that Barry had been informing on them to Scotland Yard.

Jack 'the Fibber' Warren: the gentle humorous conman, beloved of his mates, adored a dishonest dollar but abhorred the violence that often came with it. An all-round thief and crook, his courage was sometimes questioned, but he had the last laugh, amassing a multi-million dollar fortune.

The law made the task of catching shoplifters even more difficult. In a big department store like Harrods, a shopper could walk with merchandise for hundreds of yards without leaving the store. It was only when they stepped out on the street that an offence was committed. Even a wandering shopper who concealed goods in bags or coats was given the benefit of the doubt until they stepped across the threshold. Later, an informal regulation was established maintaining that if you strayed more than 100 yards from the counter where an item was located you could be deemed a thief. But the store detective was still loath to make an accusation unless he caught a suspect red-handed.

And the stores could expect little assistance from police. It was a lot of effort to chase a shoplifter, even an organised ring like the Kangaroo Gang, if the heaviest penalty they faced was a £400 fine. If they did arrest one, the thief would be back on the hoist the next day. And the Old Bill knew that most stores, if they did report the thefts, were just going through the motions for the sake of insurance.

In any case, the Metropolitan Police had much bigger fish to fry than the Kid, Arthur or the Fibber. A vicious underworld war had erupted in the East End between the Kray and Richardson gangs. The Kray twins, Ronnie and Reggie, were prosperous West End nightclub owners but their Establishment and celebrity network covered an evil empire dealing in fraud, drugs, protection and murder. They were unlikely crime lords. Ronnie was a paranoid schizophrenic with homosexual tendencies while Reggie was a long-suffering character who claimed to be dominated by his brother. The Richardson gang were less well-known but just as dangerous, gaining the sobriquet the Torture Gang for their practice of pinning victims to the floor with six-inch nails or removing their toes with bolt cutters.

As the quarrelsome Krays and Richardsons stabbed, slashed, shot and bludgeoned their way through 1965–66, the Australians quietly got on with business. Some English villains had lost their fear of the police. On 12 August 1966, a gang led by small-time crim Harry Roberts murdered three police officers in cold blood in East Acton near Wormwood Scrubs. The Massacre of Braybrook Street caused public outrage as a massive manhunt went on for months. Two of the murderers were captured in the week after the killings, but Roberts used his military training to stay on the run, hiding in Epping Forest for three months.

At this time, the Kid and his associates were having a golden run. Their dingy flat was an Aladdin's cave of stolen goods, racks of clothes, jewellery, watches and household appliances. One night in September 1966, the boys were holding a raucous party at home to celebrate their latest success. After midnight one of the lads (let's call him Mick) was coming to grips with a comely maiden in the front bedroom when there came a knock on the door, barely audible over the music and commotion. No-one answered, and the knocking became louder and more insistent. Irritated that the knocking was putting him off his stroke, Mick leapt up and ran to the door. When door swung open, a pair of uniformed coppers was confronted with Mick, stark bollock naked.

The cops didn't know where to look, but Mick wasn't fazed at all, his enormous erection waving at them comically. 'What the fuck are you blokes doing here?' he exclaimed. 'Shouldn't you be out with the rest of your mates chasing Harry Roberts?'

'Well, we're here about the noise actually,' said one of the constables as Mick's curious lover came out wrapped just in a sheet.

'No worries, mate,' said Mick cheerfully. 'I'll gag her for the rest of the night, okay?'

The bobbies were still digesting that as the door swung shut.

By now the other lads had come out to see what was going on. The Kid was gobsmacked that Mick had been so casual. They had a house full of stolen goods and Mick was telling the cops to get lost. Confidence was one thing, but this was reckless. One drunken moment like that could bring them all undone. He resolved to associate with people who viewed the hoist as a profession not just a lark to finance drinking and partying.

Later Fibber invited the Kid to move into his place in Paddington. It wasn't much—a dingy walk-up fifth-floor flat off the Edgware Road, a few minutes from the heart of the West End. It was so close to the railway line, the place shook when trains clattered by every few minutes. The flat smelt of boiled cabbage and damp old socks. The plumbing would roar when they turned on the taps. But it was home for the Kid for the next couple of years with Fibber, Sue Powlesand and Barry.

Barry was a year younger than the Kid and they got on well. It was like living with Mum and Dad in a family of thieves. Fibber was certainly a father figure, passing on his knowledge to the Kid, the willing pupil. The glamorous Sue worked as a bunny at Hugh Hefner's London Playboy Club and never came out on jobs with the boys, preferring to sleep all day or work on her tan whenever the pale summer sun allowed.

Meanwhile, a new woman had joined the team. Grace O'Connor was petite—she looked more like a middle-class housewife than a thief, but she came with a solid reputation. And even a catchy nickname—'Grace The Case' had a criminal history stretching back to the 1950s. She had been married to one of Sydney's leading gunmen, Raymond 'Ducky' O'Connor. She had pedigree.

Grace had been part of a successful shoplifting team in Melbourne until one night she was collared leaving a department store on Bourke Street by legendary detective Sergeant Brian 'Skull' Murphy. She had maintained a dignified silence during the interview, giving away nothing despite Skull's best efforts.

Finally Skull lost patience. 'Now listen, madam, I know you are hiding some stuff on you. We've searched your person and found nothing. Which takes us to the next stage,' he said, glaring at Grace. 'Do you know what an internal body cavity search is?' he asked. She rolled her eyes as if to say of course she did.

'Well normally a policewoman would perform this on another woman, but guess what, there's no-one from the Crack Squad in the station tonight,' he said. He licked his fingers and rubbed his hands together with a lascivious grin.

She wasn't to know it was an idle threat. Grace blanched at the thought. 'That won't be necessary. Give me a couple of minutes in private,' she murmured. The cop complied.

When Skull returned, Grace was sitting demurely with her legs crossed. On the table was a set of diamond cufflinks, some earrings, a bracelet and a small notebook.

'Is that all?' Skull demanded. She glared at him and nodded.

To the cops, the notebook was the most valuable item. In it Grace had recorded the telephone numbers of numerous associates. Murphy took the numbers to the Pigs Meat and Gravy (the Postmaster General's department) and within 48 hours they had addresses matching the numbers. They carried out 40 raids over the next fortnight. The raids yielded little in stolen property, but helped police map out the network of shoplifters and thieves operating in Melbourne. With suspicion amongst Melbourne crims that Grace had lagged them to the cops, she drifted up to Sydney. Her husband 'Ducky' O'Connor was in jail in New South Wales at this time so she had to earn a living on her own.

'Ducky' was released from jail in February 1967, but his days were already numbered. Author Tony Reeves, in his book on crime boss Lennie

McPherson, suggested that McPherson, known as 'Mr Big', had been displeased with Ducky after he had bragged that he would take over Sydney when he got out. Reeves wrote that McPherson had visited Ducky in jail, pronouncing a death sentence on him after a brief kangaroo court there.

In the early hours of 28 May 1967, Ducky visited the Latin Quarter nightclub in Sydney's Pitt Street, where McPherson and a couple of associates had been enjoying the Las Vegas style girlie shows. Some New South Wales detectives were at another table. One thing led to another and, when the house lights came up, Ducky was dead, lying on the floor with a hole in his head. No-one, not even the cops, had seen who killed Ducky.

By this time Grace was already in London. If she was grieving for Ducky, she didn't show it. Grace was ready to work. She was warm and funny, a joy to be around. The Kid had known few women of such poise and refinement. She was no great beauty, but her elegance and warmth just put everyone at ease. It's what made her such a great take—there were few her equal.

For the next 18 months, Fibber and the Kid would meet Grace in town every morning and go off to work. They would bring in others to make up the numbers as head pullers and cockatoos, but this trio was always the nucleus. Grace's role as minder was crucial. When everyone was getting set for their individual tasks, pulling heads, stealing keys, providing smothers or blocks, getting ready for the take, the minder kept an eye on everyone in the shop. It would be the minder who finally set the job in motion, or sounded the retreat in the event of trouble. And they never came unstuck when Grace was on the case. If you could stay calm and think your way through it, there was always a way to earn.

The Kid had learnt his most valuable lessons at Arthur's side. Early in his English education, they had been preparing to enter a jewellery store in Mayfair where the team was already in place. 'If no-one approaches me within the next minute, then I am invisible,' said Arthur.

The Kid had looked puzzled. How could someone be invisible inside a store full of staff with people streaming past the front window?

'I will show you. Stay outside and block the window for me. Watch and learn,' he said with a wink. Arthur had looked immaculate—shiny even—from the Brylcreemed hair and the silk tie to those sparkling, darting eyes.

Four head pullers were at the counter occupying all the staff members. A fifth man, a big bulky bloke named Awful Allan, was standing in the centre of the shop, his hands on his hips so his coat and mackintosh fanned out like a cape behind him. Awful Allan looked like he was a customer waiting to be served but in reality he was Arthur's minder. The Kid watched Arthur slip into the store and move unseen into Awful Al's shadow. Up close to the minder, there was no way the staff could even get a glimpse of the diminutive Arthur. Awful Al was so big he could block a brick wall and, even if someone twigged, no-one would get past him. Of course Arthur couldn't get too close to the minder or risk the staff seeing his shiny crocodile shoes.

It was up to the Kid to block the door and the window from the outside. He would watch where Arthur and Awful Al went and keep his body between them and any nosey onlookers. If someone attempted to enter the store, the Kid was to drag them away, pulling out a street map of London to ask directions.

The Kid watched Awful Al and Arthur begin to edge their way over to the gap in the counter at the left hand corner of the shop. All the while Awful Al was making sure the heads were still pulled. When they got to the counter, Arthur just scooted straight under and seconds later he was back behind his minder with a set of keys for the showcases. From there they went back to the front window, moving to the showcase with the pieces he wanted. The Kid saw Arthur scoop up half a dozen big diamond rings then carefully rearrange the remaining items to conceal the theft. The staff might not even notice the merchandise was gone for hours, much less realise who took it. They might be able to come back next week and pull the same gag again.

It was over in less than two minutes and Arthur was out of the shop without ever being spotted. It was a performance of breathtaking genius. What amazed the Kid even more was the fact that when they whacked up the proceeds, everyone got the same share. There was no hierarchy in this team, every member was as crucial as the next to its success, whether they pulled heads, minded or played the taker.

Invisibility was a team game, but the retailers were gradually opening their eyes. In the sales of 1966, Harrods had trialled closed-circuit televisions for the first time, but the system was far from perfect. There were no inventory control tags back then. If the staff were wrangled effectively, you could manipulate reality for long enough to strike unseen. Even if they were watching through their grainy black and white monitors, the store jacks might not even spot what you were doing.

At Harrods the décor at that time suited the hoisters. Sir Hugh Fraser, the second Baron of Allander, had ascended to the leadership of Harrods upon the death of his father, the first baron, in 1966. The 30-year-old chairman of the House of Fraser decided that the old shop needed an update as the Swinging Sixties gripped London. To help change its fusty image, Fraser ordered the lighting at Harrods be lowered and more modern music played at higher volume. On the fourth floor, Fraser had created a youth emporium he had hilariously tagged 'Way In'. The lighting was even lower there. The dark colours and the try-hard rock music didn't find favour with the hip set, but the thieves loved the new atmosphere. Fraser had even put in a sandwich bar there for the weary hoisters to rest and congregate.

In late 1967, Harrods was proudly displaying a beautiful five-carat diamond ring. It was distinctive for its teardrop cut and brilliant clarity. The Kid was learning plenty about diamonds but this one was a quantum leap in his education. Arthur had previously failed with a team of ten to hoist it. The Fibber was doubtful it could be done, given the position of the counter and the shop detectives milling around the floor in disguise. But the Kid was mesmerised by the stone and spent hours watching the movements of the staff, pondering how to get it.

Finally, in a dream the answer came to him. The Kid had learnt to believe in his dreams. A few years earlier he had dreamt that a 100–1 roughie named See The Light was going to win at Melbourne's Moonee Valley racecourse that weekend. He had been sceptical and only put ten quid on it. Still, he had collected £1000 when it romped in and so from then on he had backed his dreams.

The Fibber was the boss, but he was always game for a lark. He had pulled off bigger earners than this with less than a dream for comfort so he resolved to let his protégé have his head. The trio were driving past Harrods one morning when the Kid reminded Fibber and Grace about his dream—how he had hoisted the Harrods diamond and got away scot-free. They had all laughed. Minutes later, they were walking in through the revolving doors of the store. This was how the Fibber operated—little planning, no dress rehearsals, just straight into the performance.

Grace and Fibber, as husband and wife, walked into the jewellery department carrying a large model train set they had bought, wrapped in Harrods gift paper. They engaged a couple of staff in animated conversation.

There was now no-one watching the prize, or the Kid. This was still a high risk gaff, but he was up to the task. He stood back assessing the scene, confident the cloak of invisibility was upon him. He could re-emerge when the moment came.

The layout of the jewellery area was imposing. There were three or four magnificent mahogany showcases arranged around two desks with leather and gold inlay where staff would show pieces to the customers. Directly behind the desk was the centrepiece, a double showcase about eight feet wide, standing atop a platform with three or four steep steps leading up to it. Harrods' security must have thought the raised platform made the showcase impregnable—the perfect place to securely display the beautiful five-carat ring.

The Kid was waiting for the cleaner he had seen come to dust inside the jewellery cases every Saturday. She was there on time as always. She got the keys from an assistant and began her little routine.

She began to open the smaller showcases from the back. She cleaned the brass with a rag and dusted inside with a feather duster. She was carefree, moving easily among the gleaming counters and displays, her duster flicking this way and that. The Kid waited for her to get to the biggest showcase, where the five-carat ring was on display. When she leant into the showcase, the Kid made his move.

'Excuse me, madam,' he said in a whisper so soft she had to crane her ear to him. 'My wife is just over there,' he said, smiling and drawing her even closer. He pointed to a young woman he had never seen before.

'That one, sir?' the cleaner replied.

'Shh, don't look at her—you'll give the game away,' he said.

Meanwhile, Fibber and Grace were working their way to the front of the showcase, holding their train set parcel as a block. It covered most of the front view, the Kid had the back. Now no-one else could see what was about to happen.

'It's our first wedding anniversary and I really want to give her a big, big surprise, you know what I mean?' said the Kid. The cleaner smiled and the Kid knew he had her. Every girl, even a middle-aged cleaner, goes soft for the romance of diamonds. 'I just need to know the price of that lovely diamond ring there,' he said, looking furtively over at his 'wife'.

'But, sir, I'm just the cleaner, I'll get a sales assistant to help you,' she said, starting to close the showcase.

'No, no,' he said, gently gripping her arm reassuringly. 'Oh please, it won't take a minute,' he whispered imploringly.

She could get into trouble for this but, looking into the Kid's melting blue eyes, she just couldn't say no. She leant in and reached for the three-carat ring the Kid had pointed at. The idea now was to get her as far away as possible from the object of his desire, the big tear-shaped sparkler ring in the centre of the display.

'No, not that one,' the Kid whispered. 'The one right down the front,' he said.

The cleaner wasn't very tall and the case sloped steeply down to the front. She had to stand on her tiptoes to reach right in. Even then she couldn't quite get a grip on the ring. As she was teetering, the Kid had leant in alongside her. Using her body as a block, he had two fingers on the five-carat ring, gently wiggling it out of its display. It was tighter than it had been in his dream.

He had just freed it when the cleaner happened to glance down. She saw the empty block and then the glittering ring between his fingers. 'Oh, sir!' she exclaimed in surprise.

Time froze. Then, with a flick of his fingers, the ring disappeared up the Kid's sleeve, like it was never there. It took just the tiniest nudge in the back and the cleaner overbalanced and toppled into the showcase, her feet waving in the air. By the time she had struggled upright again, the Kid was on his way to the door.

'We've just been robbed!' the cleaner cried out. 'Did you see which way he went?' she asked the nearest customers.

'I'm sure the scoundrel made off that way,' said Fibber in his best English accent, pointing in the completely opposite direction.

'Oh yes, that young man in the overcoat, I'm sure that's where he went,' Grace chimed in.

Pandemonium broke out as staff and store detectives rushed off in vain pursuit of the thief. The Kid was now 50 yards away and heading for the doors. Only a doorman in his snappy green livery stood between the Kid and the surging crowd outside on Brompton Road. The doorman was looking over the Kid's head at the drama unfolding in the jewellery department. Then he stared hard at the Kid for a second trying to see what part he might have played in the fracas.

Time froze again. This was a dash-defining moment for a thief. The slightest hesitation would betray him. There's many a fabulous take lost in the travel. Adrenalin was pumping through the Kid, but he kept his breathing nice and steady as he approached the door. An asthma attack could have left him wheezing on the carpet.

'I say, my good man,' said the Kid, not missing a beat. 'It looks like they need you down there immediately—there's been a robbery,' he said earnestly, pointing back into the store. 'The blighter's getting away!'

The bewildered doorman just stepped aside, opened the door for the Kid and then ran back to help collar the thief. The rort had gone just as the Kid had dreamt. He was on the street slipping into the throng, not game to look over his shoulder. 'Sweet,' he said to himself, a rush of ecstasy going through him.

The robbery made the newspapers, even down to the description of the Kid in his Eton tie and overcoat with the velvet collar. Stealing a new overcoat and tie for the next Harrods job was a small inconvenience for the £20 000 the ring brought them.

Of course, not every job was such a dream run for the Fibber and the Kid. Their success was based on keeping each other's backs. One day in Harrods, filling an order for clothes, they became separated. But the Kid had just carried on—the Fibber often wandered off when something caught his eye.

Soon, however, there was a commotion on the other side of the floor. Two shop jacks were struggling with the Fibber, having caught him tucking some cashmere jumpers under his overcoat.

Without hesitation, the Kid strode over and roared: 'UNCLE JACK! I TOLD YOU BEFORE, DIDN'T I?' delivering a stunning back-hander to his astonished partner in crime. Even the shop jacks were taken aback.

'Thanks so much for looking after my Uncle Jack,' said the Kid. Then he turned to the Fibber. 'Now, Uncle Jack, you promised me that if I took you out of the sanatorium for the day, you would behave yourself. Now look what you've done, causing trouble for these nice people,' he scolded.

The Fibber tumbled to the plot straightaway and was instantly transformed into a drooling simpleton, albeit a very well-dressed one. 'Gentlemen, thank you so much, I am terribly sorry,' the Kid said to the shop jacks. 'It's so sad, when I think of what he used to be . . . But since the accident, well, he's like a child, he just can't help himself. But I'll take care of him from here.'

The shop jacks were completely taken in and released their grip on Uncle Jack. The Kid took him by the hand; as Uncle Jack shuffled away, he was still trying to steal, to keep the act going.

'See what I mean? I'll take him straight back,' the Kid said.

Another winter's day they had been after Swiss watches in Knightsbridge when the Fibber wandered off again. Undaunted, the Kid pressed on, planning to hit the target solo. His partner would catch up soon enough. Besides, there was a special satisfaction in pulling off jobs solo. He manoeuvred the shop assistant to the front window, but she was proving difficult to position. Every time he thought he had her head pulled to the left, leaving the right unguarded, her eyes would dart back. This went on for several minutes, until suddenly the Kid was aware that she was staring straight ahead, a curious look spreading over her face.

There was the Fibber staring through the glass at her from the street. It was the dead of winter and icy sleet was falling on his hat and overcoat, but in his hand the Fibber was holding an ice cream cone. It was such an incongruous sight, this deranged man pulling faces and licking his ice cream, that she entirely forgot what she was doing. The Kid had no idea either what the Fibber would do next, but he steadied himself. 'Wait for it, wait for it,' he told himself.

The Fibber stepped up to the window and reached high up the glass with his ice cream. The woman's eyes followed the Fibber's hand as if they were attached with string. Smiling like a lunatic, he began slowly drawing a wide curve on the glass. She was mesmerised and oblivious to what the Kid was doing.

By the time the Fibber had finished his big smiley face on the window, the gold Swiss watches were safely inside the Kid's overcoat.

The Kangaroo Gang

5

A giant shop lifting spree is plaguing Britain. Foreigners carry a share of the blame, particularly a gang of Australian and New Zealand professionals who are driving Scotland Yard mad . . .

United Press International/*Los Angeles Times*, 4 October 1968

As she watched the thunderstorm break over the Mayfair Club's tropical lagoon, Paddy Burridge reflected on the movie she had been living in.

Six months earlier, Paddy had been as square as they come—a convent-educated girl from St Peters, a middle-class suburb in Sydney's inner-west. But then she had met Arthur Delaney holding court in the Rose Bay hotel one night. He was the dashing thief just returned from overseas, celebrating three years of plunder. The Duke had become the King, the conquering Arthur returned from his realm. Paddy was the first to call him that. She was just 21 and Arthur 36 when they met.

In the autumn of 1966, Arthur had come home to Sydney briefly, more to brag and show off than anything else. At this time he was on the move almost constantly between London and the Continent, and as far away as America. If he wasn't the best thief going round, then he was certainly the busiest.

He was the most dashing and debonair man Paddy had ever met. She was taken aback when she first learnt Arthur was a thief, but she soon got over that. She fitted right in. Soon, like so many other 'nice girls', she was pulling heads for the King. It felt like the most impossibly thrilling thing she would ever do. That such a dangerously dashing character as Arthur could fall so madly in love with her completed the fantasy world.

'You're too good for a Duke—you're the King,' she would tell him.

Arthur would bathe in the flattery, smiling and preening. 'Thank you, my little drop of morning dew,' he'd say. 'What size are you in mink?'

'Oh, you know I'm a size eight, my honey tongue,' Paddy would reply.

Whenever he took her out to dinner, there would be a gift on her chair—a diamond brooch, a pendant or the most expensive perfume he could steal. Or if they walked on the street after lunch, she might comment on a dress in a shop window. That evening it would be hers. She never imagined such a man could exist—one who lived like a millionaire entirely on his wits. Some mornings she would awake to find Arthur had already been out and stolen thousands of dollars from who-knows-where. There was never a plan, just instinct and a nose for money—like a fox on the hunt, he could smell it. To Paddy, it seemed like he could make it materialise.

Then it would vanish in the illegal casinos of Kings Cross, where Arthur played baccarat compulsively—losing, drinking and big-noting. Sometimes she could hide some of the cash during the evening, so they could get a meal in the morning. He would be furious if he caught her, but grateful the next day. She sometimes hoped maybe they could sleep in, have a day off from the job; but no, it was always back on the hoist for Arthur.

Arthur had squired Paddy all around his favourite haunts, showing her off to his friends. But Alexis wondered whether a sweet little square-head like Paddy knew what she was getting herself into with Arthur. At 29, Alexis was already an accomplished thief, supporting herself and a young daughter through shoplifting and a little bar work just to fool the Consorting Squad she was employed. She was known and respected by the milieu that ran Sydney back then. Unlike Paddy, she was a name to be reckoned with.

Alexis would see Arthur, with Paddy in tow, come into the Rex hotel in the Cross, bragging and big-noting himself with his cronies in Sydney. Against her better judgement, she had risked a quiet fling with him now and again since the late 1950s, but still she thought him the most sly, untrustworthy man she had ever met. She ultimately decided she didn't want a bar of him and concluded that, no matter how good he was at the hoist, as a boyfriend or husband he would only bring misery. No matter how much he stole, he and any girlfriend he had would end up with nothing, probably not even a house. The girlfriend would have a roof over her head alright, but it would be inside a penitentiary. Paddy would find this out soon enough—silly girl, Alexis thought.

Still, Arthur had a kind of charisma and energy about him she found unusual. One night he had come into the bar on Oxford Street, Darling-hurst where she was working. He had tried every line he could and she had completely ignored him. Finally, in desperation, Arthur told her he could give her anything she wanted. 'Just name it, darling, and it will be yours,' he said with a flourish of his hands.

'Well, it's raining outside, so get me an umbrella,' she said, happy to shake off this sloe-eyed Lothario.

When, a few hours later, he returned triumphantly with somebody else's umbrella, Alexis regretted that she hadn't asked for something more expensive.

Soon Alexis heard he was back in England with his new girlfriend. She didn't want to finish up with a thief: this life was a means to an end. Unlike Paddy, she had begun life in a working-class suburb—Maroubra—but she had always dreamt of better things. One day, she vowed, she would raise a family in a nice suburban home. Soon after, she began seeing a dashing handsome airline steward and hardly gave Arthur another thought.

Meanwhile Arthur had endured pain for his art. While home in 1966, he had undergone surgery to remove his youthful tattoos, now faded into indecipherable blobs on his arms. He hated these reminders of where he had come from, and even more because they distinguished him in a crowd. He wanted to saunter down summer boulevards in Europe in pastel short-sleeved shirts, to blend into the cultured crowd. The ink had to go, but the best method was still primitive torture back then. Skin was peeled from the back of Arthur's legs and grafted over the tattoos. He was in agony for weeks and left Sydney with a patchwork of scars on his forearms, but it was worth it.

Few people knew that Arthur had been nicked in Amsterdam for robbing a jewellery store in early 1965. He had spent nearly a year in jail there before being deported to Australia. As he bragged of his European exploits, this part was usually left out. And it had been the witness ID of his tattoos that had sunk him. Now with a forged passport he was going back to the Continent a new man, if not a cleanskin.

In May 1966, to the horror of Paddy's parents, the love-struck couple left Australia on a first class round-the-world trip which lasted seven months. It included a grand tour of the European capitals, no expense spared. He had fallen deeply in love with the vivacious blonde—and she was easy to love stretched out sumptuously in a tiny bikini by hotel pools from Paris to Lisbon and Rome to Madrid. He adored her, spoiled her and obsessed over her. If there was a ladder in her stocking, she couldn't leave the restaurant table they were sitting at—he would pay a waiter the equivalent of $100 to run off and buy her a fresh pair. Every night was a performance for Paddy and anyone else who was near. He exuded love, laughter and relentless charm.

In private, however, it could be different. Under pressure, Arthur could change suddenly and lash out. It was only ever physical—short, sharp and unexpected. There was never verbal abuse—no nasty mouth, it wasn't in him. But if he was backed into a corner, if he felt the forces closing in, he would take it out on those around him. Paddy put up with it at first. It wasn't so bad to get hit by Arthur, because diamonds would appear the next day; the charm would return, as if time had folded over. But eventually the violence became too regular to ignore. The endless compulsive thieving had worn thin too, not to mention the philandering and gambling that went with it. When they returned to Sydney in early 1967, Paddy ran away from him, hiding out until she heard Arthur was on the move again.

Four decades later, when I met Paddy Burridge, she had lost nearly all the jewellery Arthur had given her—some of it stolen, some of it pawned. But one small, exquisite diamond brooch remained in her possession. 'It was all stolen, he said. Considering how it was acquired, you could call it karma,' she concluded.

But Arthur had left his mark upon Paddy. She never returned to the square life: the middle-class family, the values she learnt in the convent school. Living outside the square, she had flirted with her darker side and, like so many 'good girls', found it irresistible. It wasn't long before she returned to London, where she ran with thieves well into the 1970s.

By the summer of 1967, the Australian contingent in London was coming to notice. Word of Delaney's exploits had encouraged others to come try their luck. Scotland Yard began to speak of a 'Kangaroo Gang' operating in the West End as more high-value stores were being knocked off. Now even banks weren't safe.

One morning the Fibber and Arthur had robbed a high street bank of more than £20 000. As usual, there was no violence, no firearms, not even a raised voice. They had simply lined up with the staff at a side entrance before the bank opened, explaining they had been sent from head office to relieve for the day. They were so cheerful and confident, no-one suspected a thing. Once inside Arthur had hidden in a storeroom while the Fibber had prepared for the day, opening up the spare teller cage which he knew, from reconnaissance, would be there. He got his cash float just as the other tellers did.

At nine o'clock, when the doors opened, Arthur emerged from his hiding spot to be the first customer of the morning, filling out a withdrawal slip for £20 000. 'How would you like that, sir?' asked the Fibber as he prepared to count out the cash. They dined out on that story for years.

In reality, the Kangaroo Gang consisted of multiple gangs—a group of up to fifty mercenary thieves working stints in cohorts with a small number of master takes. There was Arthur and the Fibber, who worked together occasionally, and then there was 'Wee Jimmy' Lloyd, a former pickpocket who had learnt his trade on racetracks in Melbourne. As his name suggested, Wee Jimmy was a small wiry man who looked more at home trackside than on Bond Street, but he was regarded by many as the best take of them all. He had none of the polish and poise of Arthur Delaney, nor the flamboyance and magnetism of the Fibber. He was quiet and modest, but Wee Jimmy was relentless and highly skilled. He knew where to strike and when. He had method.

Wee Jimmy had been an apprentice to a legendary racetrack thief named Mickie Mutch at home in Melbourne. For a generation Mutch, a dapper little man with a feather in his hat, had worked Melbourne's racetracks and marshalled an ever-changing team of young assistants. For a generation, cadets at the police academy were shown photographs of

Mutch and told to be alert for him and his men at the racecourse, and also on the trains and trams taking shoppers back and forth to Melbourne's Queen Victoria Market. In those days, shoppers could still carry their live chickens and ducks home on public transport and the tram would be a colourful crowded place to work on market days.

A lot of 'good crooks'—numerous Kangaroo Gang members among them—had worked with Mutch on their way up. Wee Jimmy had learnt from Mutch that you had to work hard at this thing and save your money. Mutch would end up with the respect of all, plus a lovely home in the suburbs. Wee Jimmy wanted the same and England was the place to earn it—he had been working 25 years when he got there yet few in Australia, outside the police, had ever heard of him. Even today only hardcore crime buffs know anything of William Lloyd.

In one of his first London jobs, Wee Jimmy and his team knocked off the retailer Watches of Switzerland, in Knightsbridge. They had broken into the store on a weekend and erected hoardings around the windows with signs apologising for any inconvenience during 'the renovations'. They had cleaned the store out—Rolexes, Patek Philippes, Longines, every last watch went. And Wee Jimmy was versatile—from Swiss watches right down to haberdashery, you wouldn't go hungry working with Wee Jimmy.

Then there was gorgeous Georgie G, a Rock Hudson lookalike who had as much dash as anyone. Tall and charismatic, with flowing dark hair and a film-star smile, Georgie had made a name as a housebreaker in Melbourne.

Georgie's speciality was banks—the foreign exchange counters in particular. A series of violent robberies of English banks in the mid 1960s had led to a tightening of security. Teller positions were now being protected by cages but, as a cost-saving measure, the foreign exchange counters were still open. Georgie had developed an ingenious method of relieving the banks of their traveller's cheques and foreign exchange.

An accomplice would join the queue, making sure he was standing to the extreme right of the person in front. When he got to the counter, he would make sure the teller was drawn to the extreme left of their cubicle, leaving the till on the right exposed. Then he would barrage the teller with questions—highly intricate queries on exchange rates in far-flung countries, requests for Russian roubles or new Polish zlotys. Doling out traveller's cheques for tourists all day was a tedious job, so the teller would welcome the opportunity to display his knowledge.

When the head puller had the conversation flowing, Georgie would step forward; he would place his briefcase on the counter, open it and start looking through his papers. Then, in another queue, a distraction would be set up. It might be a fight between two 'drunks', a woman fainting, or a man throwing an epileptic fit. Ian Leeds, known as Mr Distraction, could simulate a very convincing *grand mal* fit, thrashing and twitching all over the floor; in fact he really was an epilepsy sufferer. The distraction would be carefully thought out to provide enough time for the take to do his work. A man urinating in the corner could provide up to a minute if required. A fight between two drunks could last for much longer.

When all the heads were pulled, Georgie would strike. He would whip out his telescopic car aerial with a hook attached to the end. Combining his height of over six foot, with the five feet of aerial, Georgie had an amazing reach. He could hook the bundles of currency or traveller's cheques by the rubber bands that held them and whip them back into the briefcase. He was so fast and deft that he was never caught. When the commotion died down, the teller would look back to find his till had been emptied.

Within 24 hours, the cheques would have been cashed as far away as Glasgow or Manchester. In the days before computer security coding and tracking, American Express relied on circulating lists of stolen cheques to retailers and banks. It might be weeks before such stolen cheque numbers were distributed. In 1967–68, it was estimated by Scotland Yard that Australian thieves had stolen more than a million pounds worth of cheques and foreign exchange. And Georgie G accounted for the greatest share.

William Herbert Hill's first conviction was in 1936 in the South Melbourne Children's Court for stealing, when he was fifteen. By the early 1960s, he had racked up more than 30 convictions, mostly for shop stealing, at a rate of three or four a year. It was all minor stuff—electric razors, blankets, shirts and sheets—but by 1964 he was spending more time in the dock or the boob than on the street. In October 1964, Hill had received a three-year good behaviour bond in Sydney's Paddington Petty Sessions. He was to report to Paddington police once a month and behave himself or face twelve months' hard labour.

Then he disappeared off Australia's law enforcement radar. For four years, the longest stretch of his career, there were no arrests or convictions.

But Billy Hill hadn't gone straight—he had gone to London to work. A photograph stolen by UK police from his flat in the 1970s showed Hill ready for a day on the hoist. The clock on the wall showed 9:05 am and Billy was in full business attire with bowler hat, cigar and rolled-up umbrella. The lags back home would hardly have recognised him done up like the chairman of the Bank of England. He was smiling broadly; he was moving in better circles now.

Back home, he had been a minor player—a hoist, an egg flipper (dipper) and a two-up cheat. In London he was 'the General', the scourge of West End retailers. Australians were flocking to London to work with him. He was much admired and imitated. When British justice did finally catch up with Hill in February 1968, he was convicted of receiving two passports, a savings bank book, three international driving permits and two blank driver's licences. He was sentenced to two years' jail. In his British police record, Hill's personality type was noted as 'Persistent Liar'.

Like Arthur, Hill had clearly come up in the world. He was now an international thief. At the Court of Appeal, his sentence was reduced to just five months and Hill was back on the hoist by July 1968. In October that year he was nicked on stealing goods worth a total of £300. Despite his long history, a Bow Street magistrate slapped him with a fine of £100 and a six-month jail sentence, suspended for three years. He would do regular short stretches in English jails for the next fifteen years, but the time was worth it for the money he earned when he was free. When Billy Hill was finally deported in 1985, it was discovered he had salted away £157 000 into a Royal Bank of Scotland account in a false name, Claude Lewis.

Hill specialised in robbing big department stores like Harrods and Selfridges, having concluded they were virtually indefensible to mob-handed thieving. The General would position a few of his troops in the Harrods banking chamber, then on the ground floor, where the cosmetics counters are located today. In those days, the banking chamber was a large open area with teller cages situated around the walls. There were numerous staircases and passageways leading off to the rest of the store. It was a popular meeting place for shoppers and thieves alike, who would wait on the green leather chairs in the centre. The shop jacks would also be there trying to blend in, watching the comings and goings.

Some decoys would hang around the chamber, trying deliberately to raise suspicion. It might be a Harrods silk tie or a scarf peeping from a pocket or a bulging bag under an overcoat. Sometimes, just acting sinister was enough. They then took off in different directions for a rambling tour of the store before returning to the banking chamber. They would do this over and over, until someone began to follow them. If that person was still following when they got back to the banking chamber, he or she would almost certainly be a store jack. Then the decoys would lead them all over the store again. With security identified, occupied and dispersed, the hoisting would begin. Whole racks of clothes, suits and fur coats would walk out the door. One morning a policeman driving past Harrods on Brompton Road saw Hill and his accomplices in the window, stripping shop dummies of the latest fashions. It was becoming that brazen.

There was something about Harrods that inspired hatred in ordinary Britons and thieves alike. Maybe its overt exclusivity rankled; perhaps Harrods and its owners, the House of Fraser, symbolised the outdated class structure that oppressed the people. From modest beginnings in 1849 as a small grocer's shop, Harrods had grown exponentially and was now the largest store in Europe. In its Edwardian splendour, Harrods now presided over a whole city block of 1.8 hectares (4.5 acres) with over 5.5 hectares (13.5 acres) of sales space on its five floors, 214 departments and 4000 staff. Its motto—Omnia, Omnibus, Ubique (Everything for Everyone, Everywhere)—seemed to mock the working class, still recovering from post-war shortages. It had everything for everyone who could afford it—or who could steal it.

The Fibber, having been nicked in Harrods on his first day in London, had a special contempt for Harrods thereafter. Often, when they had finished their hoisting in there, the Fibber would suggest to the Kid that they go have some fun. They might go to the menswear department and cut the sleeves off a rack of expensive suits; or they might slip into the book department and rip out the last page of a few classics of English literature. But the Fibber's favourite mischief spot was on the second floor, between the pianos and carpets. Harrods Zoo could supply its clients with almost anything exotic—from bush babies, toucans and five-guinea bullfrogs to African lion cubs. The Fibber would scurry up and down the rows of tanks and cages, setting all the birds and animals free and standing back to enjoy the chaos. Another pair of associates had once stolen a young chimpanzee from the Harrods Zoo on behalf of a buyer. They dressed the ape in baby clothes and pushed him away in a pram.

Each Christmas, after trading hours, Harrods would open exclusively for members of the royal family or (as they were trying to attract 'the hip set') the latest pop idols and movie stars. For two or three Christmases, Fibber and the Kid hid in cupboards until the store closed, and then emerged to have their pick of the store as the Beatles or Princess Margaret wandered around with their entourages.

The heavy toll the hoisters were wreaking on Harrods had become a topic of conversation amongst financial types in the City of London, though the House of Fraser was keen to downplay the matter. Sir Hugh Fraser, after enjoying business success early in his career, was under close scrutiny now. *Time* magazine had commented that Fraser could frequently be seen 'in the casinos of London and Monte Carlo, always at the roulette wheel and usually on a massive losing streak'.

'At one time Sir Hugh Fraser, at 40 one of Britain's more powerful businessmen, played back-to-back tables at Ladbroke's and lost the equivalent of half a million dollars in a single evening. To cover his losses, Fraser has been forced into selling an estimated US$2.4 million worth of stock in Scottish & Universal Investments Ltd, an associate company of the House of Fraser Ltd,' *Time* reported. The London Stock Exchange had investigated him for insider trading, such was his reckless gambling habit; he was cleared but excoriated in their report, which accused him of a 'lack of judgment' and 'inefficiency and ignorance of financial matters' in running the company.

'I think I have been a bloody fool,' admitted Sir Hugh, promising to swear off roulette. But he just switched his plunges to the racetrack. Sir Hugh must have thought his luck had changed when he backed a long-priced winner at Royal Ascot. That is, until the Kid stole the ticket from his waistcoat pocket.

This was getting right out of control now. In the *Guardian* of 15 August 1968, Baden Hickman wrote of a 'Vast shoplifting ring operating in Britain':

A highly organised gang of Australian shoplifters is at work in Britain stealing goods worth hundreds of thousands of pounds a year. New members of the gang are flown from Australia whenever the organisers want replacements. The Australians' activities are well known to the British Police and to security staff in large stores but the gang's organisation, outstanding for its professional thoroughness, has still to be beaten. The Australian shoplifters began working as a team seven years ago. There are sometimes as many as 60 working at one time in this country. They have carried out shoplifting at Newcastle, Sheffield, Liverpool, London and many other cities.

When Mr TWS Bowman, chief security officer for the John Lewis Partnership, addressed a conference in Manchester, he could hardly conceal his admiration. The Aussies were worthy adversaries: 'They are experts. They have some wonderful techniques. They have a highly organised set-up and are absolutely professional.'

What had been dismissed as 'shrinkage' or 'wastage' was now acknowledged as 'pilfering' as the cost hit a record £120 million per annum in 1967. Losses which had been traditionally around one per cent had quintupled to five per cent in many stores that year. Staff had joined in the fun, accounting for 40 to 50 per cent of the losses.

According to Bowman, the only way to head off the thieves was to have 'alert assistants, efficient management and security men and detectives who were encouraged to feel part of management'. This was a war against staff, customers and career hoisters. Store detectives had to be 'professional ratcatchers', 'highly inquisitive and answerable only to the head of the store . . . They should never take the same day off or work the same hours. They're people who trust nobody. It is a terrible way to go through life. It is the only way.'

Through constant vigilance the Aussies could be brought to heel, Bowman asserted. The traditional store signs of 'cashier' and 'wages office' should be removed: they were 'unnecessary aids to wage snatchers'. There should be strength in numbers—retailers were advised to set up group warning arrangements, so that the arrival of a suspected shoplifter in an area could be made widely known.

The retailers, horrified that their vulnerability had been laid open to the public, quickly responded by setting up bodies like the West End Retailers Protection Association. Arthur Delaney, who was an avid reader of newspapers, must have noted the new security arrangements with great mirth. By this time he was a veteran well-known to retailers and police, but his notoriety would be a plus. He began to wander into various stores and strut around, challenging security staff to notice him.

In panic, shopkeepers would call in shop detectives from other stores to help monitor the King.

Some just came to watch him work, but Delaney wasn't there to steal. He would walk the store for hours on end, picking things up, putting them down, asking questions of staff and generally acting as sinister as he could. As the massed detectives followed him round, comically trying not to be noticed, Delaney's team would be cleaning out the stores they had left unprotected.

As they all worked together at one time or other, there were techniques common to all the Kangaroo Gang members. They even brought their criminal argot to England, which allowed them to communicate freely in shops or even in custody. It was common to buy some small items in shops they intended to rob, to get the staff out 'the hammer and tack' (back). Just how many items were to be bought (or how many shop jacks were on hand) could be relayed in code, thus:

Currant bun = 1
Nellie Bligh = 2
Mother McCree = 3
George Moore = 4
Bee Hive = 5
Tom Mix or Dorothy Dix = 6
St Bevan = 7
Mary at The Cottage Gate = 8
Tilly Devine = 9
Big Ben = 10

The thieves had also brought a kind of Pidgin English from Sydney that relied upon moving the first letter of the word to the end of the word and adding the suffix '-ar' to the end. For example, *bus* would become *usbar* and *twice* was *wicetar*. Full sentences were rendered in this code. For example, 'Be lively and get on the bus' became: 'Ebar ivelylar and etgar noar hetar usbar'. This could also be further muddied by the use of rhyming slang. 'Look at those sheilas' tits' in rhyming slang was 'take a butcher's hook at that three-wheeler's Boston bits'. But in Pidgin it was virtually indecipherable: 'Aketar a utchersbar ookhar ta-ar hattar hreetar heelerswar ostonbar itsbar!' A shop detective, or some other adversary, would be an 'enryhar hetar hirdtar', derived from the rhyming slang for *a turd* being *a Henry the Third.* Whole conversations could be carried on in front of bewildered police, who never learnt to crack the code. As long as gang members could understand each other, it could be as complex as they liked.

It wasn't all smooth sailing for the lads, however. When the Fibber and the Kid hit Selfridges on Oxford Street in early 1967, the upmarket retailer had been compiling a dossier on the Aussies. When the Kid tried to walk out with a crystal bird inside his coat, the shop jacks were right onto him. Two shop jacks, a copper passing by and the little Asian shop assistant gave chase down Oxford Street. It was a freezing cold day, so the Kid was dressed up in a singlet, shirt, waistcoat, jacket and overcoat. Running was almost impossible in this clobber—he could also feel an asthma attack coming on—but he gave it everything as he bolted down Regent Street heading east.

At Wedgewood Mews, with the posse still in hot pursuit, he turned right. For a moment he was out of sight, so he dropped the crystal bird down a manhole straight into the mud. An onlooker joined the parade at Soho Street so the Kid desperately pointed ahead: 'Quick, he's getting away! After him!' But the man wasn't to be fooled: 'I think it's you they are after,' he said, grabbing the Kid's collar as they rounded into Greek Street. It was time for desperate measures.

The Kid always carried in his pocket a silver aluminium comb, sometimes two. They were perfect for lifting the lids of glass cabinets without leaving fingerprints. He whipped the comb out. He was banking on the hope that, if he gnashed his teeth and slashed the air violently enough, the man would think it was a knife and back off. But he didn't; instead, he threw a bear hug on the Kid who, now exhausted, was relieved the marathon was over. He had run nearly a mile. Soon the posse caught up and the shop assistant delivered a couple of painful kicks to the Kid's shins.

Just then the Fibber caught up and joined the throng gathering around the Kid. A double-decker bus had just pulled up and the Fibber, as always, had a plan. In their code language, he suggested he was about to belt the shop jacks and they could leap aboard the bus and make an improbable escape. But the Kid was done in and told the Fibber he was going to accept his fate. He was dragged back to Selfridges and deposited in the security manager's office while the bobbies were summoned. Having ditched the crystal bird in the manhole, he felt confident he was in the clear. He told security he had only run away because people had been chasing him. Perhaps they knew his visa had expired, he said, full of sorrow. Not sure what to do next, the security manager locked the Kid in the office and went off to consult his colleagues.

Left to his own devices in the citadel of the enemy, the Kid decided to use his time productively. He began ferreting through an unlocked filing cabinet. The first drawer he opened contained security dossiers on prominent shoplifters, complete with photographs. The first head he saw was Arthur Delaney's, and a good likeness it was too. Better do something about that, he thought. He took the photograph and shredded it, letting the pieces fall like confetti to Oxford Street below. He went back to the cabinet and did the same to as many of the Aussies' pictures as he could. Then he heard a commotion going on outside the door, so he quickly jumped back into his chair.

The security manager and some of the store jacks burst through the door, wrestling with the Fibber, who was protesting loudly. Not knowing that the Kid had ditched the bird, the Fibber had tried to sneak in to liberate his protégé. Now they were both in the soup, but the Fibber was facing two and a half years in jail, courtesy of a good behaviour bond from an earlier misadventure that he had not managed to break down with a bribe. The Kid was torn—he had never pleaded guilty to anything in his life, but his mate was looking at a lengthy stay in the boob. He confessed all; the bird was recovered and the Kid faced court fully expecting to end the day in jail. To his amazement, the magistrate not only accepted his false name but, as the accused was a first offender, he handed down the lightest sentence possible: a £15 fine.

But even as they enjoyed victories like this, a picture of the Kangaroo Gang, which in fact consisted of a number of separate gangs, was finally emerging. As Mr Bowman told the Manchester conference: 'They work in teams of up to ten. There are one or two Australian women and also one or two English girls involved.' The chance to work with the gangs provided a novel alternative for Aussie girls looking for a working holiday in Britain, and Australian police began to monitor the social pages as Bright Young Things from Sydney and Melbourne announced their departures. Liaison between English and Australian police was patchy and inconsistent, but occasionally gems of intelligence were shared.

In June 1968, New South Wales detectives sent a newspaper cutting from the *Sydney Morning Herald* to intelligence officers at New Scotland Yard that was headed 'Extra, Extra—Dixie Wants A Job'. It continued:

Dixie Day, of Elizabeth Bay, nearly 6ft tall and strikingly attired, left Sydney for London yesterday with three other models who hope to become professional film extras—at least. Resplendent in wild fashions and huge sunglasses, the four girls left by Qantas with bags of clothes, wigs and a large collection of cosmetics. Dixie has a film test in London next month. She said: 'It's for a Warren Beatty film—but I don't know what part it will be for. We are all looking for film roles—extras if nothing else. You get paid quite well, and if it fails, we could do some modelling.

Certainly, working as a hoister's helper was a little like modelling—but it was more like acting. Women turning heads in Sydney were now pulling them in London. It must have felt like appearing in the movies. What became of Dixie Day's film ambitions is not known. She never got a part in any Warren Beatty film, but she and her companions quickly fell in with the hoisters, as predicted by the New South Wales police.

Not every girl got a start in London with the Kangaroo Gang. You had to come with references and a certain appeal to the bosses of the individual gangs, like Arthur, Wee Jimmy, Georgie G and the General. But once in, they wouldn't give you up. There would be fake IDs, accommodation and clothing organised. You would always get your share of the booty, even if you were only a head puller. A woman scorned could bring down a whole team and they knew it. And if you were caught there would be bail money and legal representation.

In those early years, it rarely got that far. Just like in Sydney, you could pay the bobbies to drop off. A 'monkey' (500 quid) was what it took and it became standard kit for all the Aussies. By 1966, the Metropolitan Police was so corrupt that Home Secretary Roy Jenkins had considered replacing up to 70 per cent of the CID and other specialist branches with CID from Manchester, Kent, Devon and Cornwall, and Birmingham. And in 1968, it was just getting worse.

6
A treat for the eyes

'London is turning out to be the dumping ground for crooks from all over the world, pickpockets, shoplifters, the lot . . . Make no mistake there is an Australian gang. There is no Mr Big, the operation is run more like a committee but they are getting caught across the country.'

Richard Brindley, 28, security chief for one of the
big stores on London's Oxford Street

As reports of the Aussie crime wave circulated through Scotland Yard, Detective Constable Mike Pearce reflected on the fact that he had not joined the Metropolitan Police to sit behind a desk. From his father and grandfather, he had learnt that a good copper was always out and about—walking, talking and listening. His grandfather had been a village bobby in Cornwall in south-west England. Of his seven sons, five (including Mike's father) were policemen.

Mike had two other cousins in the cops, but he was the first of the

Pearces who had gone up to London. As the Kray and Richardson gangs battled for control of London's underworld, he had expected to find himself in the thick of the action, not trapped behind a pile of hard wood in a back room at New Scotland Yard. He had been assigned to C11, the Yard's criminal intelligence branch. It sounded glamorous, in a James Bond kind of way, but C11 was the poor relation of the secret squirrel family. Under-resourced and mostly overlooked, it had been operating only since March 1960. C11's role was limited to supporting operational units like the Flying Squad, which operated solely on intelligence. It would collate data on targets from the Criminal Records Office and carry out limited surveillance on the crooks before handing over the file to the field squads.

Around the Yard, C11 was known as 'The Gurkhas', an ironic reference to the famous Nepalese regiment of the British Army. Like the Gurkhas, C11 took no prisoners. But the squad had slowly evolved from its clerical origins. Now C11 boasted a detective chief inspector, a first class sergeant, and two detective constables, equipped with three vehicles. There were also four area teams—comprising a detective inspector and a sergeant—who visited stations around London to gather information and photographs. Four indentikit officers made up the photofit profiles of suspects from witnesses. There was a tailing team too—a chubby constable on a motor scooter who followed the villains through London, snapping a few pictures and doing his best not to fall off. Two officers were formally assigned as photographers. They usually rigged up their own gear at home, relying on an assortment of concealed cameras inside box files, briefcases or mounted in the rear of a Morris Minor van for long-range work.

As crude as their gear was, the C11 snappers posed the greatest threat to the Kangaroo Gang. Many of the gang's real identities were unknown to police in the early days. Many held multiple Australian passports—it was a simple matter to front an Australian High Commission in, say, Papua New Guinea or Fiji, to claim you had lost your passport and then obtain a duplicate. A thief could travel to Europe and back on the duplicate and present his real passport to London police; it would show he had never left the UK, no matter how many eyewitnesses claimed to have seen him stealing in Paris, Rome or Basel.

The Aussies were also heavily involved in a thriving illicit trade in false British Visitor passports—one-year travel documents designed for people making short trips to the Continent. Georgie G and Normie Seddon had stolen wads of the blank passports from post offices and government benefit offices. They were the key to the free movement of the thieves across the world and they had just been sitting on the counter, begging to be stolen. Once in possession of the blank visitor passport and a couple of bodgie stamps, the thief could establish a new identity simply by opening a bank account in a false name. He would rent an 'accommodation address', a sparsely furnished flat in that name to satisfy the bank, while living elsewhere.

In those years, before closed-circuit video, gang members enjoyed the most perfect anonymity in London. The scam enabled them to shuttle personnel unseen to and from Australia for years. A guy would disappear from Sydney and bob up in London on a different passport. Only a photograph could help the English and Australian cops join the dots, but at that time their modus operandi was far from well-understood. So valuable were their real passports that Seddon and Georgie G never risked the police stumbling upon them in a search of premises. They stored all the gang's real Aussie passports, plus a host of other fakes, in a safe deposit box in the St James Square branch of the NatWest Bank.

With the gang wars raging in the East End and armed robbers running amok, the hard men of the Flying Squad—known in cockney rhyming slang as the Sweeney Todd or the Heavy Mob—got the glory of making the arrests, and each time the clerical cops of C11 would return to their paperwork. While this was going on, there was little interest at the Yard in chasing the Aussies—it was only shoplifting after all. There was no violence, no fuss and there was often a quid in it for the Old Bill. C11 was remote from the corruption as they never dealt with the crims in person or 'felt their collars' (lest the unit's undercover identities be revealed), but C11's snapper could have brought the Aussies undone early in the piece. Instead, the Kangaroo Gang was left to run wild.

Pearce aimed to join the Heavy Mob as soon as he could, but in the meantime he wasn't going to spend his time solely on paperwork. As he walked briskly down Bond Street on a summer afternoon in August 1967, he remarked to himself how nice it felt to be out the door. At 26, he was a tall slim man, but barrel-chested and straight-backed. With his suit immaculate and shoes shined to a mirror finish, he looked the very image of a copper. The detective sergeant at C11 had suggested he take a look at the scene of the latest in a string of jewel robberies on Bond Street.

Twenty-three gold and diamond rings—each set with a stone ranging from three to five carats—had disappeared from a window display at Bensons of Bond Street, one of the leading jewellers of the day. The theft had come as a complete surprise to the staff. They had been busy that day, so they hadn't even noticed the loss and had only raised the alarm when one of them bumped the display door and it swung open. They had then noticed the padlocks on the displays had been cut through. Just when that had occurred was a mystery.

All they could remember was that a very well-dressed couple in their thirties or forties, possibly accompanied by a younger man, had lingered by the display some three or four hours earlier. Staff couldn't remember much, except that the pair had been carrying various large parcels and perhaps they were Australians, Pearce was told. Staff had been busy with other customers at the counter, so they hadn't paid attention to the trio; and now they couldn't help much. Pearce concluded this would be just another unsolved jewel theft.

Even when I met the long-retired Pearce—accompanied by another C11 veteran, Brian James—in a Knightsbridge pub in March 2009, he remembered that job with a certain admiration: 'It's not often you can admire the handiwork of the opposition,' he chuckled. He had always wondered how they had pulled it off. I was able to tell him. In a Sydney café a month earlier, the Kid had explained how he, Grace and Fibber had done it. 'We were eight-handed that day,' cried the Kid, through peals of laughter. 'Just about everyone in the shop at that time was with us!'

To get away with a job is, of course, the object of the exercise. The 'tom' (short for tomfoolery, rhyming slang for jewellery) had fetched more than £20 000. However, there is always a part of the thief that craves recognition. He doesn't want to go to jail but he wants people to know how he pulled off the big jobs. He wants the respect that's due to his skill and dash. And the Kid was no different.

'It was the bunch of flowers,' he said. Grace had bought a bouquet of flowers and made a sturdy cardboard cone, wrapped in gift paper. She had stuck flowers around the edge of the 'bouquet' till you couldn't tell it from a real one. Then, in the middle of one of the busiest trading days, Fibber, Grace and the Kid had hit Bensons. When all the heads were pulled, the Kid dropped down on one knee before the display window, blocked by Fibber, Grace and their parcels. Grace opened a flap of her bouquet and the Kid eased out a pair of bolt cutters hidden inside. *Snip, snip, snip.* Within a few seconds the Kid had the display open. They were in and out of Bensons in less than ten minutes. This was so easy it was getting ridiculous, the Kid had thought at the time.

But the Bensons job was the turning point. Until then, police had shown little zeal in their pursuit of the Aussies. But Mike Pearce could see an opportunity here. He believed that, if he could compile a catalogue of the Aussies operating in the UK, the police might have a chance of collaring them. If existing mug shot photographs were compiled and compared with any new surveillance pictures, they would create thumbnail sketches that could be circulated across the country and the entire Commonwealth for that matter. As a result of that insight, in time a pile of assorted files on the Australians would plop down on Pearce's desk and from that would grow a full-scale intelligence operation, at that time unique in the history of UK crime fighting.

In the early sixties, Arthur Delaney and the early Kangaroos had operated below the radar, hitting stores and shops which didn't care to report their thefts in any great detail. Wee Jimmy and Billy Hill had turned this into an industry, hoisting vast amounts of clothes and luxury items to order. There was so much stuff being nicked that it could not all be fenced in England, so a large amount of contraband found its way to Australia and New Zealand. Through his old wharfie connections, the Fibber had organised for some of this surplus to be shipped to Sydney via the government-owned Australian National Line. It was landed at the Port of Balmain and then stored in a warehouse in Sydney's Haymarket. If a New South Wales police officer were deemed to have 'done the right thing', he would be handed a key to the warehouse so he could take his pick in this Aladdin's cave of London fashion and luxury goods.

But when Georgie G and Seddon began brazenly hitting English banks for traveller's cheques and foreign exchange, the attitude of police changed. A relative of one of the senior commanders at Scotland Yard was a director of Lloyd's Bank. The word came down from on high that it was time to put some work into nabbing these bumptious Australians. Pearce was overjoyed to be let loose—this was going to be a treat for the eyes and ears.

Pearce had a contact—an Aussie named Billy Broughton, who worked at a Paddington pub in west London as a bartender and knew all the

Kangaroos. Through Broughton's tips, followed up with physical surveillance, Pearce began to create a picture of their network. The leaders were highly skilled at counter-intelligence, but the troops were often less disciplined.

In the winter of 1967–68, the tail team motorcyclist followed a yellow Lotus Elan driven at high speed by an Aussie hoister named Barry 'Verbal' Muir. Apparently Verbal was oblivious to the tail—this was just how he drove all the time. They had followed him from his house through the West End and he had smoked the tyres at every opportunity, challenging other drivers to race him, and generally throwing the Lotus about to annoy or terrify. After Verbal shot through a red light on Regents Park Road at 90 mph, the tail was discontinued. But they caught up with the Lotus later, parked at a café by the Serpentine, a lake in Hyde Park. It was just a stone's throw from Harrods at Knightsbridge.

Pearce worked out that a group of Australians with a few English associates were meeting at the café every morning of the week. It was like a staff canteen for the girls and boys clocking on with the retail teams Wee Jimmy and Billy Hill had working Knightsbridge relentlessly every day. It was a place where Aussies just off the plane could try to get a start in the trade. There by the lake they would discuss the day's thieving ahead, taking the specific orders to be filled, finalising tactics and personnel, sharing news of security arrangements and shop features before setting off in smaller groups. They would often return later in the day to divvy up the day's take. It was a well-worn routine—a job.

In the evenings, the Aussies would meet at small private clubs like the Court Club on Bayswater Road, Paddington, or the Embassy at Hammersmith. Restrictive licensing laws back then meant that pubs closed at 10:30 pm, but a loophole allowed alcohol to be served at all hours in private clubs, so they had flourished across the city. Over a period of weeks, the C11 photographer managed to snap more than 50 of the gang at different watering holes or on visits to each other's homes. But without confirmation of the true identity of the subjects, the value of these pictures was limited.

Interpol, first known as the International Criminal Police Commission, had been set up as a liaison between national police forces in 1923 with its headquarters in Vienna, Austria. During World War II, the Nazis had taken over and deposed the secretary general and moved the headquarters to Berlin. After the war, the organisation was rebuilt and a new base established in Paris, but by the 1960s it was still struggling for relevance. Pearce regarded it as virtually useless—nothing more than a post office box in those days. The official protocol required Scotland Yard to send information, including fingerprints and photographs of Australian nationals of interest to Interpol Headquarters, which then relayed them to Interpol Canberra. It usually took months to get the wheels turning, unless the suspect was accused of murder. Shoplifting, even on the scale now evident, barely roused the interest of Interpol.

So Pearce made direct contact with 'Ozzie' Morris, an officer from the Modus Operandi Section of New South Wales police in Sydney, and suggested they set up a formal joint intelligence sharing effort to track the movements of the hoisters between Sydney and London. Morris just laughed: 'For Chrissakes, don't go through formal channels, mate. We'll never get anywhere. Let's just work this out between ourselves, eh?' That was fine by Pearce and C11. Morris sent mug shots of all the suspected Aussie crims travelling to England and the Continent, along with their fingerprints and criminal records. Pearce then matched the surveillance pictures to the mug shots, to work out just who was plying their trade in the United Kingdom.

Pearce also informally made the acquaintance of Len Nelson, a consular official at the Australian High Commission in London. Pearce was convinced many of the Aussies were carrying false passports, or at least multiple copies of their own. He took all his information about the passports to Australia House in Sloane Square. Nelson was overjoyed— finally someone shared his own concerns: 'I've been telling these fuckers back in Australia for rather a long time this lurk has been going on. And now you've got proof of it. Can I please have a copy?'

Through Nelson and Ozzie Morris, Pearce developed an early warning system for Aussies who were coming to England to work as thieves. In return, C11 supplied the High Commission with details of English criminals who were planning working holidays Down Under.

The first 'Australian Index' was published as a supplement to the *Police Gazette* in December 1967. It was the first time UK police had created a database of criminals sorted by offence. It would be an invaluable aid in bringing the Aussies to heel and the only costs would be a few rolls of film plus the printer's blocks. 'Attention of Forces is drawn to the after-described Australian criminals and their associates', the preamble read.

> [They] are known to be domiciled in the United Kingdom and actively engaged in stealing from shops, travel agencies and banks.
>
> All are accomplished shoplifters who concentrate on high-value articles from department stores, jewellers and travellers cheques from agencies and banks, throughout the United Kingdom and the Continent. The method employed by these persons is to visit premises in groups and while the assistant's attention is distracted by some members of the team either making fictitious enquiries or small purchases, others steal valuables and often bulky items of property.
>
> These persons are never resident in any one area for any length of time and this creates difficulty in recording their movements and those of their new associates. It is requested on the arrest of any Australian shoplifter, full details of passport(s) where possible be forwarded to Criminal Records Office for transmission to Australian Authorities. Any information in respect of these or any other Australian criminals should be forwarded to local criminal intelligence officers and collators.

For the first time, English cops could peruse the entire motley gang in one eleven-page document, rather than sifting through thousands of files from the Criminal Records Office. Those of interest were listed according to the date when their file was created at the Criminal Records Office. Anyone who was anyone in hoisting at this particular time is recorded here. Pearce and his successors at C11 were meticulous in the compilation of the names.

There has long been debate about the identity of the first Aussie hoisters to hit England. Even today there are old lags still propping up bars in Sydney and Melbourne who claim to have been members of the Kangaroo Gang. The publication of the Australian Index for the first time in this book should settle those debates—if you don't get a mention in the Australian Index, it probably means you weren't there. I am prepared to consider cases for inclusion if applicants present compelling evidence for the next edition of this book!

If you Google 'Kangaroo Gang members', only a couple of names pop up. Legendary armed robber Raymond Patrick 'Chuck' Bennett is credited as the leader of the gang—with an associate, Brian Leslie O'Callaghan, he supposedly robbed jewellery shops all over Europe. While Bennett and O'Callaghan did serve a sentence on the Isle of Wight over a housebreaking in the early 1970s, neither rates a mention in the Australian Index.

For the sake of accuracy, it should be pointed out that the first name in the Australian Index was in fact a New Zealander—Richard Marshall alias Richard Johnson, Richard Mongovin, Richard Chapman, Richard Campbell, Leslie Campbell, Eric Campbell and Richard Charles Marshall. He was otherwise known by the nicknames 'King' and 'Dinkum Dick'. His English record began in 1955 after a solid career in Sydney and New Zealand, which included convictions for larceny, dangerous driving and false pretences. It's understood that Dinkum Dick came to London with some other associates after a racing scam went wrong—a doped horse took a terrible fall and angry punters were after him.

At numbers five and six in the *Gazette*'s hoisters parade were Arthur Delaney and his original 1962 shipmate, Kevin Leo Conway, also known as Frank Collins. Arthur was described in minute detail: his alias Charles Bourke (the name was borrowed from a famous Sydney dog trainer-cum-standover man who was machine gunned to death in 1964; Arthur had lived with Bourke's widow at one time); five foot seven, dark complexion; the scar on the bridge of his nose; his tattoos—the woman's face on his left arm captioned 'Betty' (the name of an early love with whom he had a daughter). There were eagles on his left arm and wrist. By this time, he had convictions for assault occasioning bodily harm and he was a 'suspected person' in pickpocketing and larceny in England, Australia and Amsterdam. He was travelling well—his last conviction had been three years earlier—but police were now seeking him for obtaining a British Visitors passport by false statements.

'Wee Jimmy' Lloyd and his brother Cecil 'Mugsi' Lloyd had come to notice a year later, occupying numbers 8 and 20 in the gallery. In five years, Wee Jimmy had accumulated a long list of aliases through the use of false passports, including: William Ritchie, Thomas Lee, Peter William Lloyd, James Edward Wilson, Harry Lee, Arthur Jessop, William Edward Lloyd, Peter Lloyd, William Itchie, James Wilson, George Wilson and, with an indigenous touch, James Edward Marrumburrah. The only constant during his years as a travelling crook were the nicknames—'Wee Jummy' and 'Jimmy Wee'. He could be identified through his fresh complexion (though he was already 47), his receding hairline and a deformed fourth finger on his right hand. He had convictions for larceny and pickpocketing in Australia and Switzerland.

At number 17, the Fibber had persuaded British justice that he was Eric Martell. The real Martell had worked with the Fibber and Billy Longley in Gang 83 on the Melbourne wharves back in the 1950s. Longley had married Martell's sister. 'Bubba' Martell and the Fibber had studied under the master conman Jack Craig. Martell had been a skilled two-up cheat and had passed on knowledge to the Fibber, so to use his name as an alias was a fitting homage.

The Fibber's real name, Patrick William Warren, was listed as an alias with another, Lawrence Edward Callaghan. He was described as tanned with brown/grey thinning hair and brown eyes. His tattoos included a sailor girl on his right arm and two nude women on his left. No C11 profiler seems to have been brave enough to test the story that Fibber had the number 1 inked on his penis, though its power to identify him would have been irresistible. Remarkably, they had allowed him to be photographed in his wig. His nicknames included 'Pat the Liar', 'Leo the Liar' and 'The Fib'. It was believed he was usually accompanied by Margaret Linda Warren, who claimed to police that she was his daughter. There was also an unnamed son born in 1952, the apprentice Barry. 'When in custody will attempt to bribe police officers', his entry concluded.

Just making the Top 50 at number 48 was 'Ray Gilson', otherwise known by the alias Athol George Mulley. The Kid had been at school with Ray Gilson and his name served the Kid well—he was never known to police under his own name. He was barely 21 in his mug shot, but he looked much older. Though he was stick-thin, the Kid had a malleable, fleshy face he could contort to produce any impression he needed. Witnesses could swear they had been robbed variously by an Eton schoolboy or a Scottish lord, such was his mastery of accents and dialects. If you measure success by the ratio of jail time to riches, the Kid could lay claim to be the best of them all—he was way ahead. Despite some very close scrapes, the heaviest punishment the Kid suffered for his time in England was a £15 fine.

Georgie G didn't make the Top 50, but at number 63 was still a high profile target for C11. It was believed he was the leading player in a wave of bank robberies taking place across England that had netted the villains one million pounds in one year. Australian police supplied his record, featuring convictions for larceny, robbery, assault, possessing housebreaking implements, receiving stolen goods, and breaking of shops, houses, offices and garages. He was described as six foot one with a dark complexion, distinguished by scars on his arms and fingers from tattoo removal. At 27 he was the youngest of the leaders of the Kangaroo Gang, but he enjoyed the respect of both villains and police alike.

His sidekick, Norman Richard Seddon (number 73), was easier to identify. A stout man of medium height, his fellow hoisters thought he bore a striking resemblance to US comic Lou Costello of Abbott and Costello fame. He was also liberally inked in tattoos, which included 'Rose of My Heart', playing cards and a donkey's head from Shakespeare's *A Midsummer Night's Dream* on his right arm and, on his left, two hearts with a padlock, Mum, Dad, a rose, an Australian flag (though he was a New Zealander by birth), a sailing ship and an eagle. Across his knuckles he had the words LOVE and BABY. The English police always knew Seddon by his alias, John Noel Jones, rather than his given name. His string of names included Allan Ronald Richards, Joseph William, Norman Richard Harrison, Ronald Richards and Norman John Jones—just some of the names in which he held passports.

When Grace 'The Case' O'Connor made her *Gazette* debut in 1967, she had racked up only a couple of larceny charges during her year in England—the last, in June 1967, had been dismissed. She was among 28 women to be included in that first edition. Most of the females were supporting players, making up the numbers as head pullers or girlfriends along for the ride, but not Grace. Officially the 29-year-old was known as Grace Ann Wilkinson; her aliases included Grace Campbell, Rita Dalzall, Grace Anne McKenzie and Grace Duckworth. From her grainy photograph, it's easy to see why she was so popular with men. Though not classically beautiful, there was something magnetic about her fair complexion and dark smouldering eyes, her generous mouth and plump Cupid's bow lips, accentuated by a thick gloss of lipstick. She was listed as five foot six with dark brown hair, born at Colchester in Essex, though few back home knew it. Grace had convictions for 'larceny, housebreaking, robbery, soliciting prostitution etc', the *Gazette* summarised modestly, underselling her form.

On page 12, a hard, thin-lipped woman, whom we shall call Susie for legal reasons, looked through the camera with studied belligerence. The 27-year-old had no form in England, only convictions for larceny back in Australia. Grace O'Connor had never met Susie, but their lives were to intersect tragically later in this story.

The publication of the Australian Index yielded results almost immediately. When Dixie Day and her fellow 'models' landed in England in August 1968, they were surprised to find the bobbies were already acquainted with their history, courtesy of Ozzie Morris and the MO Section in New South Wales. Day, the aspiring actress, had prior convictions for larceny and used the aliases Jacqueline Ann Croft and Diane Croft. Carmel Shipley came up as Carmel Marshall Smythe, with a history of thieving back in Australia. Helen Ruth Williams, alias Helen Ruth Todd, didn't even set foot in England—on 29 August 1968 she was refused entry on the basis of her Australian convictions.

The Australian Index also included English villains who were known to associate with or assist the Kangaroo Gang. Forty-seven-year-old Peter Robin Meadows had convictions going back to 1949, but he wasn't a shoplifter. He made the list as the owner of Instant Car Hire, a source of untraceable rental cars for the Aussies. Whenever the team needed to quickly off-load stolen cheques in another regional town or grab some wheels for a hoisting tour, it was straight to Instant Car Hire they went.

David William 'Glasses' Barry had befriended many of the shoplifters, including the Kid. He was always there with tips on where to fence stolen goods; he would hook them up with English helpers when they were needed, or occasionally participate himself. They respected him as a major league criminal in his own right. The Aussies might not have been so friendly had they known he was a double agent. His entry noted that, behind the horn-rimmed spectacles and the mild demeanour, Barry 'was a cunning and violent individual who when previously arrested offered to assist Police recover stolen property and supply information in respect of other thieves. Care should be exercised when dealing with this man who avers that he is friendly with senior CID officers and makes suggestions tantamount to bribery.'

In September 1966, English thief Morris Spurling had returned to London from two years' jail in Switzerland for 'professional fraud' (nicking diamonds from jewellers in Zurich) and found his old stomping ground was now overrun with Australian hoisters. Rather than beat them, he resolved to join them—'the best of my kind or ilk or whatever you like to put it', he wrote later. He was introduced to some of the Kangaroo Gang at the Mount Club, then London's biggest gambling club. It was a fortuitous meeting—the Aussies never readily accepted English thieves, but clearly Spurling had something to offer.

'I was to get fortunes with the Australians. They knew more stings and scams than I'd ever imagined,' Spurling wrote in his autobiography, *A Diamond Fell in My Pocket*. In his view, the Aussies had the dash to exploit opportunities that few Englishmen would tackle. 'Years ago the West End was a gift. It was an absolute pension. You used to go out broke in the morning and get whatever money you needed until you wanted to stop. It was "Help Yourself".' The Aussies 'were the crème-de-la-crème of all the shoplifting and hoisting gangs that ever worked in Britain'.

Every day in the newspapers there were stories of their exploits under headlines like: 'Australian Gang Strikes Again'. Spurling had seen plenty of good thieves in 20 years on the hoist, but the Aussies had an esprit de corps unique in London's underworld. 'They were what we call "Good People" and you don't see the likes of them nowadays in this drug-related society . . . As a group they were very staunch people . . . If one of them happened to get arrested and it cost money to get him out [immediately] they chipped in and put in what they considered was their share. They would look after each other. Money wasn't their abiding thing in life. They would always help someone who was broke or in trouble,' he wrote.

And Spurling was always in trouble or broke, or both. Gambling is not a disease (life being a calculated risk for many), but there are diseased gamblers and Spurling was chronic and self-destructive. Whatever he took in the morning would end up in the bookies' bags or with croupiers at the Mount Club or Victoria Sporting Club before bedtime. To feed this ferocious habit, Spurling had developed some skill as a taker in England and Europe, 'palming' diamonds or 'switching' genuine stones for fawnies or cubic zirconia. He had some skill, but he was such a desperate scrounger. He would always come unstuck eventually through poor judgement—a lone strike at a well-guarded store, or returning to the same stores with a risible disguise.

But Spurling was useful to Arthur and the other gang leaders. He looked and acted the part. The French newspapers had once described him as 'Un Anglais Très Comme Il Faut' (The Perfect Englishman) for his courtly manner, a legacy of his upper middle-class Jewish upbringing in Tottenham. He had the arrogance of the rich man used to getting his own way. Slim, tanned and almost dignified with his prominent bald head, he looked a man of substance. He became one of the best head pullers the Aussies ever used. So 'Morry the Head', as he became known, and his partner in crime, Brian 'The Swan' Kutner, got a start with the team.

By Morry's own admission, the two Englishmen were the most unpopular thieves in Western Europe, if not the world: '[The Swan] has burnt more bridges than I have and I have burnt every one. I've got no friends, no family, he's got no-no friends and no-no family. We're birds of a feather,' he wrote. Spurling wasn't trusted enough to be the taker—he was also judged to be too nervous and anxious. Only Arthur, Wee Jimmy, Georgie G and a few trusted protégés were considered skilled enough for that.

'During those years I had run into all the top gangsters and thieves through meeting them at these gambling clubs. But the Australians were the weirdest bunch of crooks I ever came across. They elevated shoplifting to an art form,' according to Morry the Head. He idolised Arthur. The Duke was 'like a young edition of Robert Redford. Blondish hair, very smart, always immaculately dressed, medium built, he was very good looking and he was actually the governor. He was in charge of the whole Australian shoplifting gang. He used to go to any town where they were going to work the next day, walk the streets, prepare everything. He was really an extraordinarily good planner. He used to boast of his exploits, calling himself "The World's Raffles", the best thief in the world.'

EW Hornung, the brother-in-law of Sherlock Holmes' author Arthur Conan Doyle, created the character of Arthur J Raffles in the 1890s, but the Duke was playing him to a tee in the 1960s. Raffles was a clever inversion of the Sherlock Holmes character—he was a gentleman, a man about town, residing in salubrious London digs called The Albany while playing cricket for the Gentlemen of England. But he led a double life, carrying out daring and ingenious burglaries with the help of Harry 'Bunny' Manders, an old school chum Raffles saved from disgrace and suicide. Raffles shared with Holmes a mastery of disguise—in a studio apartment leased in a false name he kept a vast array of disguises and he could mimic the regional dialects of the United Kingdom flawlessly, despite his lack of skill at foreign languages.

But whereas Raffles occasionally needed the help of the faithful Manders to extricate himself from strife, the Duke was a cool and calculating master, a pioneer in his art. The distraction method was almost unbeatable, when executed with the confidence the Duke's team possessed. Spurling watched with amazement as the takers, Arthur's protégés, cleaned out entire shop windows of jewellery on Bond Street. One busy Saturday afternoon, he watched Keith Low leave a store with two suitcases full of jewellery: 'I started to laugh because I couldn't believe it. As I walked out the shop I noticed the windows were bare, not a single piece of jewellery left in the windows.'

Morry the Head would alert Arthur to new targets, such as jewellery shops inside the expensive hotels—the Grosvenor, the Dorchester, the Ritz and the Hilton. They did all the best hotels in London, over and over. Morry the Head would brief the Aussies on the prize on offer and they would think their way through how they might seize it. Morry's local knowledge was useful but, when creditors were pressing hard, his judgement of an earn could be somewhat awry. 'Gentlemen,' he would coo at the Fibber and the Kid reassuringly, 'this is going to be a doddle, this one—an absolute pension. For blokes like you,' he would add adoringly.

Morry would encourage the Aussies to hit the small exclusive jewellers in the Burlington Arcade. They were heavily fortified and well-manned— a steeplechase of locked doors, narrow staircases and suspicious hawk-eyed jewellers. The Fibber would take one look at the intended target, roll his eyes and push his toupee back on his head: 'Well, I gotta hand it you. This is a beauty, Morry—a bloody monte,' he would say, clapping the smiling Englishman on the shoulder.

'Oh yes, Jack, I knew you'd love it, old chap. You really are the governor,' Morry would say fawningly, licking his lips.

Then the Fibber would turn to the Kid and exclaim: 'Right, Kiddo, you man the machine guns and I'll bring the bloody hand grenades. We'll be doing five years for larceny and grievous bodily harm before our feet hit the pavement, Morry. Think again, son, okay?' Morry, now crestfallen, would have to find money for the croupiers another way but, fortunately, the next plot was never far away.

One day Morry the Head boarded the Underground at Victoria Station and read in the *Evening News* that society jeweller Lady Selina Jones was opening a shop in the Brompton Arcade, just off Sloane Square, with a champagne party. He got in touch with Arthur and soon ten of them had invited themselves to Lady Selina's soiree. To Arthur's delight, there were millions of pounds worth of baubles on show. As Morry later recalled: 'There were all sorts of Aussies there, including Aussie girls and Aussie wives, but they were all workers. Shortly after their arrival . . . not a jewel or a diamond remained in sight. Not one.'

Afterwards, when Morry the Head knocked on the door of Arthur's suite at the luxurious White House in Regents Park, Arthur bade him welcome ostentatiously. 'And as I came in, I saw a sight I'll never forget. There was the Duke with a girl, both of them nude, lying on the bed and in between them was every bit of jewellery and diamonds this lord's daughter had put on show in her shop.'

The sheer volume of work meant that Morry the Head was hard pressed to blow his share on the punt, but he managed it. Every night, he would be given three or four thousand pounds—his share of the day's profits—and every morning he would roll up broke, not even his cab fare left. Working with Arthur and the other Aussies, Morry the Head's fortunes rose. He wasn't getting pinched as often and he was getting a name as a dandy. He started calling himself Mayfair Morry. 'I was a top Mayfair jetsetter. I would be walking about in Pinet shoes, Turnbull and Asser shirts and Huntsman suits.'

There was a cost to all this finery though. Morry the Head and the Swan were both picked up by surveillance snappers and they both made the Australian Index, at numbers 67 and 22. Soon their faces would be known all over the United Kingdom and Europe, even as far away as Canada and Australia. Worse, as 'Mayfair Morry' paraded up and down the West End, blowing his ill-gotten gains in the finest casinos and clubs, he would lead the police right to the Aussies.

And when things got tough, he could be downright desperate, putting the bite on anyone and everyone. Morry the Head had done his dash with the Aussies by 1969–70. The last straw came when he was left in a West End flat for an afternoon by one of the Aussies while he ran some errands. When the bloke returned, he discovered Morry had sold his furniture and by afternoon tea time he had blown the proceeds gambling in the Colony Club.

In compiling the Australian Index, Pearce and the C11 photographers had blindsided the Kangaroo Gang for the first time. They had built a comprehensive picture of the gang's members and their movements. They were gathering informers who would fill in the gaps.

Gang members' love of a drink and a punt would also play a role in their eventual undoing. The Court Club on Bayswater Road had been a favourite haunt of the hoisters and C11's snapper had bagged nearly all of the gang there. One by one, the heads in the pictures were compared with fingerprints and mug shots sent from New South Wales. Only the non-drinkers, like the Kid, had escaped having their pictures taken.

Meanwhile, through wire taps, C11 investigators discovered the Aussies had a crooked international operator working for them at London's central telephone exchange. This West Indian fellow would connect the Aussies through to fellow villains back home and they would talk for hours for free, calls that should have cost £1 a minute. The operator was quietly arrested by the City of London police, rather than by Scotland Yard, so as to avoid big headlines. The post office, which ran the telephone exchange, then passed on all the numbers and the addresses of the Aussie callers, which enabled Pearce to pinpoint where the Aussies were living. The arrested operator gave information to Scotland Yard on the London network while also providing important intelligence to New South Wales and Victorian police on who was coming to join the team. They were careful not to share too much with the Australian cops.

Unaware that they were now under closer surveillance, the boys continued to plot and connive, constantly working on travel itineraries for the next recruits. They enjoyed free air travel—a connection in London's Qantas office in Sloane Square helped them to steal and validate wads of blank air tickets to move people all over the world. On the phone, they talked of massive shipments of stolen goods leaving Southampton Docks bound for Australia or New Zealand. They traded gossip and bragged of their exploits. There was evidence of basic training in theft and pickpocketing going on back in Sydney.

What had started as a two-man operation was now an industry with its own shipping fleet. They had bought off shipping clerks and managers within the government-owned Australian National Line, to ship vast quantities of booty undetected. The Federated Painters and Dockers Union controlled the waterside and they were some of the best crooks in Australia. They had offered Billy Longley the job of running the receiving operation in Sydney, but he was too busy with wars in Melbourne and so he declined—a life-long regret.

The police had not shown their hand yet. So there could be no conduit for corrupt officers to tip off the Aussies, the covert officers never met any of the villains they were shadowing. But still the Gurkhas of C11 weren't going to make their move too soon. They knew that, as soon as the Flying Squad got involved, the serious romancing would begin. He feared the Aussies would scatter all over the world, thanks to corrupt detectives suddenly dressed in Savile Row suits and wearing gold watches, courtesy of the Kangaroo Gang. In England, the crooks could be counted on to establish a network of bent police, just as they had done in New South Wales. At that time in Sydney, the corruption went right through the police up to parts of the judiciary and ultimately to the state premier, Sir Robert Askin. Once a political hero, Askin's legacy would be his business partnership with thieves and illegal casino bosses—in Askin's Sydney, you got justice when you ran out of money.

To have any hope of success against this, the coppers would have to maintain utmost secrecy and discretion. In May 1968, C11 had five leading targets—Arthur, Wee Jimmy, the Fibber, Billy Hill and Georgie G—well-covered with surveillance. And when the raids on their hide-outs began in mid 1968, the lads had no idea how they had been shopped.

At a lunch in London in 2009 I asked my two companions, former C11 men, whether we could pop out for a photograph in front of Harrods. They both politely but firmly declined. They said that, even after being retired for 20 years, there were habits and superstitions best maintained.

7
The Fiddler's Elbow

I suppose people will say I'm potty, a kleptomaniac. But those shops are really selling things at enormous prices. Who is potty really? Me or the little men in little suits taking home little wages from huge stores?

Australian shoplifter after conviction

For much of 1967–68, the Aussies were easy to find, if you knew where to look. They were regulars—the life and soul—of pubs like the Crowndale, and other notorious watering holes in North London.

On a cold spring morning in March 2009, I stood in front of the address I had been given in Australia for the Crowndale—except it wasn't a pub anymore. It was now a new block of apartments, built from what looked like Lego bricks. There was still a shape reminiscent of a London corner pub, but the 'luxury apartments' (the description on the agent's banner) were cold and uninviting, more like a modern jail block. Except for the English weather, everything had changed since the sixties. There was nothing of the old London to be found here on Chalk Farm Road.

Immigration had completely swept it away. As the cabbie told me en route from the city: 'England for the English? That's long gone, mate.' The passing faces were from all corners of the globe—a parade of Somalis, Lebanese, Indians, Poles and Pakistanis. The high street shops reflected this new population—kebab shops and ethnic grocery stores with the wafting aromas of foreign spices. Only when you looked up above the shopfronts did you see reminders of the past. Old neon tubes spelt out long-departed merchants: 'CW & AE Thomson Jewellers, Cash lent'; a Truman's Bitter sign above a pub that was now an Indian restaurant.

I suddenly wondered why I had believed that any of the old crew from 1968 might still be about. I stood there with my little bag on wheels—full of cameras, tape recorders and notebooks. All redundant now. I could hardly believe I had come so far with so little information. At least I had had hope when I set forth from Melbourne. Now that was gone too.

But I had one shot left—an address I had scrawled in a notebook during a boozy dinner in Sydney. A former Kangaroo Gang member had pulled it from her memory, almost like a party trick. I had written it down, but without a suburb or a postcode. There was only a slim chance the thief had remembered it correctly, or that anyone of note still lived there. It could have been anywhere in London, but it turned out to be just a block away.

The housing estate, built of dark liver-coloured brick, was cold and forbidding: the lower windows were covered by security screens, and there were signs warning that no ball games would be tolerated. Young mums in grimy tracksuits pushed baby carriages across the forecourt, throwing suspicious looks in my direction. I must have looked like a travelling salesman with his sample case on wheels or, worse, a council officer chasing up fines.

I rang the buzzer, but there was no answer. I rang it again, shivering as the icy wind picked up. As I was about to leave, a neatly dressed middle-aged woman came down the stairs. As she opened a heavy steel security door, I just had a feeling that she was somehow connected to this.

'Excuse me, madam, I'm looking for the people in number 28,' I said. She was taken aback, her manner immediately frosty. I was sure it was her bell I had rung. When strangers called around here, it usually meant trouble. I probably wasn't the man from the lottery, come to tell her she had won a fortune.

'Can I help you?' she asked, politely. Though, from her tone, I expected no assistance.

'I'm looking for John,' I answered.

'He's not around,' she said blankly.

'Oh, I see. Is he still alive?'

'Yes, of course. He's just not here right now. Who are you?' she asked, slightly anxiously.

I explained I was writing a book about Arthur Delaney. I had been sent here by Arthur's people.

Her demeanour changed completely. 'Oh, why didn't you say?' she said, unleashing a broad smile. 'I'm John's wife, Larry. He's up the pub,' she added warmly, extending a hand for me to shake. I could have hugged her and jumped up and down.

The mention of Arthur seemed to bring back happy, long-forgotten memories. She beamed back at me and, as I felt my anxiety disappearing, she directed me to a pub called the Fiddler's Elbow nearby, where John was usually encamped by this time of the day.

'If he's not there, try the Man in the Moon up the other end. Orright?' she said.

Luckily she got it right first time—the prospect of a long cold walk before a beverage was quite unappealing. Like many local pubs, the Fiddler's Elbow was halfway through a transition from traditional English pub to rock'n'roll venue. With its bare wooden floors, black walls and dim lighting, it had all the charm of a bomb shelter, but it was surviving where most pubs weren't.

I bought a beer and asked the barmaid where I might find John. She directed me to a door at the end of the bar. 'He's through there,' she said.

'But that's the Ladies,' I protested, pointing to the sign on the door.

'No, just go through,' she said, slightly irritated.

I gingerly pushed the door and was relieved when it didn't open into a ladies' lavatory but into a small private bar. The Ladies sign obviously offered select clientele a little seclusion. Casual visitors wouldn't know the bar was there; regulars who weren't invited simply didn't venture in there. It was the opening day of the Cheltenham Festival, the biggest steeplechase event on the British racing calendar, and on the TV the runners were approaching the barrier for the first race. A slim middle-aged man sat at the bar talking into his mobile, the form guide spread out in front of him.

Through his thick North London accent, I could hear he was getting set for the day, perhaps not on the tote but with the kind of bookies who gave better than official odds. He was dressed impeccably, much better than anyone else in the pub, but his was an older, outmoded style—an apricot Lacoste pullover, fawn trousers with a sharp crease and a pair of well-polished brogues. He topped his vodka with a dash of Perrier water and this completed the rather 1970s flavour to the scene.

As I waited for him to finish his call, another middle-aged grey-haired man entered the bar. 'You wouldn't be John, would you?' I asked, though I sensed I had my man.

'Depends who wants to know,' he replied suspiciously. 'Who are *yew* then?' he asked in a voice I had heard in every English crime show from *The Sweeney* to *The Bill*.

I told him who I was and my business, and he smiled just as Larry had done.

'Yeah, I'm John too. But that's the John you're after, my son. You're a long way from home, ain't ya?' he said, shaking my hand vigorously. 'You got a drink? Susie! SUSIE! Another Stella, love!' he yelled out to the barmaid, ignoring the full beer in my hand.

The other John had been listening to this exchange with one ear and, when he finished his call, he too greeted me warmly. 'Arthur Delaney, eh?' he said slowly, rolling the words around on his tongue. 'Now there was a man who never paid for nothing,' and he broke into a rasping laugh. There wasn't a lot to smile about these days, but Arthur could still change the mood.

'He was the King!' said my John. 'We was together all the time back then,' he recalled fondly. 'What a generous bloke he was too.'

'Wiv other people's money, course!' the first John chipped in. They both laughed uproariously.

'Hoisting was a way of life then. Everybody had a fiddle, just to survive in them days,' my John said. 'It was all quality merchandise in them days. Not like the rubbish you get down at the Camden Market today,' he snorted. The Stables at Camden Lock, a couple of kilometres away down Chalk Farm Road, had long been a market for goods acquired both legally and illegally, but now, with the influx of the 'ethnics' and the 'alternatives', it wasn't worth a hoister's time anymore, said John glumly.

'You get a pair o' trousers home from there and the arse'll be fallin' out of 'em in a coupla days,' he said bitterly.

'Arthur liked the finest things in life,' said my John. 'French champagne, best scotch . . . Nothing but the best for the King. Even when he was in the nick, Arthur was always turned out beautiful. He always had a crease in his trousers like a razor blade,' he said.

'And he spoke better than most Englishmen, even the toffs.'

I had to resist the urge to pull out my tape recorder and camera; to turn off the television and start mining this rich resource of memory. This scungy old pub was the treasure room, and I was standing on the threshold. But I had to be patient—to press hard would be a big mistake. They had never welcomed a journalist into their midst before. There might still be danger, even in pursuing stories from 1968—the London underworld was just as dangerous now as in the days of the Krays and Richardsons, but today the violence was more random and unpredictable.

The assortment of people wandering into the bar hinted at the existence of secrets that must be kept even today. A regular came in with his neck swathed in bandages—he had been attacked with a screwdriver as he pushed through a crowd of Middle Eastern men on the street in Camden. The weapon had narrowly missed his jugular vein and now he was recruiting volunteers for a bloody reprisal. If a Lebanese kid turned up dead in Camden Lock, I was going to pretend I hadn't heard this conversation.

I needn't have worried—the crowd at the Fiddler's Elbow turned out to be the most welcoming I found in all my travels. Soon Larry joined us at the pub, and we drank away the afternoon and much of the evening. After the first beer, I didn't put my hand in my pocket again. It was like standing in for Arthur that day, being repaid all those drinks and laughs from 40 years ago. Because of our animated conversation, some of the others in the bar assumed I had just returned home from a long stretch in jail in Australia.

Between races, I tried to swing the conversation to shoplifting, Harrods and even Asprey, but it was impossible and everyone, including me, got steadily drunker. So I gave up and toasted the winners, and commiserated with the losers. Larry promised she would gather up the rest of the old Crowndale mob that Friday night, and I would have more stories than I could handle.

I left after 7 pm, completely hammered and swaying. I switched on my iPod and began to belt out Tom Jones' 'Help Yourself' at the top of my lungs as I weaved my way to the Tube station. When I had begun this research two years earlier, the Kangaroo Gang had been a throwaway line in other people's books and articles, a passing reference to 'the fabulously successful group of shoplifters' who had torn up the UK and Europe. No-one had taken it any further and, as the old members began to die or lose their marbles, the story was rapidly becoming a myth.

Now Arthur and the rest were born again. I had heard their voices and seen their faces in the stories I had just heard. I fretted that I had been too drunk to take many notes. I had scrawled a few mysterious hieroglyphs as I balanced my notebook on the ledge above the urinal in the pub toilet. But I would hopefully have another session that Friday and I resolved I wouldn't get as drunk. Looking round for the Tube station, I realised I had taken the wrong direction out of the Fiddler's and was now hopelessly lost.

When Friday night rolled around, John and Larry were as good as their word. There was a crowd of old Crowndale people in the pub waiting to meet me. There were men and women who had been on the hoist with Arthur and the rest of the Kangaroos; there were barmaids who had served them drinks and watched their antics. There were old villains who had travelled the Continent with the Aussies.

They had brought with them photographs of trips long ago to Monte Carlo and Paris. Here were John and Larry in their younger days, tanned and smiling, sitting at tables overflowing with fine food and drink. They had posed for photographs with Petite Philippe, with his dazzling white smile and dark eyes. Here was Petite Philippe with Arthur, both resplendent in pastel casual wear—a white fedora was perched rakishly on the Frenchman's head. In every picture Arthur seemed to have his arm around another girl, with a different gold watch on his wrist. He never kept anything for long.

And with the pictures, memories came flooding back—the days of wine and roses that would never return. Arthur and the other Aussies had made everything special. When the Crowndale gang thought of their youth, it was to the days of the Kangaroo Gang they returned. The Aussies had brought an optimism that few—not even the very rich— enjoyed in London at that time. Arthur had taken them all aboard and paid for everything. No wonder these people were being so nice to me, connected as I was to this man whom they regarded as the veritable saint of shoplifters, a talisman for fun and positive thinking.

There had been hard times since then. John and Larry's boy had fallen into drugs and was doing yet another stretch for armed robbery. He had pulled a cigarette lighter shaped like a pistol on the bloke who ran the betting shop. The bloke had laughed but the judge didn't, and gave him three years.

There was one person I especially wanted to meet. Molly Gunner, the publican at the Crowndale in 1968, had come all the way from Hertford-shire, despite the heavy load of grief she was carrying. She had lost a son in mysterious circumstances in South Africa and was fighting for justice for him. Another son had recently returned from jail in Australia. At 70, she was raising her grandson Billy, her late son's boy, while helping her other son settle back into life as a free man. Now living quietly in a small home on the edge of a park, she had put those wild days behind her; but, for Arthur's sake, she would talk to me. I resolved to stay sober and professional to record this, the most important interview of my research to date.

By midnight, I was rolling drunk (again) with Molly, Larry and a few others at a nightclub. Under the influence of memories and strong liquor, we danced around like it was 1968 all over again. My last memory of the night was of Molly re-creating the Age of Aquarius for the startled onlookers.

The Crowndale had been the unofficial headquarters of the Kangaroo Gang, and there had been a constant stream of Aussies coming and going. It was an eclectic crowd—on any night there might be a team of skinheads in the bar, alongside actor Peter O'Toole and assorted thespians from the rehearsal space around the corner. There would be hoisters, fences, thugs, mugs and drug dealers.

Molly had seen it all from behind the bar. The flamboyant Georgie G sweeping into the pub with his shambling sidekick, Normie Seddon. Or the dashing Keith Albert Collingburn, another of the Aussie hoisters. They were all decked out like rock stars—in mink coats and lime, purple or orange flares, dragging their latest female conquests behind them. They were loud and charismatic, exuding the confidence that brought success in their business. In London they had discovered cocaine, amphetamine-based pills and barbiturates. These drugs worked by hooking into the areas of the brain that control the production of natural opiates, but, in the right combination, they matched very closely the euphoria experienced on the hoist—that thrill became habit-forming, hence the relentless need to work every day.

Criminal activity can become compulsive—the kleptomaniac may be neither criminal nor a nutter, but merely a drug addict. The reward of taking greater risks went beyond the money. It was an ever more intense high, followed by the customary celebration. The party never ended— washed down with copious amounts of alcohol, stimulants saw to that. And this would be the moment for creativity, for planning the next auda- cious heist.

The schemes reflected not greed or ambition, but the pure thrill of mischief—like the group that turned up to Selfridges in dust coats with a couple of stepladders. Under the supervision of a man in a suit holding a clipboard, they took down a crystal chandelier on display and walked out with it. They used the same scam to hoist a priceless Persian rug from a display in a gallery on Bond Street. Some members of the gang had begun to feel invincible.

There was competition between the thieves. When the Kid had arrived in London, Billy 'the General' Hill had shown him a few tricks in a store, but the protégé had been unimpressed and thought the General overrated. The Kid judged Hill to be more like a corporal, and he aimed to prove it with the sheer audacity of some of his hoists. The Kid and the Fibber each acquired an oversized overcoat, 'Big Bertha'—customised with an extra panel of cloth stitched horizontally inside at the mid-section, which acted as a rail for stolen garments. It could take a whole rack of stolen garments and on a big man there would be no outward signs. Unless you got sloppy. Coming out of Aquascutum one afternoon with a full load, the Kid looked at the Fibber and noticed the different coloured sleeves of more than a dozen cashmere pullovers dangling below his overcoat like cats' tails.

Soon after, in Piccadilly Circus, the Kid and the Fibber were out filling an order for cashmere jumpers. There were half a dozen of them working and they suddenly hit on the idea of passing the garments from hand to hand under their overcoats and out of the store. This conga line method proved highly effective.

Sometimes the staff were in on the gag. The Aussies had been hitting an exclusive men's store at lunchtime so regularly a staff member had been setting his watch by them. One day they had been delayed, robbing another store, and the staff member, who was a proper English gent, looked over his glasses at them as they entered the store: 'Gentlemen, you're late today,' he deadpanned. He always took his cut after that, even preparing specific orders wrapped in gift paper.

One group formed an alliance with a well-known pop singer, whose father had been something of a villain. Whenever the star went into a West End boutique, at least three members of staff would descend on him—he was the perfect head puller. While the obsequious staff members were sucking up to the star, the lads would be cleaning out the store. Speed was the crucial factor at such moments.

The Kid's favourite rort of all time was not a big job, but a piece of pure theatre. A famous tie maker had set up an exhibition of his most exquisite silk ties in a shop on Savile Row. A head puller was assigned to flatter and gull the proud couturier who, mindful of thieves, stayed close to his sumptuous display. Even so, the Kid was able to find the right moment, when he stripped the entire display of 300 ties and stuffed them straight into the half lining of his overcoat.

As Mike Pearce circulated the Australian Index around the West End, shopkeepers began to become paranoid about the Aussies. One afternoon, five leading heads were in a Bond Street jeweller. The proprietor was terrified of being robbed again, having already suffered the indignity of several raids. He watched everyone like a hawk. He inspected the group one by one and noticed that, despite their fine clothes and posh manners, they were all chewing gum. He watched them with increasing terror as they prepared to choreograph their robbery. Finally, even before they had struck, the proprietor was in a state of near collapse. He ran to the door and bolted it. Turning to the startled thieves, he wailed: 'I know who you are and what you're here for. Just leave please, and I won't ring the police. Just GO!'

During these glory days, the Crowndale was often full of Aussie thieves—their endless telling of yarns such as these became part of the entertainment as they egged each other on to greater feats of daring. If Delaney was in, there would be a crowd of courtiers, which now included a couple of conspicuous heavies. Arthur's success and his well-known cowardice had left him vulnerable to attack from other thieves, so he moved around with a big unsmiling ogre by the name of Scotch Bob and at least one other. Scotch Bob would melt into the scenery when the King was holding court, but he always watched Arthur's back. If Arthur had a good day, everyone would know it. With a quiet word to Molly, he would buy drinks for the pub. Despite a growing fondness for cocaine, Arthur remained circumspect even under its thrilling influence.

Wee Jimmy and his brother Cecil and their crew would be plotting and muttering in a corner. Molly thought Wee Jimmy too sly by half—his unctuous manner made her skin crawl. Always on the make. That described most of them, she used to say, but there were also some true deviants among them. There were many with a voracious sexual appetite, and some with a disturbingly perverted edge, which Molly cared not to dwell on when she spoke to me. She admitted to affairs with a couple of them—Georgie G and Keith Collingburn. She reckoned there was something different about the thief to other men. They were exciting, spontaneous and magnetic to be around; but they were also utterly unreliable, and serial philanderers to boot.

When they had a good win on the hoist, a room upstairs would be turned into a showroom for their plunder. The English receivers and fences would come to the pub to choose from rack upon rack of stolen clothes and luxury goods. Molly never said anything when she noticed the Aussies cheating the locals. The Aussies knew the fences were tight, only paying 25 per cent of the ticketed price of a stolen garment, so they nicked boxes of blank price tags and attached them to their goods after applying their own professional-looking mark-ups.

If the Crowndale was quiet, the boys would head down to Soho to rub shoulders with London's hip set in bars like the famous Bag O' Nails on Kingly Street. Georgie G would announce 'We're off to Sack O' Tacks, who's comin'?' and half the bar would spill onto the street and into cars. There they might catch a late night set from rhythm and blues man Georgie Fame or US guitar hero Jimi Hendrix. They could bump into Paul McCartney after a gig with the Beatles, dropping in with friends for a plate of steak and mushy peas. From there, they might hit any one of dozens of clubs or casinos—from the Victoria Sporting Club to the Colony Club—to gamble till dawn with the likes of Hollywood stars, foreign potentates and industrialists.

Every Aussie in the pub seemed to have his own little scam going. Sydney crook Doug Wardle never made the Australian Index—he was not even a thief. But 'Doodle Doug' hit on one of the best earners of them all, even if it wasn't to everyone's taste. To put it bluntly, but Doodle Doug had an enormous doodle—so well endowed was he that the Fibber used to call him 'Wotawhoppa'. It hung down to his knees, so the legend went.

'Hey, Wotawhoppa, how's it hanging?' Fibber used to ask Wardle. 'I know a policewoman who could throw a saddle on that thing and ride him for three furlongs!'

It had been his doodle that had sent Wardle to London in the first place. A notorious Consorting Squad detective in Sydney had discovered Wardle was knocking off his wife—he warned Wardle that, if he ever caught him in Sydney again, there was a bullet with his name engraved on it.

Doodle Doug 'wasn't so much a shoplifter as a cock-lifter', according to the Kid. He earned his money by taking his prodigious member into public toilets around Mayfair. When he spotted his mark—one of the upper-class gents who indulged their guilty pleasures in such places—the doodle would make its dramatic appearance. Wardle would sidle up to the urinal, smiling at his mark. He would give his member a wristy flick, and all but put it in the gentleman's hand.

But, as soon as the mug took the bait, Doodle Doug's demeanour would change. 'You're borrowed, you dirty bastard,' he would say, coiling his bits back into his trousers. 'Detective Sergeant Robertson of Scotland Yard. You will be coming along with me, sir.'

Dragging the horrified man out by the collar into the busy street, Doodle Doug would admonish: 'This is a very serious offence—this is public indecency! Imagine when your family and the chaps down the club find out about this. You may even do time!'

The mark would usually be a Sir So-and-So, a lord or a wealthy legal eagle. By the time they got halfway to West End Central police station, the mark would be begging, often crying, trying to make a deal with 'the police'. Inevitably, Wardle would soften and suggest the whole thing could be cleared up by making a discreet donation to the Police Youth Club. With the terms agreed, they would then change course and head for the nearest bank branch, where the grateful offender would hand over up to £3000 in cash.

But it never ended there. Doodle Doug would later back up with more demands for donations, and this might go on for months. He claimed to have pulled this stunt on about 50 mugs—he had a dozen regulars paying him hush money. A voracious card player, Wardle would pull out bundles of money still in its bank wrappers.

Of course, it couldn't last. Finally one of the marks plucked up the gumption to complain to police. A West End magistrate, the butler to a peer and a visiting US rear admiral were among those who finally testified against Wardle. Doodle Doug got the heaviest lagging of any of the Australians—seven years for impersonating a police officer.

At this time, everyone assumed the Crowndale was under surveillance. Some were convinced that Scotland Yard had posted a surveillance team across the road in the Indian grocery shop there. Or they were peering down from the tower block, a mile away, with long lenses. The summer of 1968 had been a vintage season for the Kangaroo Gang, but by September there were evil portents in the autumn shadows of North London. In reality, there had been no surveillance in the Indian shop or the tower block. Brian James had carried out physical surveillance on the pub looking for Australians, but never had any luck catching up with the suspects he was after. He gave up eventually and the pub became a safe haven again, though the gang never knew it.

When I originally convinced my publishers to take this book on, I sold the idea to them on the premise that I knew the story of what happened on that much-fabled day at Asprey. At the time, I didn't really—I didn't even have a date for the incident, just a vague idea something truly spectacular had taken place between 1989 and 1991.

When I approached Asprey in my researches, they had been no help at all. Their PR team, after ignoring my numerous emails and phone calls, had curtly dismissed me with a 'we don't comment on security matters' and cut off all communications. On the broader topic of shop stealing, there had been a little help from London's retail establishment. I persuaded the archivist at Harrods to let me look at their mid 1960s press cuttings for a 'social history' I was writing. After much security screening and frisking I was admitted to the Harrods back offices, where I was shown the newspaper archives from 1967. Maybe I was too eager, or asked too many questions about thieving—the nervous archivist must have worked out what I was really doing and then cut off any further contact with me.

I had trudged up to the British Newspaper Archive at Colindale in the northern reaches of London, trying to get access to Mike Pearce's Australian Index in the *Police Gazettes*. When I phoned, a staff member told me they had *Gazettes* going back to 1870 and I was welcome to have a look at them. But when I got there, a stout and red-faced woman indignantly told me I would do no such thing. A 75-year confidentiality rule applied to the *Gazettes*—if I came back in December 2042, I might have a chance of getting access, she said, with a thin sadistic smile. Then my mobile phone rang and she scowled at me, and loudly ordered me off the premises. I was starting to feel like a thief myself, so I stole a pen from her counter.

As usual, the underworld provided a much better alternative to musty reading rooms and blurry microfiche films. As I soon found, even in cold and miserable North London, Arthur's name could still bring a smile. Maybe he did have a little of the charisma his mates in Sydney had talked to me about. His exploits, as people had previously recounted them to me, had seemed so outlandish as to be barely credible, but now I was picking up his trail again on the other side of the world.

Maybe, I told myself, I was getting closer to what happened on the day of that extraordinary heist at Asprey.

A summer of love ends 8

Crime fighting is rarely guided by science or reason. For its success it often relies more on happenstance than planning. The promotion of Detective Constable Mike Pearce to the Flying Squad on 19 February 1968 was one such occasion. As a C11 man, he had gathered the evidence; now he was on the Heavy Mob, he would put it to good use. Without this link between the Gurkhas and the Flying Squad, the hoisters would have run amok for years longer.

The Flying Squad was the only unit that could chase travelling criminals like the Aussies around Great Britain but had shown little interest to date. The squad had been originally established as an experiment—a mobile patrol to counter pickpockets and thieves travelling across police boundaries. In October 1919 a dozen officers were recruited to move anywhere within the Metropolitan Police district, carrying out surveillance from a horse-drawn canvas-covered Great Western Railway van with spy holes cut in the sides. If known thieves were spotted, officers would leap out of the van to make the arrests.

According to Met Police historians, the mobile team did so well they became a permanent squad and were issued with two Crossley motorised tenders from the Royal Flying Corps, capable of a top speed of 40 mph. In 1929 the squad got their own fleet of six cars, including a Lea Francis coupe, an Invicta, a Lagonda, a Railton four litre and a Bentley coupe. Their greater speed and mobility quickly brought results and criminals and the public soon became aware of this new 'flying squad'. Its officers would frequent known criminal hangouts, observing suspects and gathering information.

The Flying Squad worked solely from information and intelligence to collar crims engaged in serious and organised crime. This meant tackling armed robbers in particular, and monitoring the associated handling of stolen goods. Its focus was now on lorryloads of high-value goods, often going to or from the docks at Southampton. Flying Squad officers would learn from informants what was on offer—it might be whisky or razor blades, anything that could be sold on the cheap. Though World War II had ended 20 years earlier, the black market it had spawned was still thriving. It was up to the Heavy Mob to follow the money and the goods through the system. The Flying Squad never dealt with reported crime cases requiring investigation; it only took over a case if officers arrested a person for a previously reported crime.

Pearce did not know why he had been promoted. This was a posting that most senior officers got just before ascending the ladder. But he had never imagined a career in the Met's top brass and, having escaped the confines of the desk at C11, he was in fact destined to become a career investigator. There were a few on the Flying Squad, like Pearce, who never rose above the rank of Detective Sergeant—hard heads, who wouldn't cop a quid to back off, often found themselves fending off complaints lodged by vengeful crims. If you copped 15 years' jail, there was nothing to lose in making bogus allegations against the arresting officer. Bent cops might even lend a hand. To ascend the ranks, you needed to pay attention to the politics. Anyway, police work was about making arrests, Pearce reasoned, and, even if he never mastered the politics, on the Flying Squad he would get to feel the collars of some of the country's best crooks.

The Flying Squad, under legendary Detective Chief Superintendent Tommy Butler, was a tough school. Small in stature but a formidable force, Butler expected his officers to be fearless and resourceful. If the ends justified the means, Butler's Flying Squad didn't think twice. Butler himself was wanted in both Ireland and Canada for cutting corners in the making of arrests.

He had gone to Dublin to pick up a well-known safebreaker and prison escapee, Alfie Hines, but hadn't waited for the papers to be processed—he bundled Hines into the back of a car and drove over the border into Northern Ireland, beyond the Irish Republic's jurisdiction. In February 1968, when he arrested Great Train Robber Charles Wilson in Montreal, Canada, Butler seized the jewellery of Wilson's wife, describing it as 'proceeds of crime'. She alleged theft—generating another 'Wanted' poster for Butler.

Under Butler you were expected to get on with the job. His man management consisted of occasionally walking into the muster room, home to a hundred officers, and asking those present if there were 'any problems other than financial'. Then he would walk out. When a young detective constable piped up that he had a problem with his auntie, he was transferred back to a divisional station by the end of the week.

Butler was obsessive about security and confidentiality, fearing other squads would sell out his men to the villains. Officers were ordered never to use their own names on the radio, only call signs. Butler would listen to Flying Squad cars on the radio and, if a car gave its location, he would find the culprit and kick them off the squad. Uniformed units listened in and tried to guess where the squad was working. It was only after arrests had been made that the Sweeney might ask for uniform assistance at a scene, and only then was a location given.

Compiling the original Australian Index had provided Pearce with a ready-made list of crooks to work on. He also had a pipeline of new information from the officer who replaced him at C11, Detective Constable Brian James. From 1968 until 1970, James was responsible for the updating of the Index and printing the revised edition each December; he was more than happy to help. Together they would rack up some arrests from all the hard work C11 had put in.

At the top of their list of likely lads were Georgie G and Normie Seddon (otherwise known as John Noel Jones). The Natwest Bank had some concerns about the contents of a safe deposit box in its Sloane Square branch, and the people who held it. The top brass in the CID were very interested in the safe deposit box and ordered Pearce to get a result as soon as possible. Pearce got a search warrant at Bow Street Magistrates

Court and the box was opened by force. Inside were all the tools of trade of the professional thief—numerous passports for both Jones and Georgie G, rubber stamps for forging entry and exit visas, bank stamps for endorsing traveller's cheques, a couple of guns, not to mention the keys to all the safes at the Dunlop Rubber Company.

If Georgie G and Seddon had been planning to rob Dunlop, Pearce and James' timing was immaculate—a Dunlop manager confirmed to the police that, with the keys found in the safe deposit box, the crooks could have laid their hands on £10 million worth of bonds and negotiable securities. This was a major blow to the villains. More was to follow.

Pearce had an address for Seddon in north-west London—a block of flats in a private estate. At 6 am one morning in May 1968, with Flying Squad officers surrounding the block, Pearce knocked on the front door. He caught Seddon completely unawares, just waking up with his girlfriend Sally Mary Farrelly, a pretty 25-year-old Liverpool girl. When interviewed, Seddon seemed shocked the police knew so much about him.

More incriminating evidence was found in the flat, including a tube of green oil paint linked to £10 000 worth of stolen traveller's cheques that had been cashed in Scotland. When presented with his photo likeness in several passports in different names, Seddon said glumly he was a dead duck. When arrested over the safe deposit box, Seddon was already on bail over the theft of British Visitor passports from a post office. While on remand in Wormwood Scrubs prison, he was identified in a line-up by a female witness over the passports. It was a definitive pick to say the least. The doughty postal worker walked up behind Seddon and whacked him hard on the back of the head, outraged at his audacity in thieving from her counter so brazenly.

Pearce was confident Normie Seddon would get up to five years' jail. And his mate would too, but first they had to catch Georgie G. Even holding on to his dead duck wouldn't be all that simple.

In March 1969, Mike Pearce arrived at the Wells Street Court in central London, carrying a voluminous brief of evidence for the trial of John Noel Jones (Seddon). He had 41 witnesses waiting at the court to help send down the prisoner, who was charged with, among other offences, conspiracy to forge under a statute that hadn't been used since 1850. Pearce had certainly done his homework and this would be the first of many Aussies, he thought. He puffed his chest out and entered the building.

Then a superior officer came running down the stairs, yelling at him: 'Where have you been, Pearce? John Noel Jones has escaped and you're the only one who knows what he looks like. Get out there and help them.'

Just minutes earlier, Jones had been in an anteroom on the fourth floor waiting to enter the court for the day. He wasn't dangerous—a shambling amiable wombat, pleasant and compliant. The prison guards who had brought him from Wormwood Scrubs didn't bother with handcuffs. He asked to go to the toilet and the guards agreed.

As an unrehearsed escape plan, it was one of the best and certainly one of the most comical. Onlookers saw Seddon's chubby form burst through the four pane window of the bathroom and lose altitude rapidly. Normie wasn't built for gliding. Fortunately he managed to grab hold of the fire escape ladder of an adjacent building or he would have fallen four floors to the street. Collecting himself, the surprisingly nimble Seddon descended the fire escape, clambering, slithering and finally careering like a sack of spuds to the ground. It wasn't stylish, but it did the job. He ran into the morning traffic, a gaggle of angry prison officers on his tail.

But he didn't get too far. Apparently, he was supposed to rendezvous with some mates waiting in a car a couple of streets away. But there had been a bogus 999 call and the area was teeming with cops. Thinking their plan had been exposed, the back-up team abandoned Normie and drove away. Seddon, with police and prison guards in hot pursuit, had nowhere to run. He ran into a building and up the stairs, but he was tiring now. He grabbed the lead officer and banged his head against the wall before being overwhelmed. When he returned to the court, in addition to the bumps and scratches from his daring fourth floor plunge, Seddon complained that he needed treatment for sore ribs. Allegedly, on the way back to court in the prison van, the guards had exacted a little revenge.

Seddon had engaged a prominent barrister to handle his defence, but Wilfred Fordham QC was well past his best. The ageing barrister could hardly follow the evidence and was continually mixing up the exhibits. It was painful to watch. Pearce was embarrassed for the advocate and began to feel sorry for Normie. Even the jury was squirming and shaking their heads as Fordham bumbled his way through the case. Seddon was duly found guilty and at the sentencing Pearce expected to hear a jail term of at least five years for his various crimes, including his ill-fated escape attempt.

When the judge gave Seddon only two years, Pearce nearly fell off his chair. After all the man hours of work, the surveillance and the long wait to nab him, with good behaviour the felon would probably be out in 18 months. This might have been a £10 million robbery if Seddon and Georgie G had got around to using the keys they nicked for the Dunlop Rubber Company. This was the lightest possible sentence—nicked for three counts of conspiracy, larceny, making false statements, procuring bank stamps with intent to commit forgery and endless counts of receiving, he got just four sentences of two years and they were all to be served concurrently.

Afterwards Pearce went to visit Normie in the cells below the Old Bailey, to tell him how lucky he had been. Particularly with that bumbling old barrister and all, he said. 'Ha! That was me strategy all along!' chortled Seddon. 'I knew if I had a barrister who couldn't tell his arse from his elbow, the jury and the judge would feel sorry for me. And it bloody worked a treat. Two years! I couldn't believe it meself.'

Pearce and Seddon laughed together. The policeman couldn't help but feel admiration for these ingenious rogues who operated with such foresight and finesse. Of course, Seddon would be deported back to Australia or his native New Zealand at the end of his time, but, with a new passport, he could be back again a week later. And who knows how many passports he had stashed away for a rainy day?

A few weeks after Seddon's eventual deportation, a Flying Squad officer was on holidays with his wife in the Canary Islands, a Spanish possession off the coast of North Africa. One morning, he noticed lounging on the beach a very pale fat man who matched the description of Norman Richard Seddon. He crept up close and identified some of Normie's very distinctive tattoos. He had been part of the crew that had arrested Seddon, so he was certain it was him. But being out of his jurisdiction, the cop could do nothing except watch Seddon's skin turn pink in the summer sun. The thief was back in London soon after, and moved from team to team until the late 1970s.

A few months after Seddon's conviction, Georgie G had also turned up in the Canary Islands. The Spanish police nicked him in the capital Las Palmas, and then notified British authorities. Pearce was overjoyed— Georgie was the biggest fish he had yet landed in his career. So he started the process for Georgie's extradition immediately. Just as he was about to jump on a plane, Pearce got a message from Las Palmas. Georgie was gone—there had been a mistake and they had let him go, destination unknown. They had even handed him back his false passports.

This 'mistake' was a fiddle for sure—a back-hander for the local *policía,* thought Pearce. Frustrated that Georgie had evaded him, he applied a little pressure on Wee Jimmy to come and have a chat. Wee Jimmy, to his surprise, was more than happy to, but only over a pint.

In a series of meetings, Wee Jimmy filled Pearce and his partner in on the details of the goings-on in Las Palmas. Georgie had negotiated a payment of £40 000 to the Spanish police for his freedom. They agreed, but Georgie didn't have the readies—a desperate call went out to London. Wee Jimmy, Arthur and Billy Hill weren't happy about it, but the hat was passed around and the money was sent to the Spanish police.

There was drama over the incident for some time, tension between two factions in the gang. Seddon, Georgie and the others doing traveller's cheques had brought everyone to notice. The retail hoisters argued they could have kept knocking over jewellery shops and boutiques forever. Hitting banks had put the spotlight on all of them.

The Australian Index in the *Police Gazette* would now ruin all the fun, Wee Jimmy said. He intimated there were a few rogues that needed packing home. If he could help, just ask, he would say as he ordered yet another round. He had a way of speaking softly and confidentially, giving the impression that he was imparting his deepest secrets, and they would return to the station with notebooks full of ancient history. Wee Jimmy kept everyone sweet, but he never told them anything they didn't already know.

After a long amiable drink in a Paddington pub in the winter of 1969, Wee Jimmy had a question: 'I s'pose you've got a driver out there, to take you home after this, right?' he asked. Their driver had indeed been waiting in the police car, freezing his arse off all night. 'Well, get him a drink, wouldja? Compliments of Wee Jimmy!' he said, dropping a five pound note on the bar.

'You bend a bloke little by little, don't you? You clever bastard . . .' thought Pearce, looking into Wee Jimmy's mild and pleasant countenance. He was a past master.

In fact, Wee Jimmy had endless ways to influence police. If he was questioned, he would maintain a customary no-comment throughout the interview, until the tape stopped. Then he might reach over and take a grip on the coat sleeve of the earnest investigator, plying the cheap fabric between his thumb and forefinger. 'Tut, tut, Guvnor. A man of your cut deserves better than this . . . What size are you? I'd say . . . 42 or 44 regular? Come down to the Crowndale Friday after work, okay?' There would be half a dozen Huntsman suits, with the Harrods tags still on, to choose from. If the cop took one for free, he'd crossed the street. There were plenty of Wee Jimmy's suits walking around Scotland Yard.

Later Georgie G turned up in Dublin, arrested by the Irish national police, the Garda, on Pearce's information. Pearce couldn't believe his luck; he dusted off his old warrants and prepared to rush to Dublin to pick up Georgie. However, it took him a couple of days to get the authority to go to Dublin. And the other problem was that, even before he had set off, the Irish police had already released him.

'Oh you should have come by yesterday,' said the charge sergeant on duty. 'We let him out on £100 bail. He's only a shoppie after all.'

'*Only a shoppie!*' Pearce cried. 'This bloke's made off with more than the Great Train Robbers, and you gave him bloody bail.'

What had cost Georgie G £40 000 in Las Palmas had been achieved legally for £100 in Dublin. Pearce put away his warrants with a growing sense of foreboding that they wouldn't catch Georgie G again. And so it turned out—they never came close ever again.

Forty years later, Pearce's warrants are still open. Last I heard of Georgie, he had given up the hoist and was living in Sydney, working for a pest control company. In Melbourne, retired cop Brian Murphy extended his sympathies to Pearce: 'Tell him not to worry. I'd reckon my warrants— for possession of housebreaking implements and attempted escape from lawful custody from 1955—would still be kicking around,' he said.

Frustrated and angry, Pearce ripped into the remaining Aussies. Wee Jimmy was hauled in and charged with larceny and passport fraud. In contrast to their earlier convivial meetings, Wee Jimmy maintained a brick wall defence of 'no comment' to every question:

'You like a cup of tea, Jimmy?'

'No comment.'

'Nice weather we're having, cobber?'

'No comment.'

He was 'doing his time'. From the moment they were captured, this was how the smartest of the Aussies handled themselves. Forget the court case. Forget any long-winded defence. Silence was Wee Jimmy's best tactic. He wouldn't incriminate himself and he could test out the police case against him. He might also ascertain which cops he could bend later on. In the meantime, he would do his time.

When busted in Switzerland, Wee Jimmy had done two years' jail—every day of it in solitary confinement, at his own request. He didn't need the company of other prisoners, nor did he trust them. In custody, a number of other Aussies had opened like watermelons falling off a truck, but not Wee Jimmy. Nearly 50, he was the elder statesman of the group—he set the example.

When the interview finished, Wee Jimmy's face softened: 'Guvnor? A minute of your time, if you please.'

'Yes, Jimmy? What now?' asked the exasperated Pearce.

'I really don't want to insult your intelligence, or upset you after all the hard work you have done gathering witnesses and evidence, sir,' he said apologetically, clasping his fingers on his chest. 'But I feel it my duty to inform you that on the days in question, I was in fact not present at the locations that have been put forward.'

'And where were you then, Jimmy?' asked Pearce, his face reddening with anger.

'Why, sir, I was in Sydney, of course,' said Wee Jimmy. 'And there are some New South Wales police that will attest to that fact,' he said, a half-smile appearing on his face.

If that didn't beat all! A dozen witnesses could pick out Wee Jimmy from photos, but there were cops in New South Wales who were prepared to swear he was 6000 miles away.

'Yes, I had elderly relatives I had to visit,' said Wee Jimmy, the very image of the dutiful son. 'Like I said, sorry for the inconvenience, Guvnor.'

He was rubbing it in now. On the perjured testimony of New South Wales's finest, Wee Jimmy ultimately walked free. Afterwards, he couldn't apologise to Pearce enough.

'We thought we had really slowed them up, but they were back at it with a vengeance not long after,' Pearce told me 40 years later. After deriding Georgie G and Seddon for their bank jobs, Wee Jimmy was soon knocking over those same targets using the same modus operandi.

Despite such setbacks, information continued to flow to Pearce. Until Christmas 1969, he was fairly certain his informers were unknown to the gang, but perhaps they had their suspicions. Pearce had for a long time been meeting with his Aussie contact, Billy Broughton, on a semi-regular basis. Broughton never told Pearce a great deal, but he kept the investigator in touch with who was who in the zoo. One night, Broughton met Pearce in a bar and they had a cordial, if insubstantial, chat before the Aussie went off to work. But the next day, Pearce was called to identify a body at the mortuary. Cleaners at the Paddington pub where Broughton worked had found his corpse behind the bar at 4 am; he had died sometime after 11pm when the pub shut. According to witnesses, it had been a quiet incident-free evening. But there, cold and stiff, lay Pearce's informer, dead of a drug overdose.

It was a wake-up call for Pearce. He grudgingly admired the Australians for their dash and ingenuity. By comparison, English thieves often seemed brutish and uncivilised; and yet it was easy to forget there were at least five suspected killers amongst the Kangaroo Gang, according to intelligence from Australia. On the hoist, however, they had behaved themselves impeccably. Thugs didn't last five minutes in Arthur or Wee Jimmy's teams. Arthur had one conviction for assault occasioning bodily harm, but that had been years earlier. While violence was almost always bad for business, nonetheless the Aussies would never let anything, or anyone, threaten their criminal enterprise, and certainly not one of their own—a dog, an informer, was fair game whether in England or Australia. An Aussie, Frederick Kidd (alias Gerald John O'Neill), who was believed to be fizzing to the Flying Squad, was found dead with his head in a gas oven. Yet another gang member inexplicably stepped into the traffic in Knightsbridge and was run over. There was a whiff of something nasty creeping into this story.

The Kid and the Fibber continued to work hard into 1969, but times they were a-changing. In 1966 they had had their pick of West End shops, but now they often needed to travel further afield. Security was tighter and more determined than ever before. The little old lady detectives had been replaced by big burly athletes in many stores.

In Ilford on one occasion they had nearly come badly unstuck. They had hoisted more than 20 Patek Philippe watches, but on the way out the shopkeeper had twigged. He had thrown a switch locking two sets of security doors. The Kid and the Fibber had made it through, but Fibber's son Barry was trapped in the space between the sets of doors.

A huge West Indian security guard, built like decathlete Daley Thompson, had dashed out of a side entrance to give chase. The Kid and the Fibber ran as they fast they could, but a chubby middle-aged man and a young asthmatic were no match for the fast-closing security guard. The Fibber had to buy some time. He stopped and shouted back to his pursuer: 'Mate, if you want your watches here they are!' He took one £20 000 wristwatch from his pocket and flung it high into the air behind the guard.

The West Indian skidded to a halt on the pavement and doubled back, his eyes skyward and his arms outstretched, like he was trying to catch Bradman on the boundary at Lords. When he made the catch, he smiled, gritted his teeth and resumed the chase. But The Fibber lobbed another watch, then another and another, till the pockets of Big Bertha were empty. And still the West Indian kept coming, shouting for passers-by to grab the thieves.

They ducked into a crowded shop and zigzagged through the aisles, turning over racks and boxes of stock into the security guard's path. As they burst back into the street, 20 metres ahead of their maniacal pursuer, the Fibber spied a double-decker bus just pulling away from the kerb. They scrambled aboard.

Seeing this, the staff and customers from the store behind them yelled out to the security guard: 'Quick, the blighters have got on the bus.' The security guard emerged from the store, striding out to full pace as the bus gained momentum. Like a long jumper, he took off effortlessly and landed on the open back platform of the bus. There was no escape now, he must have thought, as he vaulted the stairs to the top deck.

But there was no sign of the Fibber and the Kid. They had leapt on the bus certainly, but they hadn't stayed on for long—they'd jumped straight off before it got to the corner and run down a side lane. The security guard was running up and down the lower deck, furious he had been duped. As the bus disappeared over a bridge, the Fibber and the Kid waved at the security man, slapping their arses and brandishing the last of the Patek Philippes, which the Kid had stashed in his coat.

In all the confusion, the shopkeeper had accidentally let Barry out. It was another hair's-breadth escape, but it seemed these were happening much more than when the Kid had originally arrived in England.

On another occasion, the Kid and Hughie Maher (otherwise known as 'Humour') had been dipping at Royal Ascot but, after relieving a few gentlemen of their winnings, they were recognised and the racetrack police gave chase. Most teams had a system worked out for moments of crisis like these. If you got separated, you would proceed to 'the short meet', which might be the getaway car or a certain pub; but if your accomplices didn't turn up promptly, you didn't linger there. The long meet might be in another city six or twelve hours later, where you would front up at the airport or a train station.

When you made the long meet, you would alert the others you were sweet and on site. If the Kid heard an announcement saying 'Could Mr Terrence McSweeney Williams please come to the information counter,' he knew it would be Fibber or Humour directing him to the appointed spot. This day, however, Humour hadn't made either the short or long meet, and the Kid had returned to London on his own, disconsolate that Humour must have been collared.

But later that night Humour turned up, slightly the worse for wear, smelling to high heaven. When they had been chased off the racetrack, Humour had run into the greenkeeper's yard and dived into a massive pile of horse manure. He had covered himself in the muck, leaving only a hole to breathe through, and had waited there. He had stayed there all afternoon till the track cleared; after dark he had finally crawled out. It wasn't too bad, once you got used to the smell, said Humour. It was probably the warmest place on the course that bleak day. Humour had a way of seeing the best in a bad situation.

In February 1969 the Kid, 'Little Carmel' Shipley, Nicholas Davitch and a handful of others travelled to Farnham in Surrey to do a job on a jewellery store. It went off without a hitch and then the team jumped into the cars to head back to London, an hour or two away. They kept to the back roads, just in case.

The Kid was enjoying the ride, watching the snow-dusted hedgerows flying past and recollecting his many adventures. Most of the team only stayed in London a few months at a time before heading home, but the Kid had been there since 1966. He felt like a veteran, though he was only 21. During these few years he had seen this caper blow right open—the place was just crawling with Aussies now, many of them green and inept, a danger to their mates. Where were all the old hands he had known from 1966?

The Fibber was in and out of Britain on various escapades in South Africa, America and Europe, with occasional trips home. The Kid missed working with the Fibber, who had been about as close to a father as he had known. People just dropped in and out of your life in this game, he thought. It was like living a gypsy lifestyle—you would be tight with someone, spend every minute of your time together, and then one day they would be gone. No goodbyes, no tears, no forwarding address. Someone else took their place and the business went on.

That's how it had been with Grace O'Connor. In 1967–68 they had been on the hoist together every day—she had been as tender and sweet as any woman he had ever met. She had cared for him and laughed with him. Then one day in early 1969 Grace hadn't turned up for work, and that was the end of it. There were snippets of gossip about her occasion-ally—she was working with some new Aussies in town, someone said. But it wasn't like the old days, when you knew everybody. There were so many Aussies now, and plenty of bad and desperate men among them. He missed Grace, and hoped she was doing okay.

It was now only 3:30 in the afternoon, but the sun was already gone as they sped along the country lanes. How he had put up with this English weather he didn't know, he mused. Millions of pounds had run through his fingers like sand. He had saved a little, sending some back to his mother, but what had happened to the rest was a mystery. Hardly anyone he knew had ended up with much—maybe only one in ten of them had any more than their airfare home. He would only stay in Old Blighty long enough to put together a stake, and then he would be off home.

It was then he noticed the headlights of a Jaguar a few hundred yards behind them in the lane. He told Nick to make a few turns, to check if they were being followed. Sure enough, the tail stuck to them. There could be no high-speed escape—there was no telling how many cars were in the area and, if they ran, any doubt about their guilt would be removed. This wasn't *The Italian Job*.

Finally the Jaguar closed in on them and two plain clothes detectives pulled them over. They searched the car and found nothing. They ordered the Kid to turn out his pockets one by one. Little did they know the pockets of his overcoat were all joined, so he could move the tom from hand to hand and appear to be clean. Reluctantly the coppers let them go, even though they surely recognised them as notorious thieves.

The crew in the other car weren't so lucky—they were nabbed in possession of stolen goods from the robbery. Carmel Shipley, according to the *Sydney Morning Herald*, had come to England with her girlfriends in 1968 for modelling. Her trip was to be extended with two years' jail for theft. The Kid was now wanted for the same job (the police, after consulting the Australian Index, picked him out after their brief roadside meeting) and would probably get more jail time than the others.

An intermediary, Richard 'Dinkum Dick' Marshall, made an appointment on the Kid's behalf with the detective in charge of the investigation, to see if this could be sorted out. They met on a golf course and Dinkum Dick offered the detective £5000 to drop off. But a bribe wouldn't do it this time—the Kid had been getting away with too much. This was now a matter of pride and ego. 'I want that young bastard, and his mate Davitch too. You tell him that,' the detective told Dinkum Dick.

It was time to come home, but not on his passport. The Kid visited a cemetery and found the tombstone of someone around his age and stole his identity. It had been an extraordinary adventure, but now it was over. Soon most of the Aussies would follow him, the Kid thought. A golden age like this could never last forever.

For many, this had been a youthful lark and now they would return home to a more sedate life. Some developed respectable business careers, while others used their overseas experience and contacts to become involved in the international drug trade. Many, like the Kid, returned to what they knew—the hurly-burly of the racetrack, two-up schools in back rooms in Sydney and a lucrative trade in 'second-hand' goods.

However, very few got to love the place as much as Baby Bruce did. Through his work in King Solomon's Mines (the Tube) he became a well-known figure in the ganglands. He teamed up with remnants of the Kray and Richardson gangs, and soon he was speaking like a native South Londoner. At one time Baby Bruce and his team were nicked stealing jewels in Amsterdam and got five years' jail. But, fortunately, Bruce 'made restitution' (he gave the loot back) and got out after only nine months. He ended up spending 40 years in England, eventually running a famous nightclub, the Trianon, in the West End.

The Fibber's South African adventures finally came to a screeching halt when he did a stretch in the infamous Cinderella Prison in Boksburg, South Africa, in 1970–72. Just how he got there was a matter of debate. Some, like Baby Bruce, said that 'Morry the Head' Spurling had persuaded the Fibber to go down there to steal diamonds from the dealers in Commissioner Street, who took delivery of stones direct from the rich Kimberley mines. Unfortunately, they had come unstuck. They had got the stones but the dealer, armed with a pistol, had run them down.

The Kid had another version—that the Fibber had stolen cash from over the counter in a bank. Knowing the Fibber, maybe he had done both. Either way, he had got a couple of years in one of South Africa's worst jails.

At first the Fibber found Cinderella terrifying. Even inside jail, apartheid guaranteed that white inmates received more humane treatment than the blacks, but nonetheless they all lived amid cruelty and savagery. The Fibber had never seen such abject misery. To survive, he would have to ingratiate himself with the biggest and nastiest of the black inmates. To show his racial tolerance, he made up a story that he had trained Aboriginal boxer Lionel Rose in his successful bantamweight world title fight in 1968. Soon he was passing on Rose's 'secrets' in the exercise yard to adoring groups of young Africans. Being busy made the time pass more quickly. After the daily excitement of hoisting, jail must have been incredibly tedious.

Hangings of African inmates were commonplace in South African jails. It ground away at the souls of everyone, as Benjamin Pogrund recalls in his best-selling book, *War of Words*:

> Executions were held about every ten days. Days beforehand the condemned began singing and, being Africans most of them, they can't help singing harmoniously. But as the time wears on the singing becomes more and more ragged. The last two days and nights they just sing right through. 'Nearer My God to Thee' and stuff like that. I never want to hear such hymns again. Then you would hear the condemned walking to the gallows cells singing hymns. You would hear the door shut. Later, you would faintly hear the sound of the trapdoors opening. I would feel a tremble run through the part of the building where I was as the trapdoor fell.

The Fibber dealt with the horror in his customary manner. He had been assigned to the prison radio as the announcer. To lighten the mood (or to drown out the piteous hymn singing), he would dedicate to those due to be hanged in the morning the song 'Bye Bye Blackbird'. To those unacquainted with jail, this might seem insensitive, but to the wretched souls awaiting the noose, it must have come as a moment of light relief. The Fibber just couldn't bear the sadness of those nights. And despite the macabre humour, the Fibber felt real compassion for the plight of the blacks.

He noticed some of the condemned men were bent over and hobbling, their toenails so ingrown they could hardly walk. So he made a special plea to the warden for a pair of clippers, and he gave them all a pedicure. The other inmates and screws could hardly believe it—a white man on his knees before a black man. This just did not happen in South Africa, but to the Fibber it was natural. He had lived high on the hog in the UK and Europe, but he had been down and out too, and people had looked after him. At least, with their toenails clipped, they could walk upright to the executioner with some dignity restored.

9

A practical affair

The Australian Index of 4 December 1969 recorded the fact that Arthur William Delaney had obtained a British passport by false statement and was 'now in Australia'. This intelligence rather undersold the King's meanderings at that point. With the heat increasing in London, the King was on the move. Sure, he had been home a few times—just long enough to seal the most important relationship of his life—but, if anything, his wanderlust had intensified. That was probably a good thing—as charming as he was, Alexis would probably have strangled him if they had spent all their time together.

Arthur had worn Alexis down over a long period. Despite her original misgivings—she had thought him too full of himself, vain and arrogant—they had started working together in Sydney and she had never seen a better thief. Also, he was generous and awfully persistent—a character even. As part of his campaign, he had wooed Alexis' mother, taking her out for dinner and buying her flowers. Under this all-out charm offensive, Alexis had finally begun to look at Arthur in a different light. But she never got carried away with romance. First and foremost, she wanted stability and a home for herself and her daughter, Debbie. Maybe Arthur might come in handy after all, considering what a great money getter he was.

As a single mum surviving on the hoist, she had to be very careful. To fall blindly in love with Arthur would be a very foolish thing to do—if he went down, so too would she. It was important she keep her bets hedged. Officially, she was in a relationship with another hoister, 'Skinny Fred' McKinnon, but increasingly she was spending time working with Arthur. And Arthur was living with an off-and-on lover named Barbara Bourke, but that would never inhibit him at all. Their professional relationship flourished, even as Alexis kept Arthur at arm's length as a lover.

Skinny Fred was a tall, amiable fellow—not a bad sort of a thief, but not a patch on Arthur. Eventually, it dawned on Alexis that Skinny Fred would never take her round the world like Arthur would. Her relationship with Arthur would always be a gamble, but by now there was enough trust to take the risk. Their relationship, one of Sydney's worst kept secrets, came out in the open when Alexis invited Arthur to move into her place, or at least stay with her on his forays through Sydney. Suddenly Skinny Fred was history.

Alexis hoped that, if she rode Arthur hard enough, the two of them might end up with something—a house even, a place to call her own. But most of her friends told her she was mad—Arthur would gamble every last cent they had, and then some. If he had his way, their life would be lived from day to day, from job to job. There would never be enough money to satisfy him; his quest had nothing to do with cash.

But it would be the same for any woman who chose a crook for a lover. There would be regular unexplained absences, infidelity and lots of time on the run. There would be no white picket fence in the suburbs for Mrs Arthur Delaney, if she could even drag him to the church. The only certainty was that she would do lots of boob for Arthur. It went with the territory and she knew that. Arthur simply represented the best of a bad set of choices. But still, Arthur gave her hope. Every day brought new opportunities for change. If you went with the flow, perhaps everything would work out in the end. Whatever this life would be, it would not be dull. At the very least she would see the world.

Forty years later, sitting in her modest Sydney bayside unit, Alexis could hardly believe she was the same person as in the photographs. How on earth had she lived through those amazing times? She put on her gold-rimmed glasses to take a closer look at the youthful faces in the pictures. There they were in Paris, walking down the Rue Royale; there they were in Italy, arriving at Lake Como for the jewellery auctions, or floating down Venice's Grand Canal. She had loved playing tourist in the great capitals of world—it was the education she had never had as a kid in Maroubra, a lifestyle she had only glimpsed as an usherette at the movies in her teen years. After nearly 30 years at home, Alexis' accent had returned to its original 'strine'. Back then, she had blended in with all those fine society ladies and gentlemen.

Her daughter Debbie brought out her album and showed me its numerous group shots in bars and restaurants, where tables always overflowed with food and drink. There were Arthur, the Fibber and the rest with floral leis around their necks, suntanned and relaxed in white pants and Hawaiian shirts. There were so many of these shots that Alexis and Debbie struggled to identify everybody in them and where they were. That was Malta—no Rome. There's one in the casino at Monte Carlo; that's Madrid, and fishing in Cornwall. That may be Cannes, said Alexis, turning the pictures over.

Amongst the piles of photographs was a book that Alexis handed to me. It was one of only a few of Arthur's possessions she still had, said Alexis. It's called *An Autobiography*, written and self-published in 1988 by George Freeman, the late Sydney crime identity. I opened the cover and there was a handwritten inscription for Arthur: 'King, King, King, Best Wishes George Freeman'.

Until my conversation with Alexis and Debbie in 2009, Arthur had been a composite character in my mind, cobbled together from the impressions of others. His life had been lived so deep inside the underworld, there was virtually no public record of him, beyond accounts of a few arrests. Up to 1969 the only reference to him in newspaper archives had been in 1952, when a female witness testifying against the police was discredited by evidence that she had carried on a relationship with Arthur. There was nothing else available. I wondered how he would feel about that, considering his relentless big-noting and his well-known ambition to be the flesh and blood equivalent of the fictional Arthur Raffles.

In his book Freeman, who took over running Sydney after Joe Taylor's retirement, mentioned Arthur's name only once in passing—he did not reveal Arthur had been with him when they got nicked in Perth for stealing cash from a shop in 1967. While Arthur by then was playing the international man of mystery, he still wasn't above cleaning out a till or two when his pockets were empty. And he was keen to pass on the tricks of the trade to the young George Freeman. The Perth job was only $258 in cash from an open till. Freeman had been the taker and got caught, serving six months' jail while Arthur walked free.

Their relationship was extremely close. Before his international career began, Arthur had been a mentor to Freeman, a tough kid who grew up in boys' homes and penitentiaries. Through example, Arthur showed Freeman he could aspire to a decent life, or at least a life of crime a cut above the street riffraff he had been running with up to then.

The Perth lagging turned out to be Freeman's last jail stint; soon afterwards he turned to organised crime through starting price bookmaking and illegal casinos. Freeman was rough—a small intense man whose cold eyes inspired fear in even his close mates. Not a man given to subtlety, Freeman was ruthless—you were with him or against him. George had jail tattoos across his knuckles—LOVE and HATE—and that was how he led his life. Freeman was to become the most prominent crook of his generation, and the equal of his mentor as a thief. Freeman could do it all, from cutting safes and armed robbery to confidence tricks and hoisting.

In his book Freeman wrote of a shoplifting expedition to the United States with 'some Aussie mates' in 1968. Arthur was the leader of that expedition. He had previously travelled many times to the US, coming in through Canada on dodgy British Visitor passports. He had already made friends in most of the major cities. Normally, he would off-load his stolen sparklers with crooked jewellers in London's Hatton Gardens, but the larger and more distinctive pieces were difficult to off-load. So he would take them to New York, to the diamond district of West 75th Street, where they could recut or reset and sell them to American buyers. In 1966, Arthur had taken his then girlfriend, Paddy Burridge, on a whistle-stop tour of the States, travelling by road from the Pacific north-west coast right down to New Orleans in the Deep South. He seemed to know people everywhere they went—crooks and cops, even a singing rodeo star in one town.

When Freeman wrote his book, Arthur was still alive; in fact he was one of Freeman's best clients—the King would ultimately lose thousands betting with George's SP operation. Clearly Arthur's name couldn't be mentioned, so George outed himself as the taker in a job that became legend in Australia and the States. But, in truth, compared with the worldly Arthur, at that time Freeman and his travelling companions had been complete ingenues.

Freeman wrote of knocking off a large quantity of jewellery from a department store in Los Angeles:

> One day, I was walking through a big department store in Los Angeles when I noticed a woman shop worker had left the jewellery safe unattended. The safe was locked but I could see the keys just lying nearby. I signalled to the other guys to draw the attention of the other staff, and I had the safe open within seconds. There, standing up looking up at me, was a large amount of jewellery. I couldn't believe my eyes—it was a big score. I stuffed the lot in my shirt and we walked slowly out into the sunlight a whole lot richer than when we walked in.

Without denigrating Freeman's story, Arthur told a different version, which featured himself in the starring role. It must have made Arthur bleed to let someone else take credit for his handiwork, but his version seems more credible, given his personality. One evening, after a slow start to the hoisting holiday in the US, the boys had gatecrashed the opening of a jewellery store in downtown Beverley Hills. It was late and everyone, including the hosts, was half-cut on champagne and cocktails. Expensive items of jewellery were being passed around. Showcases and the safe in the back were left open. The scene just invited a massacre and Arthur had led the slaughter, cleaning out every bauble he could find.

Whichever way it happened, the boys now had a large amount of hot jewellery and nowhere on the West Coast to off-load it. A contact back in Australia suggested they look up a fringe Mafia figure based in Chicago, Joe Dan Testa, who would look after them and get the best price for their booty. Testa was more than happy to accommodate these dashing Aussies. A black stretch-limo was waiting for them when they landed at Chicago's O'Hare Airport. The tom was taken to a local police station and locked in the safe there; the cops later helped to fence the gear and the boys pocketed a cool $200 000. This was normally enough play money for a few weeks, but their gracious host, Testa, wouldn't let them spend a cent. They were taken to Testa's mansion which, according to Freeman, was inhabited by gorgeous air hostesses lounging round the pool in various states of undress:

One night Joe threw a dinner party at the mansion and it was full of Joe's business associates, most of them old guys who had swallowed Joe's tough-talking style and one or two younger guys, who were more than fringe dwellers on the Chicago scene. They were less than impressed—especially one of them.

One of the younger guys started cutting up rough. He looked mean, and he was . . . The dispute was over a business deal that had gone wrong and there was no way Joe would take a backward step. Next minute, the young guy belts Joe, sending him crashing across the room. The blood—all of it Joe's—begins to flow . . . When the rough stuff started no-one wanted to know our host. No-one, that is, except one of my Aussie mates. He yells 'fair go' and then boots the young Chicago boy under the chin. By the time the boy lands back on the ground, one of his ears and half of his nose had been bitten off. Crocodile Dundee has nothing on this Aussie bloke. His legend, and that of all us, spread far and wide through Chicago and beyond as a result of that brief blue.

Needless to say, the hero of the hour was not Arthur, though of course he basked in the glory of the incident for years afterwards. The group stayed six weeks at Testa's Chicago mansion, forging a friendship that lasted for more than a decade. They hosted Testa in Sydney in 1969, throwing lavish parties and showing him off at Sydney nightclubs and casinos. Sydney heavy Lennie 'Mr Big' McPherson even took Testa pig shooting in the west of New South Wales. Meanwhile Arthur talked up their exploits to anyone who would listen. He was enjoying a status now that no shoplifter had ever dreamt of. Finally, through Testa, he was front-page news.

Testa returned to Australia again in 1971. The media, and a couple of royal commissions, later concluded that Testa's visit was a key step in the Mafia's infiltration of Australia. The purpose of the 1971 visit had been to arrange the purchase of slot machines manufactured by the Bally Manufacturing Company, an American slot-machine manufacturer that was Mafia-controlled, and to 'persuade' Sydney clubs to purchase Bally slot machines, often through threats of violence.

Freeman always denied that Testa was a Mafia boss, but the trouble was that Testa swaggered around Sydney doing little to dispel the image. An appearance at the Moffitt Royal Commission into Mafia penetration of Sydney clubs only reinforced his heavy image. A TV interview followed that created more suspicion. 'The more Joe talked, the more he denied it, the more people believed he was a crook; because deep down Joe wanted to be regarded as a crook . . . In fact, it got that way that Joe's tough-talking mobster style was becoming something of an embarrassment,' George Freeman concluded.

News of Arthur's new friendship quickly spread all the way to England. The 1969 Australian Index included entries for George Freeman and the heroic young Aussie who had defended Testa in Chicago, though neither of them had ever set foot in England. Arthur and Alexis remained close with Testa into the 1980s, travelling back and forth to Chicago as guests of the mobster on several occasions. That is until June 1981, when Testa turned the ignition of his Lincoln Continental and was blown to smith-ereens by a car bomb.

While Arthur had been away on his global hoisting tour, Sydney had become a violent place. As the illegal casino business boomed, jealousies and rivalries had intensified. Between 1963 and 1968, there had been eight killings in the Sydney underworld, mostly the result of paranoia and bad debts. Most of the leading crime figures wouldn't move about town without a gunman or two. It was an unhealthy time and people were getting shot for the most trivial of reasons.

Arthur had made a few enemies since breezing back in from Chicago in late 1968. By now he had won Alexis' trust, if not her heart, and the pair was living in Randwick on the seventh floor of the Mile Post apart-ment block, named for its strategic view of the mile post on the racetrack directly across the road. But Skinny Fred was grieving the loss of Alexis. She was not only a highly desirable woman but also an integral part of his modest thieving operation. He would never be in the same class of hoister as Arthur Delaney, and the King had rubbed his nose in it by stealing his girl. There were curses and threats exchanged and finally a challenge. 'Meet me out the front of the Mile Post just on dark,' Arthur told his rival. 'We'll sort this out like men of honour.'

At the appointed time, Arthur stripped down to his singlet and went downstairs to wait for Skinny Fred. Alexis stood watching from their apartment's window; her seven-year-old daughter Debbie looked on from another window. This was ridiculous, thought Alexis—as a fighter, Arthur couldn't knock a pea off a chop. Skinny Fred was no street brawler either, but there was something chivalrous about a man fighting for the hand of his woman—she felt a little flattered. She imagined the pair would prance around waving their fists at each other; Skinny Fred, being taller, would give Arthur a black eye, and that would be it. Arthur didn't want a war—he was too busy sniffing out money every day to waste time killing people.

Just then Alexis recognised Skinny Fred's car coming slowly down the hill from Randwick Junction on the other side of the road. 'Good, he's by himself,' she thought. 'They're a pair of bloody fools. Let's get this over with.'

But as the car approached, Alexis saw its headlights go off. From her vantage point, she could see someone crouched in the back seat. Suddenly she realised it was a set-up. This wasn't going to be a fight—she was about to witness an execution. As the car drifted to a stop across the road, Alexis was desperately calling down to Arthur to get inside. She shouted and screamed, but the traffic drowned out her pleas from seven floors up. She watched as a figure in the back seat bobbed up at the window, and then there was the muzzle flash, a tongue of flame under the dim street lights.

There was no chance of escape. The gunman fired a volley of six shots at Arthur. In the split second between when he spotted the gun and the fusillade began, Arthur had turned and begun to run back up the drive. If he hadn't, he might have caught a slug between the eyes. As it was, the first five shots actually missed him. It was only the last that struck him—in his lower back near the spine. The power went from his legs, as if someone had flipped a switch.

Alexis watched him fall on the driveway. He was desperately dragging himself on his elbows up the drive to the front door and safety. Alexis stood transfixed, expecting to see the gunman cross the street to deliver a coup de grâce. To this day, Debbie swears she saw a figure, dressed all in black, walk up and stand over Arthur for a moment, before hurrying away. Whoever it was, he probably saved Arthur's life, because in that delay Skinny Fred roared away.

Alexis didn't see the shadowy man in black. She was now frantically trying to reach the ground floor, cursing the slow descent of the lift. By the time she got to him, Arthur was unconscious—a dark pool was spreading on the concrete, his singlet was soaked in blood. Remarkably, a passing uniform policeman arrived on the scene just seconds later. He immediately recognised Arthur's stricken form. Pushing his hat back on his head, he exclaimed: 'It's the Duke. They've shot the Duke!'

It was quickly discovered that Kevin Victor Gore had been the shooter in the back seat. Gore was a psychopath, a man who just loved killing people. He had always made Sydney's 'decent' crooks uncomfortable. 'If he was sitting in a room, you wouldn't look twice at him. He was a small thin bloke. So mild and pleasant, you wouldn't think he could hurt a fly, but inside he was as cold a killer as the Devil ever owned. He made your skin crawl,' said one old crook, shuddering at the memory.

Gore was the leader of the Toecutter Gang, a bunch of merciless pirates who favoured stealing other people's loot rather than pulling their own jobs. Their grisly moniker had been earned after they had sought a cut of a $500 000 armoured car robbery in Sydney. They had taken a blowtorch to the toes of one of the robbers, Frank 'Baldy' Blair, in an effort to find the loot. Mercifully they had eventually killed Blair, but the men who ran Sydney had marked Kevin Gore for death. Shooting Arthur had added insult to injury. Gore didn't care—he was taking the team to Melbourne to join up with Billy Longley and his forces. There was big money to be made for killers in the struggle for control of the Painters and Dockers Union.

However, he would never get there. One evening in 1971, Gore got into his car and started the engine; but before he could pull away, a gunman burst from his hiding place in the boot through the back seat and opened fire on him with an automatic weapon. The talk in the underworld was that police heard that Arthur's protégé, George Freeman, had been the shooter. The police questioned Freeman but no charges were laid. It was better for everyone that Gore had gone; no-one but Billy Longley would miss this monstrous gun for hire. It was believed the bodies of Gore and another member of his gang, who had been murdered a few days later, were weighted down and dumped at sea.

Whether by design or omission, Skinny Fred somehow escaped the same fate. But he never bothered Alexis or Arthur again. Arthur wasn't interested in revenge—that wouldn't give him back his legs. At first, the doctors feared he would never walk again—the slug had damaged his spinal cord, how badly they couldn't yet tell. His days of running round the globe like Raffles might be over, he thought. A thief in a wheelchair would get sympathy, but that was all. He could still pull heads on the hoist, but he couldn't operate as a taker, not like this.

However, during the first few days in hospital there had been no self-pity. Outside the summer sun was shining, the world was moving on without him. Yet he was philosophical. If the best days of his life were behind him, then he hadn't missed out on anything. And if there was any hope, then he would focus on that and nothing else. The thief knows all too well that 99 per cent of his worries never come to pass. So he screens them out. It's the one per cent he overlooks that trips him up. So live it up now, he says, before all is gone.

Even as the doctors shook their heads gravely, Arthur remained upbeat about his chances. From gambling to crime and romance, Arthur's life had been a victory of optimism over commonsense. Some people said he was lucky to be alive, but he disagreed. He was unfortunate to have been hit—after all, five shots had missed him before Gore's sixth shot found its mark. Arthur figured he was now due a lucky break.

10

An uncle in Manchester

'Better give this lot twelve minutes in the dish,' 'Smudger' Smith thought as he prepared to print the previous night's work in the darkroom. Detective Constable James Smith was the Yard's best covert man, and the cloak of secrecy even extended to his own colleagues. No-one would see these pictures before his boss, Detective Inspector David Woodland. From a beaker, he played the developing solution over the photographic paper. Then he carefully exposed the rolls of 400 ASA film in the solution and stood back bathed in red UV lamplight, waiting.

The light had been low and the subjects nearly a hundred metres away, so he had racked the Nikon wide open to get an effective ASA of 1200. At this stop, with the slightest camera shake the image would become indecipherable—an unusable blurry blob. But he'd been rock solid. Smudger knew how to get the best from his equipment under the most trying of circumstances. He loved his camera, like a sharpshooter might love a rifle, but this job on 7 March 1972 had been especially enjoyable.

For a couple of years before this, he had followed members of the Irish Republican Army around London. Part of him had always feared what might happen if those fanatics ever twigged to his presence. Shooting from inside his Morris 1000 van, he was virtually invisible. He would be in the back, wearing a balaclava and dark clothes. A sliding panel, which opened at the rear, was just big enough for his lens. From 300 yards away he was beyond human eyesight, but occasionally one of them had seemed to look right down the lens at him. It would make his heart skip a beat—maybe a ray of light had reflected off the lens, or maybe one of Scotland Yard's finest had tipped off the villains to the Morris. Funerals had been the worst—if you got caught there, you were a goner. They would tear you apart. Working solo could be a short, thrilling experience.

Now, after watching the Aussies down the lens for a few months, Jimmy could understand the charge they got from robbing banks and high-class jewellers, relying solely on their wits. With a camera in his hand, he felt it too and the surge of adrenalin was addictive. He had never tried drugs, but he couldn't imagine a narcotic that matched this high.

Last night he had worked at the Royal Albert Hall in Knightsbridge. He had sauntered in from the street, camera bag slung over his shoulder, hands thrust deep in his pockets from the cold. It was an imposing place, the Royal Albert Hall, as much for its design as for its size and distinctive Britishness. An epic mosaic frieze, titled 'The Triumph of Arts and Sciences', ran around the outside of the hall and proudly declared England's greatness. In one-foot-high terracotta letters, it read 'This hall was erected for the advancement of the arts and sciences and works of industry of all nations . . . Thine O Lord is the greatness and the power and the glory and the victory and the majesty. For all that is in the heaven and in the earth is Thine. The wise and their works are in the hand of God. Glory be to God on high and on earth peace.' Nice to know God's on my side, Jimmy thought. Not only was he an agent of justice, but also an expression of British destiny and ingenuity.

It was a fight night, a five-bout card of local and international pugs—a couple of title fights, so there would be a lot of money riding. Plenty of heavy London crims would be ringside to watch their investments, but the Australians wouldn't be among them. Jimmy expected to spot them in a box halfway up to the gods in the cavernous hall, from where they could see who could see *them*. So Jimmy went higher—to the gallery level, almost at the glass-and-wrought-iron dome, 40 metres from the ring below. Through binoculars he scanned the rows of well-dressed punters—and there they were!

They couldn't have posed better for him, he thought as the grainy black and white images slowly appeared on the photo paper in his darkroom. As he'd snapped their portraits, he had written their names in a notebook. Smith had knocked off all the Aussies by the time local boy Bunny Sterling stopped American Tom 'The Bomb' Bethea in the ninth round of the main event. Now he ticked them off as he pegged up the prints to dry: *Wee Jimmy Lloyd, Cecil Lloyd, Victor Edward Doyle* (alias *Victor Emond*), *Robert Spinks, James Richard White, Geoffrey Robert Willis* . . . And last but not least, *John Noel Jones*.

The old firm was still operating. The Kangaroo Gang, even without Arthur, had outlasted the Beatles. They had prospered under the rule of three prime ministers and had vexed four chief commissioners of police. Four years after their publication in the first Australian Index, these heads were still popping up. Wee Jimmy had finessed himself and his brother Cecil out of trouble in 1968, cooking up a false alibi with a crooked Australian cop. On his last trip to court, Wee Jimmy had pleaded guilty and copped a fine. He had remained in the Index every year till now, but around 1970 his list of convictions inexplicably disappeared.

Other members had also benefited from this bureaucratic 'amnesia'. 'Geoffrey Robert Willis' was in fact Leslie John Cole, a noted Melbourne standover man with a long criminal history—he was a killer some said. ('Johnny' Cole would later sire one of Melbourne's best-known crooks, Mark Moran, slain in 2000 in a drug war.) How was he coming and going so freely?

The rest had all been first identified when Mike Pearce collated the criminal records and photographs in 1967–68. John Noel Jones was unmistakeable, though he had grown a wispy moustache and piled on weight since his first appearance in the 1967 Australian Index. Jimmy Smith had made a report on his night at the boxing and attached his pictures, sending the lot to his boss Dave Woodland. By rights, Jimmy shouldn't have been at the boxing that night. The boss of the CID, Commander David Dilley, had ordered the operation be ended—there were better things to do than follow the Aussies around. But Woodland had kept Wee Jimmy's phone 'hooked up' (wire-tapped), defying Dilley's orders.

Someone in the Yard had tipped the Lloyds off to the wire tap early on and Wee Jimmy had warned callers the phone was off, making a joke of it. The Aussies were always careful on the phone after that, but still Woodland had persisted. Another surveillance unit had been watching a flat frequented by the Aussies when one of the gang came down and, with a huge smile, squirted shaving foam all over the van. They'd had to call for uniform back-up to get out of there.

Maybe, Woodland calculated, the same traitor would tell Wee Jimmy when the surveillance had been officially canned. Maybe then he would get careless. Woodland just had to make sure that no-one told the boss what he was doing. This way they would learn that the traitor was David Dilley.

Just why police had let this caper get so out of hand was a source of mystery to American Express Chief Special Agent Len Mountford. 'Mounty', a former detective inspector on the Flying Squad, had a few passions in life—model railways, antique firearms and catching crooks. As head of Amex's security, he was running his own private squad of former detectives. Despite their best efforts, they were getting ripped off blind, he thought as he sat in his backyard watching a goods train nego-tiate the elaborate track he had constructed there. The Amex team had recorded thefts of traveller's cheques worth £200 000 for that year alone. The total amount stolen ran into millions of pounds over the past five years—he didn't care to do the sums. Georgie G and Normie Seddon had preyed on Amex in the mid 1960s, and now in 1972 a new crew was hard at work.

Theft of traveller's cheques and credit cards had been a problem since their inception, but it was a highly sophisticated operation now. If the Great Train Robbers had known of this lark in 1963, they wouldn't have bothered with the Glasgow to Watford train, he thought—they would have gone out and bought a transistor radio with a long aerial and a fishing hook.

There were two main scams going on. The thieves would befriend hotel cleaning staff and pay them to provide master keys to hotel rooms, particularly those of loud Americans who had come to London to spray their money around. The thief would take half a guest's traveller's cheques, carefully cutting them from the bottom of the stack so they wouldn't be missed straightaway. Then they would create a false passport in the name of the guest, complete with a new photograph in their own likeness to use as ID to cash the cheques. On one occasion, thieves had cashed the cheques with a new passport in the same name in just 20 minutes.

A new team was practising the distraction method in banks. They were using Georgie G's trademark taking style, the telescopic aerial attached to a fishing hook with treble shanks. But Georgie was still on the run for bank jobs going back to 1968 and was only making cameo appearances in the United Kingdom. These were imitators, but very good ones—they had to be Australian.

Mountford knew that, once they got hold of the cheques, there was little he could do. In those pre-computer days, Amex would produce circulars with the serial numbers of stolen cheques and distribute them to its merchants all over the world. If a merchant were suspicious of a cheque, he could check it against this list. However, it might be a month before the circular reached all the merchants. The Amex agents had no chance of catching these crooks if they cashed the cheques within 24 hours in a different city.

If the extent of this fraud became widely known, every crook would be at it, severely denting public confidence in traveller's cheques as the new safe form of currency. Already Mounty had special agents constantly travelling all over the world following up scams and fraudulent claims. He had agitated for the formation of a Cheque Fraud Squad at Scotland Yard and held seminars for officers like David Woodland at C11, explaining that this was more than just simple fraud. There was evidence, he told Scotland Yard, that stolen cheques were being used in the international drug trade: heroin coming from Afghanistan and Pakistan was being paid for by bodgie cheques. Crooks were on-selling the cheques for a discount on their face value to the drug barons. Amex had begun to collate the particulars of the stolen cheques cashed, where they were cashed and how they were signed. A pattern began to emerge—the characteristics of the 'screevers' (forgers) became apparent—but they couldn't put a name or a face to the scammers, and that would have to be up to the police.

In David Woodland's mind, all roads led to Wee Jimmy. It didn't matter that Wee Jimmy had earlier condemned Georgie G and Seddon for taking on banks; this was an earner that couldn't be ignored. Most of Woodland's superior officers, including boss David Dilley, thought the whole thing a waste of time. They were non-violent types—good guys, who went out of their way to socialise with the Old Bill, regularly getting invites to police outings to the boxing or racing trips.

Woodland had come across them socially and found them good company, but that didn't give them any licence. When he first put a wire tap on Wee Jimmy's telephone, it yielded nothing and he assumed the operation had been sold out. In the summer of 1971, Wee Jimmy's team had suddenly gone from relentlessly working every day in Knightsbridge, Kensington and the West End to doing nothing at all. It was like they had all suddenly decided to retire. But Woodland kept the wire tap going, over the objections of David Dilley, and he kept Jimmy Smith on the job too.

Smith watched them gather every Sunday morning at the Dennis Club on Bayswater Road,' Paddington. Some mornings there were 20 or 30 of them there. As the weather got warmer, they would open the windows and sit chatting on the sills. For a covert photographer this was like a turkey shoot. After an hour or two, they might move down to the Red Lion to meet up with other Aussies. They were pissing it up all day, but there was never any evidence of crime.

On the surface it looked like a social club, but still Smith was turning up heads never before identified as being in Britain. There was a sense that something was building here—these Aussies hadn't come for the Ashes series due to start in the summer of 1972. Under other circumstances they might have stolen the priceless urn that carried the ashes from the Lords ground in London, but clearly they had other priorities.

Finally, after Woodland had disobeyed Dilley's orders and kept the tap on Wee Jimmy for another couple of days, his patience was rewarded. On the evening of 5 April 1972, Wee Jimmy telephoned his brother Cecil and, dropping his normal cautiousness, gave a big clue: 'It's the big one Saturday,' he said. 'I'm off to see my uncle in Manchester. We'll be on the 8:30 out of Euston.'

That weekend, the biggest race in the British calendar, the Grand National Steeplechase, was to be run. That was certainly a big one, but why would a mad punter like Wee Jimmy be going to Manchester when the race was being held at Aintree near Liverpool, 40 miles from Manchester? After pondering this cryptic clue for a while, Woodland concluded the Lloyds weren't going racing. Wee Jimmy's 'uncle in Manchester' could only be Lloyd's Bank. The team was back in business.

Fortunately, Commander Dilley was on holidays so Woodland called Manchester CID and arranged a top-secret briefing. He flew to Manchester and briefed nearly 200 officers from regional crime squads across

Lancashire. No-one from Scotland Yard, except for C11 members, was in the know.

Jimmy Smith and a female detective constable were at Euston Road Station at 8:30 am the next day buying a ticket to Manchester. On the platform they saw William 'Wee Jimmy' Lloyd, with other known Aussie thieves Geoffrey Willis (Johnny Cole), Victor Spinks and Gary John Roberts, preparing to board the first class Pullman carriage for the two-hour journey. The rest had travelled on another train, lest they be nabbed in one group. Jimmy Smith and the policewoman, holding only economy tickets, settled down in the carriage behind.

After an hour of watching the bleak scenery go by, Smith couldn't sit there any longer. At Hounslow Station, an hour out of Manchester, he marched up the platform and into the Pullman carriage. He took a seat right next to the Aussies and sat there reading a photographic magazine while listening in to the would-be bank robbers' conversation. There was no mention of crime or playing up. They looked like nothing more than young Aussies on holiday in Britain, skylarking and taking the piss out of each other. For months he had followed these men from a distance and now he was up close. He couldn't help but like them, with their easy manner and ready laughter. Still, the adrenalin was pounding in his temples when the train reached Piccadilly Station in Manchester.

The cops observed the group of six or seven link up in downtown Manchester. They watched them go into two banks, including 'Uncle Lloyd's', and come out a short time later with A4 envelopes stuffed with stolen traveller's cheques. They watched them mail the envelopes to themselves at Australia House in London's Strand. Then they struck. Everyone, except for Wee Jimmy, was nicked; some had stolen driving licences and blank passports, while others were actually doing the business in the banks. A blanket count of 'conspiracy to steal from banks' was eventually brought.

After a good session on the drink with the local CID, the team returned to London and then searched all the known hangouts of the associates. To prevent leaks, Woodland booked the conference room at the Yard and called in a mix of Divisional CID, Regional Crime Squad and Flying Squad members for a briefing. He divided the men into various details and assigned a C11 man to each team. The cover story for any nosey coppers inquiring what exactly they were up to was that they were a surveillance operation on a robbery team. All officers were directed to map locations and, at a given time, instructed to open a sealed envelope containing the target's name, address and a search warrant.

There had been no leaks and over a dozen Aussies, publicans and associates were nicked in London and charged with a variety of offences, from receiving stolen traveller's cheques and passports to bank and shop stealing. It was the single most successful operation ever undertaken against the Aussies, and it had gone off without the top brass even knowing. But there would be no bragging. C11 was a 'secret squirrel squad' and any publicity or other identification of its members would blow their cover. So Woodland was rather bemused to read in the *Evening Standard* the next day that a team of detectives led by Detective Superintendent Frew and Detective Inspector Woodland had collared the Aussie team.

An international arrest warrant was issued for Wee Jimmy, but they didn't expect to see him again—he was too slippery to err twice. However, much to David Woodland's surprise, he was seen to cop a feel of Wee Jimmy's collar.

The Aussie was picked up in Brussels on Woodland's warrant a few weeks after the Manchester job. Woodland and a DC from the Passport Office went to Belgium to organise the extradition. However, unable to operate in this jurisdiction, the two Englishmen sat and watched as an officious little Belgian detective tried in vain to interrogate Jimmy.

Wee Jimmy was already 'doing his time' in his customary fashion, and sat stony-faced, deflecting all queries with a mumbled: 'I can't answer that.'

Finally the Belgian, in frustration, shouted at Wee Jimmy: 'You're not in England now,' he fumed. 'I am the law inside this place and if you continue to defy me, I will have you locked away for the rest of your life. Do you understand me, Mr Lloyd? I am going to put a stop to you Australians once and for all.' His face was now close to Wee Jimmy's.

This was too much even for Wee Jimmy. 'Who the fuck do you think you are, mate?' he snarled. 'You would fucking think you were Inspector Clouseau [Peter Sellers' character from the 1963 film, *The Pink Panther*]. Or what about fucking Hercule Poirot [Agatha Christie's fictional Belgian detective]?'

Such a stream of invective flowed from Wee Jimmy's mouth, it was pointless to continue with the interview. Woodland later told colleagues he would have given a day's pay for a tape of that interview. Nonetheless, Wee Jimmy was finally extradited back to England and served three years' jail along with Cecil and the rest.

A few weeks before the trial of Wee Jimmy, Smith was in an elevator at the Yard when a well-known detective sergeant from the Flying Squad got in. The Heavy Mob always felt they were above the scroungers at C11, so this detective had never so much as acknowledged him before. Now he was acting like Jimmy's best mate: 'Well, Jock, you must be rapt,' he said, clapping Jimmy on the back. 'I hear you nicked at least one of the Lloyds and all their mates—that's a good collar, my boy. Well now, Jock, I'm going to do you a favour, okay? I've got three grand for you, if you provide a little cooperation.'

Smith's eyes widened. He had dealt with crooks from 200 yards through a lens, but he had never before been approached so openly with a bribe.

The detective pulled out a passport photograph of one of the Lloyds. 'Who's that?' he asked with a big smile on his face.

'I believe it's one of the Lloyds,' Smith replied. They were difficult to tell apart—both short with receding hairlines and green-hazel eyes. In the picture, the subject had a cap on, pulled slightly over one eye. It was impossible to tell which one they were looking at.

'You can't tell you, can you?' said the detective. He turned the picture over. Written on the back was: 'This is a true likeness of William Lloyd.' It was signed by a solicitor in Sydney and dated 6 April 1972. *The day before Jimmy Smith had sat beside him on a train to Manchester!*

With this photograph placing him 6000 miles away, there would be real doubt the man they'd nicked in Manchester was in fact Wee Jimmy Lloyd. Maybe it was his brother Cecil; maybe it was someone else entirely. All Smith had to do was say that in court and he would be £3000 richer. His stomach was churning. He had never taken a penny of graft in his career, but this was big money. His housing mortgage was only £4500 at the time. The detective said he'd already been squared off with cash and that Smith would be too after the trial, if he did the right thing.

The detective got out of the lift, leaving Smith sweating buckets. He daren't raise the offer with his boss, Dave Woodland, lest the top brass create a big fuss chasing the culprits. He feared being ostracised if he spoke out, so he kept quiet. Every time he saw the Flying Squad detective, it was like they were best buddies. Here was an opportunity to join the system.

Smith's identification would be crucial to the case against Wee Jimmy Lloyd. When he was called as a witness, Lloyd's barrister looked disdainfully over his glasses at him.

'Detective Constable Smith,' he began. 'You say in your statement that you recognised Mr Lloyd over there on the train to Manchester.'

'Yes, sir,' Smith replied.

'Now I'm going to show you a photograph—please don't turn it over,' the barrister instructed.

He was handed the very same photograph the bent Flying Squad man had shown him in the lift. His stomach tightened into a knot. The bent cop was in court.

'Now, can you recognise the man in this photograph?' the barrister asked.

'It's one of the Lloyds, but I can't tell which one from this picture,' replied Smith. He glanced over at the Flying Squad detective, who was smiling and nodding.

'So it's difficult to tell them apart, is it?' said the barrister, addressing the jury.

'Yes it is but—' began Smith, before the barrister cut him off.

'Turn the picture over, DC Smith, and read out for the court what you find on the back, if you please,' he ordered.

There was the same writing as before. Smith read the words.

The barrister was triumphant. 'Well that date puts a different complexion on things, doesn't it, DC Smith? Sydney one day and Manchester the next? Mr Lloyd would have to be a very fast mover, wouldn't he?'

'Well, yes . . .' said Smith, his face reddening.

'No further questions,' said the barrister with a contemptuous wave of his hand.

'But, Your Honour, there's one point I would like to make,' said Smith, turning to the judge.

'Proceed, DC Smith,' said the judge.

'Well, Your Honour, there is another way to tell the Lloyds apart. The man I saw on the train to Manchester, William Lloyd, was missing the index finger on his right hand,' said Smith, humbly.

The faces of the barrister, Wee Jimmy and the bent copper from the Sweeney suddenly looked stricken. Over the objections of his barrister, the judge ordered Lloyd to stand up and show his hand. Wee Jimmy's face curled into a furious sneer as he slowly unfurled his fingers. Smith counted four, just as he had on the train.

Smith never told on the bent copper who had tried to get him to lie. A few years later, that detective's capacity for duplicity was exposed in tragic circumstances—his then girlfriend, a window dresser, had threatened to tell his wife of the affair they were having, so he strangled her right in the shop window where she was working.

Despite their success against Wee Jimmy's gang, neither Jimmy Smith nor his boss David Woodland prospered at Scotland Yard, courtesy of their vengeful boss Commander David Dilley.

Smith went on to become Britain's greatest ever covert policeman — Queen Elizabeth awarded him an MBE, but he claims that David Dilley falsely accused him of leaking one of his photographs to the *News of the World* tabloid in 1974. He was cleared but quit the Met Police in disgust. When David Dilley discovered that David Woodland had duped him over Wee Jimmy, he unleashed a vendetta that resulted in this dedicated and courageous officer being drummed out of C11 and returned to uniform duties on rumour and innuendo. At least Smith and Woodland had the satisfaction of knowing they had defied the corruption of Scotland Yard to collar some of the Kangaroo Gang's finest.

11
A cold Case of Grace

The arrest of the Lloyds for the Manchester job was a major blow to the Kangaroo Gang. Wee Jimmy had been a leading employer of the Aussies who landed in London looking for a start in the gang. With him out of circulation, and Arthur in parts unknown, the Aussie crime wave finally began to abate around 1974.

Video surveillance tipped the odds back to the shop detective and the cops. Just seven years after the first video surveillance systems in shops, cameras were popping up everywhere. In October 1968 police used a temporary camera to snoop on anti-Vietnam War demonstrators in Grosvenor Square. In 1969, permanent cameras were installed in Grosvenor Square, Whitehall and Parliament Square. There were only 67 cameras operating nationally but, with the IRA waging war across Britain, video became the Metropolitan Police's new weapon of choice. By 1975, all major arterial roads in and through London were covered, as were a number of soccer grounds so police could track hooligans.

When cameras were installed in four of London's busiest Tube stations, even the pickpockets working King Solomon's Mines came under scrutiny. The best of thieves could still operate but many of them had left the scene by now. Detective Inspector David Woodland, when interviewing an Aussie shoplifter after the Manchester pinch, had allowed himself a little triumphalism: 'This game's up for you now,' he taunted. 'You will all be smiling for the birdie now, won't you?'

The shoppie was cool: 'You have got to be kidding me, mate!' he laughed. 'We love the cameras. With the cameras on, the shop assistants and store jacks have gone soft again. They think the cameras are going to catch everyone.' He then detailed how the new surveillance had changed their methods.

Upon entering a store, one of the team would now establish where the output from the cameras was being watched. Half the time the monitors would be unmanned. Or you could draw the staff member on the monitor back into the store—or even into the street. Success usually depended upon having superior numbers. To tip the balance in their favour, a female on the team would ring the store from a nearby public phone box. In a panic, she would say she had been in minutes earlier and then moved on to a shop up the street where she had left her purse, full of money. She would ask whether someone could please run up to the shop to retrieve it. It was usually the shop jack on the video that was sent. Once the team had the numbers, they had endless ways to block and smother the cameras with parcels and people.

If they didn't have the numbers, the choreography became more intricate, requiring sleight of hand that was too fast for the cameras. And they needed props. Arthur used what magicians and thieves call a shooter box—it might look like a normal gift-wrapped parcel, maybe containing a book or a box of cigars from Harrods, but it would be hollow, with a flap opening at the side. If they were after a specific piece, they had a cheap copy made, and switched it for the real one. The ring, for example, would disappear into the shooter box and, to complete the dance, Arthur would swap the shooter box for a real Harrods parcel with another team-mate as he hit the street. If the staff and security couldn't pick any of this from two feet away, the cameras high in the corners had no chance.

Some just walked straight up and disabled them. Finally, it was rare that there would be a monitor for each and every camera—therefore, having worked out the sequence, you knew when to strike as the monitor cycled through its cameras.

But street surveillance was another matter. You never knew when you were under the electronic eyes of the Old Bill—it was a far cry from the early 1960s and C11's man on a motor scooter. London would ultimately become the most closely watched city in the world. There are at least 500 000 cameras in the city today, and one study has suggested a person going about their business in its streets, shops and offices could expect to be filmed 300 times in a single day.

Yet, though the halcyon days were over, a hoister could still make a decent living. Sydney man Richard Jeakins arrived in London in September 1975, and embarked on a spree that would have impressed even the King. Police found goods worth £90 000 when they finally raided his St Johns Wood flat. Among the treasures packed into the small space were a Picasso print worth £7000, a William Blake original worth £12 000, two icons worth £14 000, a £1500 Kashmiri rug (which had been nailed to the floor at Harrods), 40 cashmere sweaters worth £80 each and numerous electrical appliances. The 33-year-old Jeakins, described by a judge as 'a super shoplifter', had been operating largely on his own. 'I just walk in and take them,' he told police. 'It is really easy.'

In earlier years, Jeakins might have slipped the bobbies a 'monkey' and walked free. However, a new Chief Commissioner of Police, Sir Robert Mark, had been appointed in 1972 and he had begun a wide-ranging campaign against corruption. The Met was so dirty that Mark had to use investigators from neighbouring Dorset for the clean-up that would eventually see 400 Met officers get the chop.

Senior officers were aware of the role the Aussies had played in police corruption and so they kept close tabs on officers who dealt with them. However, it was one particular incident more than any other that changed police opinion against the Aussies.

The commotion upstairs stopped abruptly, as though a radio on full volume had been switched off. It was late at night towards the end of 1973 and the neighbours, a middle-aged couple, had heard voices—two women and a man—punctuated by a crying baby. The argument had raged for hours before reaching an awful crescendo just after midnight. Then a fearful silence descended.

Some time later there was a rhythmic 'thump, thump, thump' down the iron back stairs of the Seymour Place building in London's Padding-ton. From their kitchen window, the neighbours watched two people in the car park struggling with a heavy rolled-up carpet. They tossed the carpet into the boot of a lime-green Ford Cortina and drove away.

The couple on the second floor had only maintained a passing acquaintance with their Aussie neighbours, who were an unusual pairing. The woman was a handsome dark-eyed lady in her mid thirties. Though the bloom of youth had faded, she carried herself like a lady, with a gloss of rich red lipstick and powder. She was courteous and polite when they passed her on the stairs pushing her baby in a pram. There was no in-depth conversation, but the woman just gave off a good vibe.

By comparison, the man was shifty and sly—younger than his partner. There were lots of Australians living in the Paddington area, so two more were unremarkable. They had been quiet and easy-going. That is, until a few days before this dramatic episode, when a second woman had arrived on the scene—she was big, brassy and loud, with the hard eyes of a prostitute. For the first few nights after she came, there had been laughter and music into the night upstairs. But tonight it had turned nasty, and now there was this deathly silence. They hadn't called the Old Bill, despite their concerns—you learn to mind your business living cheek by jowl in London's inner-city.

On this same night, the telephone had rung in the apartment of an English villain well-known in London's Australian circles. He struggled out of bed to answer it, annoyed to be woken so late. This man was the West End's top distributor of illicit pornography and adult products. He did a sideline in fencing whatever he could sell. His main business was good, but the hours were long—people just didn't buy dildos during business hours. And the Aussies kept him up late too—they pitched up at all hours, looking to fence some hot gear, or to ask his help in a jam.

What the Aussies did not know was that this man had connections in the Flying Squad. The price of his criminal franchise was a steady flow of information back to the Sweeney. He liked the Aussies and they trusted him, but he had to look after Number One. Business was business.

The caller was Tommy Wraith. A small-time thief in Melbourne, Wraith was a minor player in the West End, trading false passports, stolen traveller's cheques and credit cards. He hadn't even made the Australian Index in the *Police Gazette,* such was his lack of form and reputation.

It had been a surprise to many when Wraith hooked up with the best female take of the day, Grace 'The Case' O'Connor. Readers will recall that the Kid had often wondered where Grace had finished up—one day in 1969 she had simply disappeared out of their lives. Baby Bruce later told me that in the early 1970s Grace had made a name for herself as a take in her own right, drawing on other teams to work all over England. But by mid 1973 Grace, now 36, was living with Wraith in a top-floor flat on Seymour Place, Paddington. They had a child together, born in England just months earlier, and seemed set to stay.

It was a shame, some said—a take like Grace could make money for all of them, but she was home tending to Tommy and the baby. Of course, she was still active, but now in the service of a cruel, lazy man in Wraith. A heavy drinker, Tommy had a growing fondness for hard drugs. Underneath his easy charisma, he was vicious and unpredictable. Tommy stood over women all his life. Grace would have found that out, but he was kiting (passing stolen) cheques and trading in forged passports, so with her earns they were getting by nicely.

But now Grace was dead, Wraith told the informer. He needed to get rid of the body before morning and wanted him to get over there as soon as possible. The informer was torn. He had made good money from the Aussies but this was too hot to hold, so he rang his handler at the Yard. He recounted Wraith's story and asked what he should do. The detective told him to go down to Seymour Place as requested by Wraith. He should confirm there had been a murder, and confirm it was Grace O'Connor. But then he must beg off and get the hell out of there. He should report back and let the Old Bill take over. Nobody would ever know he had shopped Wraith.

The informer hurried over to meet Wraith. He recognised the other woman in the flat when he arrived. Susie, as we shall call her, had been working London and the Continent since the late sixties. Nicked in Tenerife, in the Canary Islands, in April 1969 for theft, Susie had slipped back and forth into London using forged passports in various names. She had just returned from a few months lagging in Germany.

Susie wasn't in Grace's class—she was just a head puller for whoever would take her on. Grace was the lady thief, living 'respectably' on her hoisting, complete with her man and baby. Grace had put away a tidy float, in case things ever turned sour; she didn't need a man. Susie, on the other hand, was entirely dependent—a survivor who had slept with many of the Aussies over the years. She was no beauty, just a big blousy blonde with a hard jaw and thin cruel lips. She was still drunk when the informer arrived there and seemed unconcerned at the scene before her. On the bed lay Grace's lifeless body, a stocking lashed around her throat.

Wraith filled in the details for the informer. He had been sleeping with Susie behind Grace's back. Grace had found out and an argument had broken out. Dead drunk, Wraith had watched the whole thing unfold, sitting by when the women came to blows. Grace had run into the bedroom with Susie in hot pursuit. The smaller woman hadn't stood a chance against an attacker of the size and strength of Susie, who had proceeded to choke the life out of Grace on the bed. By the time Wraith got into the bedroom, the murder was well under way. He could have stopped it, but killing Grace had seemed the best option at that moment, when everything that was hers instantly became his.

The informer didn't want a bar of this; as per his orders, he made his apologies and left. The following morning at 4 am, PC Carol Bristow mustered with 20 other officers at Harrow Road police station, two miles from Seymour Place. They were briefed on the information the Flying Squad had been given, but warned there could be no mention of the informer or the murder allegations. They could not risk the informer being exposed, as much for their convenience as the informer's well-being. They were to execute a ruse, pitching up to the Seymour Place flat with a search warrant for stolen chequebooks, credit cards and passports. Once in, they could search for evidence of the murder. A back-up squad of 18 members was ready to pounce if needed.

At 5:30 am, when Bristow and a detective inspector knocked at his door, Tommy Wraith was cool and calm. He ushered the police in. There was just him, the wife and their baby at home, he told them. Susie emerged from the bedroom, with Grace's baby in her arms. Where Wraith had been cool and accommodating, Susie was sneering and belligerent. Furious that the baby had been woken, she had let fly with a foul-mouthed tirade. When she calmed down, Susie was asked her name. Without hesitation, she told them: 'Grace O'Connor.'

Bristow's heart leapt into her mouth. She and the DI had to stop themselves challenging the blatant lie. They searched the flat and, finding a cache of stolen chequebooks and credit cards, hauled Wraith and 'Grace O'Connor' back to Harrow Road station. They were remanded on conspiracy charges but these were intended simply as holding charges, until murder could be proven. Clearly Susie was not O'Connor—their pictures were a couple of pages apart in the Australian Index—but the lie was allowed to remain until the demise of the real Grace could be proven. Meanwhile, detectives were secretly despatched to Australia to recover items from Grace's mother that might help with identifying a corpse, if and when they found one. They came back with dental charts, hair from brushes and some clothes.

Meanwhile a search was mounted London-wide for O'Connor's body. There was a tip that Grace had been dropped into an above-ground grave with a table-top lid in Hampstead Cemetery. Someone else said Highgate Cemetery. Officers flipped the lids on hundreds of graves, with no success. There was also a story that Wraith had buried Grace in one of London's eight royal parks, which narrowed the search area to a mere 5000 acres.

A week later, Wraith's lime-green Cortina, possibly a hire car, was located at Southwark police depot. It had been towed there by police after being abandoned not far away from Seymour Place. The carpet from Wraith's flat was still in the boot, but there was no other evidence linking it to Grace O'Connor.

Police delayed taking the holding charges to court as long as they could, but never revealed the true reason. PC Carol Bristow would sit in the back of the prison van with Susie as she went to and from court. Bristow didn't expect a confession, but she wanted to try to understand how this person could take someone's life and then steal her identity and her baby. She wanted to tell this foul-mouthed oaf of a woman what she thought of her, but she always bit her lip.

Eventually, Susie admitted she was not Grace O'Connor, but still she was never questioned on the murder. She and Wraith were finally tried on the cheque fraud and sentenced in late 1974 to only nine months' jail. The pair was deported in March 1975. With the suspects out of England, the Metropolitan Police gave up the investigation into Grace's disappearance without ever raising a murder docket.

It is not known what happened to Grace and Tommy's child. It was the fate of the baby boy that made the case stick in PC Bristow's mind, she told me when I met her in London in March 2009. Over the next 20 years she would occasionally check the file at the Missing Persons section of the Criminal Records Office. There was never any progress. On the day she retired, she checked the file one last time—still nothing. Though the police knew there had been a murder and knew who had committed it, officially Grace would remain a missing person and her file would never see the light of day again.

In 1982, legendary Melbourne detective sergeant Brian 'Skull' Murphy took a call from a junior colleague. The young policeman was in quite a state—he feared some villains were trying to harm his family over an incident that had taken place in England nearly ten years earlier. His wife was an agency nurse posted to a small psychiatric hospital in suburban Melbourne; one evening, a patient had told her an extraordinary story of how he had killed the mother of his own child.

The private hospital was one of many treating a range of mental illnesses with one brutal, catch-all therapy. Electro-convulsive therapy (ECT) involved sending an electrical charge of up to 120 volts through a patient's head in order to 'reset' the brain chemistry. It had been a popular therapy in many hospitals for treating addictions and depression, but in this institution just about every patient got a burst of ECT. Some of it actually helped, but the policeman's wife suspected nothing would help this man.

When she first laid eyes on Tommy Wraith, he was strapped to his bed in a Posey restrainer, a kind of straitjacket that kept the patient flat on his back in his bed. He was trying to come off heroin for the umpteenth time; as he went through the horrors of withdrawal, staff kept him sedated and strapped to the bed. His chart said he was 32 years old, but he looked much older. His arms were covered in track marks from needle use—most of the veins in his arms and legs had collapsed, and among his many tattoos there were dotted scars and fresh sores. The staff cut his unkempt hair short at the temples in preparation for the ECT electrodes.

After a zap or two, Tommy seemed to pick up a little. Though he was a hopeless junkie, the nurse could see flashes of personality—a charisma that few of her patients shared. He had lived another life before this descent into substance abuse. One evening on her rounds, she stopped at Tommy's room and they began talking.

Over a couple of years of working in this place, the nurse had learnt to listen without making judgements. No matter how crazy the conversation, she could let it wash over her. For the patients in that forbidding place, it seemed to help a little to have someone to talk to. Tommy already appeared a shell of a man, just waiting for death. Something, more than the heroin, had hollowed him out. He had died years before, the nurse thought, as he spoke to her of his life. She had previously nursed others getting off drugs who, in the course of restarting their lives, had purged themselves of past misdeeds and regrets. But Tommy wasn't like that. As her copper husband might have said, in making this dying declaration he had 'the hopeless expectation of impending doom'.

He had not been a good man, he told her sorrowfully. He was full of regrets and a guilt that never left him. He had killed someone in England, he told her gravely. She hadn't believed him at first but, as he spoke, the clarity of his story changed her mind. She realised that, as death approached, Tommy wanted to get this off his chest. He wasn't a religious man, so this hospital confession was perhaps the next best thing, she thought.

He said he had murdered a woman in his home and buried the body in a park or wood ten years earlier. At first, he spoke of these events as if he had been alone, solely responsible. There was no mention of Susie. But then he said there had been an argument at the burial site. Someone had been hit over the head with a shovel; he didn't say who. The nurse was confused—though Tommy was confessing to the murder, he didn't seem like a murderer at all. Not that she had mingled with murderers before, but there was something or someone missing in the story. He had certainly been on the scene and buried the body, but the nurse could sense the presence of another. She hadn't pressed him, just let him talk.

The conversation went on for nearly an hour. When she left work that night she was convinced that someone had been murdered, but that Tommy Wraith had not been the instigator. She recounted her meeting with Tommy to her husband that night and he got straight on the phone to 'Skull' Murphy, who organised a meeting with Victoria Police's Bureau of Criminal Intelligence. The story was recounted and messages sent to cold case detectives in Scotland Yard. Soon word came back that Wraith had indeed been a suspect in the disappearance of Grace O'Connor.

Murphy was thunderstruck. He had nicked O'Connor in the early 1960s for housebreaking and she had given up a whole team of her associates. She had been helpful and polite. To help find her killer, not to mention her mortal remains, was the very least he could do. But it wouldn't be easy—there was no way Wraith would repeat his confession to a policeman. So it was decided that the nurse would go back to Wraith and gently probe him for more information. If she could find out where Wraith had buried the body, Scotland Yard would almost certainly reopen the case.

Understandably, the nurse was terrified; but, with a little cajoling, she agreed. In their second chat, Tommy told her that he had taken the body to Hertfordshire. He said it was buried in 'beautiful country'. She didn't want to press him any further—he was getting suspicious. The nurse relayed the information to Victoria Police, who passed it on to Scotland Yard. It wasn't much to go on, though it had narrowed down the potential burial site to a mere 634 square miles.

In 1973, the police had been looking for Grace's body in London, so Hertfordshire was new information. It was a logical place to bury a body. From Seymour Place, the murderers could have been in the pleasant countryside of Herts County in just 45 minutes. Though only about 25 miles away from the West End, this was farmland; its country estates were the setting for Jane Austen's *Pride and Prejudice* and in his novel *Howard's End*, EM Forster described Hertfordshire as 'England at its quietest'. It was a perfect place to bury a body in the middle of the night. But without more specific information, Scotland Yard showed little interest in taking the matter further. So there it rested.

Meanwhile, Wraith had picked up enough to be discharged from the hospital. He hadn't died after all, but perhaps he now thought his confession ill-advised. It might come back to bite him. One night after work, the nurse was followed all the way home by a man in a black utility. Skull Murphy's inquiries suggested the car matched Tommy Wraith's utility. The nurse and her family could well be in mortal danger, he concluded.

Shortly afterwards, someone broke into their home; nothing was taken, but it was enough to spur Murphy into action. He rang a mate of Wraith's and told him to relay a message that Tommy had nothing to fear from the nurse, but if he kept bothering her, there would be trouble: 'Tell him that if he doesn't stop bothering her, I will personally come and shoot *your* wife and kids in front of you, okay?' That was enough for the Wraith camp to drop off.

Then, in 1983, Sergeant Murphy received a call from a woman, one Rae Elizabeth Collingburn, asking for his help. This was a surprise, given that Murphy and another policeman had stood trial for the 1971 manslaughter of her husband, Neil Stanley Collingburn. They had beaten that charge, but the widow had persisted with a civil action for wrongful death. Finally she had dropped off and disappeared.

Now, out of the blue, she needed Murphy's help. Her de facto husband, Tommy Wraith, was beating her and threatening to kill her. She feared she would have to kill him first to survive. Murphy begged her to come in and report Wraith, but she refused—our people don't lag each other, she said. Murphy resolved to pay Wraith a visit, to quieten him down; it was the least he could do. But before he got there, tragic events intervened.

It was near midnight a few days later when Tommy Wraith left Dennis Allen's 'drug house' in Richmond with a quarter of a gram of heroin. He was back on the gear so he was a frequent visitor to Allen's place. Allen, an amphetamine-ravaged killer, was operating his drug business with the help of his mother, Kathy Pettingill. Kath liked Tommy; though he was a hopeless addict he was charming and good company. At one time Kath's daughter Vicky had been his girlfriend. Tommy had told them his wife had disappeared in London some years earlier. He had showed Kath an old picture of his then five-year-old son, an unlit cigarette dangling from his mouth. She felt sorry for Tommy and had organised a birthday party for him just weeks before.

Tommy always seemed to have women around him. He had teamed up with Rae Collingburn and another woman, Lynne Williams, in a successful thieving operation. It was like London all over again.

On this night he had been reluctant to go home—problems with Rae, he had said—but finally he left. After he was gone Kath remembered Tommy had borrowed her tommy axe. She reminded herself to ask him for it next time he came around.

A few hours later Rae Collingburn had grabbed Kath's tommy axe to get square with Tommy. He had been beating her as usual but she'd had enough this time. She had caught him off-guard, creeping up behind him in the kitchen. It was too late when he realised. He had pulled his gun out but before he could shoot her, she had brought the axe down, taking his arm clean off at the elbow. Tommy looked with horror at the arm still holding the gun now lying on the floor. Then she raised the axe again and kept chopping at him until she made sure he was dead, before covering the body with a cloth 'so the kids wouldn't see', prosecutors told the Victorian Supreme Court in 1985. She then rang her sister to say: 'You know what he was always going to do to me? Well I've done it to him.'

Rae Collingburn was found not guilty of murder, but she was convicted of manslaughter. Murphy noted, on behalf of Grace O'Connor, that Wraith had ended up with his right whack. The bloke who had taken a collection to pay for Tommy's funeral ran away with the money, so it was left to his drug dealer to foot the bill. It was an ignominious end to say the least but Tommy's story may not end there.

It's my belief that someone knows where the body of Grace O'Connor still lies buried. If Tommy Wraith would tell a nurse, then he might have told others in greater detail. There is also a son, now nearly 40, who deserves to see his mother laid to rest with dignity. Moreover, there may still be a killer on the loose, if Susie remains alive.

12
Double Bay mafia

The significance of shoplifting may be gauged from the background of recognised organised crime leaders who reportedly held clandestine meetings at a home in the Sydney suburb of Double Bay in August 1972 . . . Australian police noted that [the meetings] were something of a grand council of local crime leaders . . . Four out of eight are known to be associated with organised shoplifting

The Age, 23 July 1985

It took nearly a year but, by the winter of 1970, Arthur had taken his first steps unaided. The doctors said he was a marvel and wrote up the case in the medical journals—his first appearance in print, aside from court reporting and the *Police Gazette*. He should have been a paraplegic, the doctors said. The bullet was still in his back, pressing close to the spine, but his body had repaired itself enough for Arthur to walk again.

At first he had suffered the indignity of wearing callipers to support his weakened muscles. The callipers allowed only a straight-legged waddle, but soon his confidence grew. He hated being helpless and relying on others, so Arthur threw himself into the rehabilitation with a zeal only shown previously for scotch whisky, women and stolen diamonds. Every day without fail, Arthur would turn up at the pool at Prince Henry Hospital, wading up and down, or doing weights in the gym, putting strength back into his withered limbs. Alexis was full of admiration. He was growing on her now. Having seen him shot and then nursing him through recovery, Alexis felt a connection to this roguish thief that went beyond their shared love of ill-gotten gains.

After about eight months Arthur was fit enough to go back to work, even with the callipers on. He had always said that, if a shoppie had to run, then he was in the wrong business. Now he had no option. For the rest of his life he would walk with a limp that made him sway from the hips. Truth be told, he had no choice but to return to work. His confinement had done nothing to slow his ferocious gambling habit. Each weekend, he racked up a sizeable debt backing slow horses with George Freeman's SP operation. And bright and early every Monday morning now, Arthur began meeting with the Fibber to work it off: 'Come on, Fib, let's go get some money for George,' he would say cheerfully. And they would work the whole day.

It was a far cry from the plush boutiques and jewellery stores of London. In Sydney, they plundered newsagents, butcher shops and corner stores. The Fibber would distract the shopkeeper while Arthur slipped into the back room to get the cash, the weekend's takings. The Fibber always marvelled at Arthur's nose for money—he could sniff it out, grab it and be out of the shop before most thieves had even started. This was child's play compared to what they had done in London. While they took no joy in robbing working people, a merchant was different, and a bloke did have to survive. And 'surviving' for Arthur was an expensive business.

Unlike their Sydney cohorts, Arthur and the Fibber were still pulling the same tricks they had learnt in the fifties. Their contemporaries—men like Lennie 'Mr Big' McPherson, Frederick 'Paddles' Anderson and George Freeman—now ran Sydney and had offsiders to run errands and fix problems for them. But Arthur was still a one-man band, living hand to mouth as he always had. He would always be a crook, never a gangster—that required far too much organisation.

In the early 1970s, the press was waking to up the fact that the Mob was a part of life in Australia. Joe Testa's vacations in Australia in the late

1960s had spurred the Commonwealth Police to conclude the Mafia had infiltrated local crime groups, in turn providing more incentive for local figures to get together. The Commonwealth Police admitted its information was less than solid, but still drew fantastic conclusions about what Testa was doing in Australia: 'Even though much of the information we have received is unconfirmed and from a variety of sources, the overall perspective indicates that Testa is a member of the syndicate,' the Feds wrote in a submission to the Moffitt Royal Commission. '[He] is therefore unlikely to bring anything to this country other than a totally undesirable connection between organised crime groups in this country and the United States of America.' By August 1972, a special team of New South Wales detectives was assembled to investigate the claims, in response to 'intense public concern'.

One of the most enduring images of the Mafia's history in America is the famous Apalachin episode. In 1957, a New York state police sergeant received a report that criminals from different regions were meeting at the country home of Mafia boss Joseph Barbara in the Apalachin mountains of upstate New York. The cops set up a roadblock on the only road out and nabbed 58 crooks, including some of the top Mafia figures in America. The FBI dubbed the get-together 'a meeting of the Grand Council', where crime interests were discussed and regulated almost like a parallel government. A special State Investigations Commission was set up to 'determine the purpose of the gangland meeting and whether any crimes were committed'. Despite all the hoopla, only 11 of the 'delegates' were ever jailed, and only on less serious charges like contempt of court and perjury. But ever since, Australian mafia investigators had looked for evidence of similar organisation in Australia.

In early August 1972, the authorities, with great excitement, concluded the Apalachins had come to Sydney's Double Bay. Commonwealth Police received a report that over the preceding fortnight, three meetings had been held at the Double Bay home of Sydney crook Karl Frederick Bonnette. Despite his criminal reputation, Bonnette's main income was derived from ripping off used-car buyers. His nickname 'The Godfather' was used ironically amongst knockabouts, but that was lost on the Feds. To the local would-be mafia busters, Bonnette was now Sydney's Joe Barbara. They reported the meetings 'are alleged to be called to discuss the current activities re organised crime'. It was uncertain how they came to that conclusion, but the list of delegates seemed to justify the fears. The guest list included

Lennie McPherson, George Freeman, Stan 'The Man' Smith, Frederick 'Paddles' Anderson and Milan 'Iron Bar Miller' Petricevic. Some police sources also put a New South Wales politician on the guest list—Albert Sloss a Labor member of the Legislative Assembly. Sloss later denied that he had been at the meeting.

According to the Commonwealth Police record: 'Apparently the men first meet in a bar which is located downstairs in a building close to William Street. They usually have drinks until 11 pm, when they move to the William Street address. A male person in an old Holden car is alleged to act as cockatoo during these meetings.' One policeman told the Moffitt Royal Commission that, because of the different criminal activities of those present, it was unlikely that they were meeting to organise crime. While it was likely they were up to no good, the men had been meeting to play cards, he said. This was ignored in the feverish rush to judgement. Any hope of adding to this fig leaf of intelligence was destroyed when a member of the Consorting Squad knocked on Bonnette's door and asked whether the villains had indeed been meeting there.

In his final report, Justice Moffitt was incredulous about this policing gaffe. 'Here was a group which included some of the worst local criminals, whose place and hours of apparently regular and continuing meetings were known. [This] was a chance to check by surveillance procedures one of the suspected avenues for infiltration of organised crime. This chance could not by any plan have been more effectively terminated . . .' If the surveillance operation wasn't sabotaged by bent cops, it was certainly a low point in police intelligence gathering in New South Wales. While C11 had compiled dossiers on hundreds of Aussie crooks in London since 1967 (including some of the Double Bay delegates) without mishap, the New South Wales cops had blown their first opportunity.

The hue and cry over the Double Bay meeting produced even less than the Apalachin revelations. Bonnette, the Godfather, was charged for receiving a stolen television set and barely rated a mention in criminal history after that. The entire operation was a waste of time, a blind alley. It yielded nothing more than confirmation that these men—who had been drinking, gambling and plotting together since the 1950s—were still at it, albeit at more salubrious addresses.

Lennie McPherson had harboured dreams of controlling the slot machine business in New South Wales and was already standing over the operators of illegal casinos, but there was little interest among the other delegates in such activities. Indeed, McPherson was unlikely to share the spoils. Each man was involved in his own affairs; crime in New South Wales was not nearly as connected and orchestrated as the conspiracy theorists wanted to believe. That would come in the next decade, with the drug trade, but for now crime was more haphazard and only to any great extent organised where there was involvement from New South Wales police. And yet the delegates at Bonnette's house became known as 'The Euro Milieu'—'inter-related and overlapping criminal syndicates, led by Mr Big Enoughs', as Evan Whitton summed it up succinctly in his book, *Can of Worms*.

If this was a summit of organised crime, then it was hard to see where a shoplifter fitted in. Indeed, by dint of their direct involvement in crime, Delaney and the Fibber did not meet any essential criterion of being part of organised crime, if such existed back then. It wasn't until 1983 that Douglas Meagher QC, counsel assisting the Costigan Royal Commission, had a go at defining the new structures that had then emerged: 'The intelligent and well-educated criminal would scorn . . . personal involvement in the commission of crimes. Today the master criminal stands back. He leaves it to the less intelligent followers to work to his plans . . . reaping the rewards at a distance.'

Arthur was always at the forefront of every operation. To stand back or employ soldiers would be to forfeit much of the spoils. When Alexis read the breathless accounts of these crime summits, she had to smile because whatever was going on at Karl Bonnette's place had never enriched Arthur. On those nights, Arthur would come home drunk, with his pockets empty as usual. And the next morning he would be back on the hoist. The mafia publicity just made it harder to work in Sydney.

At least as the strength returned to his legs, Arthur could travel further afield. Melbourne became a favoured destination for the Delaneys and crew back then. Although it was just an overnight train ride or a one-hour flight, a Melbourne sojourn could be a tricky proposition. If Sydney police got wind of your travel plans, they would be waiting with their hands out at the airport on your return. So, if you flew down, it was a good idea to drive back or catch the train. And Victorian crooks were likely to dob you in to the jacks to protect their turf. But at least it was better than Western Australia, where magistrates would give you a double sentence if you were from out of state.

In mid 1973, Victorian police informers passed on information that Delaney had brought a team to Melbourne. It was the cream of the crop, including the Fibber, Alexis, Ray Dwyer and Jackie Muller. They were planning to rob the Opal Cave jewellery store in the foyer of the Southern Cross Hotel. The Southern Cross in downtown Exhibition Street was the acme of Melbourne style back then, playing host to the Beatles in 1964 and other visiting celebrities. As a local icon, Melbourne's crooks decided that only locals should be allowed to rob it.

Sergeant Brian Murphy of Melbourne CIB took it upon himself to visit the Southern Cross to see what Delaney and the Fibber were up to. The plain clothes detective had watched the pair stroll through the Opal Cave, but they hadn't appeared to take anything. They were now enjoying a quiet scotch, watching the well-heeled clientele move through the foyer. Murphy announced himself to the thieves and asked how they were enjoying their stay in Melbourne. Arthur was courteous as always.

'We are having the most delightful time in your fair city, Sergeant. It's simply terrific—the weather, the people are so welcoming. And the shopping . . .' With his bespoke tailored outfit and plummy accent, Delaney could have been an English lord on holidays.

'Well I am sorry to cut short your plans, gentlemen, but if you don't make your way back to Sydney by tomorrow, you will be staying here in Melbourne for the next five years. And don't expect the accommodation to be quite so salubrious as this,' said the detective, with a half-snarl, half-smile. 'Am I making myself clear, gentlemen?'

'Why yes of course,' Arthur cooed. 'And I do thank you for your concern and attention, officer. That same information in Sydney would have cost me a bagful of money.' He motioned the officer to take a seat: 'What are you drinking, dear boy?'

'Nothing, thank you. Just heed what I have said,' said the detective, eyeballing Delaney with menace.

'But of course—our business here is complete,' said Arthur.

By now, it was pretty obvious that Arthur could never leave town without an opal or two. He proposed they stay another day and knock over the Opal Cave before hightailing it back to Sydney. But the police were watching. The next morning, police raided the hotel and arrested the entire team on conspiracy to steal. Just to top it off, when the cops burst into Arthur's room, they dropped a pistol on the bed. 'This would be yours, would it?'

Arthur was dismayed. At worst, the conspiracy charge might cost him six months' jail, but possession of a firearm was a felony and could well delay him in Melbourne for five years, just as Murphy had warned. They were remanded but received bail. The case went on for more than a year, with the team travelling up and down to Melbourne for court appearances. The conspiracy charges were nonsense—they hadn't done anything, just walked through a store—but the gun was a real problem, warned their barrister, Brian Bourke QC. Better to plead guilty on conspiracy and to fight the gun charge, he suggested.

Arthur had no history with firearms, and with his shoplifting skills he certainly had no need of them. It would be a difficult case to win but, with the Fibber on the team, Arthur had another line of defence. Though he had been away from Melbourne for nearly 20 years, the Fibber still had plenty of mates in the police down there. An extra-legal deal was arranged. The gun would disappear if they pleaded guilty to conspiracy and handed over a tidy sum of money to the arresting officers. Fibber was fluent in the international language of corrupt police—he had honed his skills all over the world.

The guilty plea resulted in a non-custodial sentence. Arthur was over-joyed to be finally free of Melbourne. The next day, he gave Bourke a gold watch as a thank-you gift. To avoid the obvious questions, the thief had thoughtfully included a sales receipt in the box. When he got home that night, Bourke found that a florist had delivered an entire vanful of flowers to his wife. Later Arthur told his legal team how he had paid their fees. In a method first perfected in London, Arthur lined up at the staff entrance of a Commonwealth Bank wearing a dust coat. He had ingrati-ated himself with the tellers as they set up for the day and simply walked out with a bag of money from the vault.

But Arthur was a victim of his own publicity. A relentless skite and big-noter could never maintain a low profile in a small place like Australia. His stories of international intrigue had become steadily embellished. Soon the bent cops would be lining up to bite him for 'a drink'. The press, convinced he was part of Joe Testa's Kangaroo Mafia, would never leave him alone. He came to realise that his future would have to be on the world stage; but first he would have to make himself scarce again.

The liaison between international police forces was finally gaining strength. Interpol, based in Lyons, France, had once been no more than a post office box, but it was now tracking crooks like Arthur more effec-tively. His mug shots, published in the Australian Index of the English

Police Gazette, had been sent to police around the globe. He needed to become an international man of mystery once more. He longed to be in London again; but it was no longer the easy get it had been in the early sixties. The distraction method was well-known now—new gangs from South America and Eastern Europe were using it on the Tube and in shops. Many of Arthur's mates in the Old Bill had been cleaned out in the corruption probes of the early seventies. It was time to explore new horizons.

Riding the escalator at Harrods in 1976, Alexis felt she had been transported to another dimension. In every direction, there was such a vista of opportunity as she had never seen before. At 39, she was the most experienced of the Aussie women hoisters in London, now that Grace O'Connor was gone. But as an international traveller, she was a novice. The sheer scale and variety of the merchandise here in Harrods dazzled her. Back home, there was nothing to compare with this. For Alexis this kind of store—full of beautiful, haughty people buying gorgeous things—existed only in movies and books. Now she was walking among them. She could be one of them, if she wanted, because the world of the rich was full of impostors and phoneys anyhow. If looking the part meant dressing up and carrying herself like a lady, then she could do that.

Alexis felt the same greedy surge of pleasure as the rest of them as she contemplated the potential spoils. But beyond that, there was a sense of destiny—a feeling that she had made the right choice with Arthur. If she had stayed with Skinny Fred, she would still be hoisting shirts and sheets in Sydney, paying off the sugar bags in the police force, worrying about the knock on the door in the middle of the night.

She could reinvent herself here, establishing the home she had never known in Australia. It wasn't just the diamonds and furs she was after, though she would take them by the armfuls. She could turn a house into a home with all this stuff, she thought. Look at all these soft furnishings—the rich velvet drapes and satin cushions, Persian carpets, silk flowers and gilded mirrors. They would live like this when she could get Arthur to stay in one place. As she walked around Harrods, she filled out a mental shopping list—her dream home taking shape in her imagination, just like a Harrods catalogue.

This wasn't her first trip to England. A couple of years earlier Arthur and the Fibber had sent her to London with a famous black opal they had stolen overseas that was too big to sell in Sydney. So Alexis had been packed off to London with the stone concealed in her luggage. As arranged, she had been met by one of Arthur's loyal fences, but he knocked back the stone as too distinctive to move. So she had returned to Sydney a few days later and her only memories had been of airport terminals, bad weather and grimy North London pubs. There hadn't been time to visit the plush Mayfair shops that Arthur had so often bragged of robbing.

But this time, Alexis was determined to enjoy what London had to offer. On her first day, she had made straight for Harrods. Arthur had encouraged her to get out while he attended to business. But he had warned her to keep her hands to herself. They were not in London to steal, he said, unless of course a red-hot go presented itself. They were to live as a respectable middle-aged couple. Europe would be the place to get money—there were still huge opportunities on the continent. And besides, Alexis' picture had been posted in the Australian Index of 4 December 1975.

Information had been passed from New South Wales of her relationship with Arthur, so they must have been expecting her. She had no form in England and the information in her entry was slight. She was described as five foot six with a fair complexion, light brown hair and brown eyes. And that was it. She didn't yet have a file at the Criminal Records Office. She was included amongst Aussies who were 'believed to have travelled to [England] and may come to notice in due course'. The mug shot was a number of years old; when it was taken, she had been scowling, eyes downcast, her hair tied back. The bobbies would be flat out identifying her now, so she could move about without fear, said Arthur, as long as she stayed out of trouble.

Somehow Arthur had managed to slip out of the Top 100 list of Aussie thieves. In 1968 he had been at number six, but just seven years later he had dropped out altogether. With a new passport and birth certificate, he was no longer notorious in England. He could transform himself once more into the Raffles character of his dreams. He could live as a gentleman in England, while in Europe operating as the world's greatest jewel thief. He would buy his shaving cream from Harrods, his suits on fashionable Jermyn Street, select gifts from Fortnum and Mason for his girlfriends, take Sunday roast lunch at the Dorchester Hotel and while away his evenings on the punt at the Victoria Sporting Club. They could live the good life here, so getting nicked in England was strictly forbidden, he warned Alexis.

But it looked so easy, thought Alexis, as she strolled through the women's accessories department. There was no security to speak of and about a thousand ways to get out. They won't miss one little piece of silk, she thought, as she slipped a Hermès scarf into her pocket. She hadn't gone six feet before she felt a heavy hand on her shoulder. A store detective had been watching her since she arrived.

Arthur had been upset, but he understood the temptation had been overwhelming. He had quickly fixed it up with a bobby he knew. With a little influence, she had got off with just a fine. They hadn't even taken her picture or created a file.

Those early days in London seemed so long ago now, thought Alexis, as the Air France jet circled over Paris' new Charles de Gaulle Airport. They were living deluxe now, she thought.

She had been caught in Harrods on her first day because she looked out of place. Her accent had given her away; she didn't belong. Now, after a year away with Arthur, she felt imbued with a new spirit of confidence. For the last twelve months they had been operating 'head to head' in broad daylight, robbing the richest jewellers in Europe. And they had done it all without a second thought, or even the slightest tremor of fear. Arthur made people feel that way when they were with him. He just knew when a job was on and when it wasn't, even if the plan was always formulated right on the threshold of the shop. After a few seconds of observation Arthur would assign each person their task and cheerily wish them all good luck. 'Righto, troops, let's get to work then,' he would say. If you did what Arthur said, no harm would come to you.

Often he would travel solo from London, pick up a car in Paris and go looking for jobs across Western Europe. A week later, Alexis would get a call from Arthur with instructions. She was to organise the rest of the team to travel to Antwerp or Frankfurt or some small regional town in Italy where Arthur had sniffed out an opportunity. They would all take different modes of transport and meet at the appointed place. Such was Arthur's expertise, there was rarely any hanging around before the strike. With the tom in hand, they would move on to the next country and the next, only returning to London if they were under suspicion or ready to unload the gear. There were trips where they would steal a million pounds' worth of jewels in less than a week.

It was actually nice to arrive with Arthur somewhere for a change, she thought, taking a fashion magazine from the plane's seat pocket. She could already sense his growing excitement—he was never more alive and intuitive than at these moments leading up to a job. He was smiling as he looked down on the grey-green patchwork of Paris below. Arthur looked like a friendly American tourist in his blue trousers and white linen shirt. He was accessorised perfectly, with matching loafers and a belt cinched around his prodigious belly. A less threatening couple it would have been hard to imagine, and that was Arthur's ploy.

The remnants of the Organisation de l'Armée Secrète, a guerilla group that had fought to keep Algeria as a French colony in the 1960s, was now financing their survival with robberies. Like the British blaggers, the OAS men relied on terror—they would burst into shops and banks in masks, waving automatic weapons. Arthur would never have dreamt of anything so crude and brutish—he wanted to leave them feeling proud to have been robbed by the King.

Alexis wondered what the afternoon would bring as she flipped through the magazine. She opened to a spread on actress Farrah Fawcett-Majors festooned in diamonds, sapphires, rubies and emeralds. Her starring role in the hit TV series *Charlie's Angels* had made her an international sex symbol, and now the finest fashion houses clamoured to drape their wares upon her. This ad was for a new line of jewellery from the top Paris designer known simply as Fred. Born in Buenos Aires, he had opened his Maison FRED Samuel on one of Paris' most famous streets, the Rue Royale, in 1936. During the Nazi occupation, Fred had fought for the Resistance. He'd reopened his store in 1944.

By the 1970s, the name FRED was synonymous with a modern dashing sense of French style. A decade earlier, he had boasted that his FORCE 10 collection had synthesised chic with sport, combining gold and steel for the first time. Now he was experimenting with multicoloured gemstones and pink, blue and yellow diamonds in lavish asymmetrical designs. Even on an all-American girl like Farrah, the effect was stunningly elegant. In the magazine photograph, the necklace seemed a part of her. The diamonds, sapphires, rubies, tourmalines and amethysts, set in a net of gold thread, highlighted the natural contours of her cleavage. When Alexis showed Arthur the picture, his eyes widened. Farrah might have been stark naked holding a card with her address and phone number, but all he saw was that necklace. 'Dear, we will have that by the end of the day,' Arthur announced as they touched down at Charles de Gaulle.

That night Alexis stood at the window of a suite in the Hôtel Concorde La Fayette, overlooking the Champs Élysées. Alexis let the lights of Paris play over Farrah's exquisite necklace, which was now dangling from her fingers. Arthur had never been a red-hot lover, but he had something extra on nights like these.

13
A dirty weekend abroad

There are many sham diamonds in this life which pass for real, and vice versa.

William Makepeace Thackeray

March 2009

I fell asleep somewhere under the English Channel. Boarding the Eurostar bound for Paris at St Pancras International Station pre-dawn had been a sobering experience. I had only booked the day before, and only first class seats were available by then. As I handed over the £300 for the return journey, I had cursed my lack of planning. But after the stewards had taken away my breakfast tray and offered me a newspaper, I began to be glad I hadn't travelled economy class.

I stretched out in my seat and dozed off before the train reached Ashford in Kent, the last English station before the Channel Tunnel to France. When I awoke, the train was hurtling through the French countryside between Calais and Lille, still an hour away from Paris. I was suddenly glad to be nowhere in particular, if that makes sense.

As adults, so much of our lives are spent fulfilling expectations and responsibilities in one place or another. Whether we like it or not, we succumb to the view that this is our life—a regimented series of appointments that we must keep. If we tick all the boxes, we hope to receive in return a sturdy form of 'happiness' that will stop us dwelling on the big questions. What should be the freedom of the here-and-now seems challenging and almost oppressive—our minds seem geared only to process either pleasant memories of the past or anxieties about the future. We strive to move from station to station, rushing to the reward awaiting us at the destination. Even if it's only a weekend in Paris, we project forward, rejecting the uncertainty of the present. To be spontaneous, to freewheel, is to be almost out of control.

Arthur knew what it was to live in the present. This is not to glorify or forgive Arthur's crimes—they cannot be excused as just a metaphysical journey—but let us not dismiss anyone's life as worthless. Perhaps even the thief has something to offer, if only an understanding of the art of living.

In Paris I would have to look for accommodation, exchange pounds for euros, find people to interview, visit landmarks vital to the writing of this book, find a place to eat within my budget, avoid getting robbed by gypsies on the Metro. There were so many things that could go wrong in this Continental sojourn of just a few days, I wondered when I would begin to enjoy myself. It would start with simply letting go, resigning myself to the fates. That's what Arthur did.

I tried to imagine sitting on this train to Paris with no plan in mind, just mischief. In the seats right behind me, two young Englishmen were discussing the plan for their business trip. With their loud South London accents and trashy suits, in a different era they might have been thieves. Perhaps their customers would not have disagreed with that. They had some shoddy Chinese-made commodity (I couldn't tell exactly what) and now they were here to flog it in vast quantities to the French, for whatever price they could manage. Their success would depend on cheating the buyers. There was an edge of desperation as they discussed how to optimise the appeal of their modest products. Deception seemed their only option, such was their pessimism.

I tuned them out with my iPod and soon all their anxiety simply drifted away as I focused solely on my day ahead. As the train slid into the Eurostar's Gare du Nord terminal, three days in Paris now seemed full of promise. If I could just find the correct change for the pay toilet in the station, the adventure would begin. Another 45 minutes decoding the colour system in the route map of the Metro and I would be right on Arthur's trail.

There are worse places to be lost than in a Paris Metro station. A troupe of Russian buskers sang and played a jaunty tune on clarinet, double bass and piano accordion as well-dressed commuters strode up and down the corridors. It was just as dirty and claustrophobic as London's Underground, but the Metro seemed so much more alive. Here people seemed to notice each other, to take an interest in their surroundings. In London everyone seemed to believe they were invisible—there was no-one else on the train but them. If the Tube stopped unexpectedly in a tunnel, English commuters would dive into their newspapers or fish in their overcoats for iPods or mobile phones. To gaze too long at them was to provoke discomfort or outright hostility. Life in London was to be endured, not celebrated.

But in Paris there was a different atmosphere altogether. In the crowded carriage, it seemed everyone was checking out everybody else. Women inspected the hairstyles and fashions of other women. Men threw sidelong glances at pretty girls. There were loud conversations between strangers. People were interested in each other in ways the pale English commuters could never be. The only sour note was provided by a young American busker, who leapt on the train with an electric guitar and portable amplifier and began massacring the Elvis Presley hit 'A Little Less Conversation'. He was pointedly ignored or jostled out of the way as people got off. I wasn't too fussed when I discovered that I was on the wrong train—this journey was an introduction in itself. And I did finally manage to arrive at Tuileries, the Metro station that disgorges tourists heading for the Louvre, the Jardin des Tuileries, the Place de la Concorde and the best shopping in France.

Today FRED's headquarters on the Rue Royale is just a vacant shop-front across the cobbled street from the famous Maxim's restaurant. Operations were moved to the nearby Place Vendôme in 1999. In its day, Maison FRED commanded an almost imperial location, sitting between the neo-classical masterpiece of the Madeleine and the splendour of the Place de la Concorde, with its fountains and monuments to the glory of France. The team would have passed down this magnificent octagonal *place* on their way to rob FRED, I thought, but I doubted Arthur had any time for history. The 23-metre Luxor Obelisk, with its hieroglyphics exalting the reign of the Egyptian pharaoh Rameses II, now occupies the place where the guillotine stood during the French Revolution, but that would have been lost on him. He would hardly have noticed the pair of grand stone buildings at the north end of the *place*, separated by the Rue Royale—the French Naval Ministry and the sumptuous Hôtel de Crillon, where Marie Antoinette once whiled away her afternoons learning the piano. All the treasures Arthur desired had been behind the glass at Maison FRED.

Place Vendôme is the Bond Street of Paris; but where the architecture of Bond Street is unremarkable, Place Vendôme is monumental. Originally laid out in 1702 as Place des Conquêtes, the square was a commemoration of the military achievements of Louis XIV. Now its Corinthian pilasters and palatial facades lend majesty to the work of the most exclusive jewellers and couturiers. It's a daunting place for a tourist, let alone someone come to steal. As in Bond Street, there is little overt security, but there's a feeling of being observed. As I passed over its worn flagstones, a single armed gendarme leant absently against a wall at the entrance to the Ministry of Justice, and at the apex of each archway the face of a satyr, each one unique, keeps watch on the square. I had no doubt there was also a phalanx of cameras trained on me, but at least the surveillance was discreet. I wondered why FRED had given up the Rue Royale for this location. The new modern showroom was sleek and beautiful—with floor to ceiling pictures of haughty celebrities like Kate Moss draped in FRED's finery—but situated as it is, at the south end of the plaza, FRED could easily be overlooked as the eye becomes seduced by the grand vista of the square ahead.

However, I had business with FRED this day. Confidently, I told the elegant young blonde assistant, Imaine, that I was looking for a present for my wife. This woman was icy and remote—middle-aged men in scruffy jeans and leather jackets didn't buy from FRED unless they were English rock stars—and she had picked me for a nobody. But I was determined to break her sangfroid, almost as an exercise, to see if it were possible. I told her I wanted to see if items from FRED's 1970s collections might still be available, specifically 'les bijoux spectaculaires' I had seen Madame Farrah Fawcett-Majors wear in a certain fashion magazine all those years ago. I rattled off a potted history of 'la Maison', reciting some crap about FRED's virtuosity and asymmetric design and the combination of gemstones, diamonds and pearls that gave an almost organic quality to FRED's work.

She was now intrigued. She was very sorry—fashion and FRED had moved on, but she had some lovely designs she could show me. Soon she had the showcases open and was displaying a sumptuous selection of jewels, five- and six-carat diamond rings, clusters of emeralds and rubies. I told her my wife's hands were very similar to hers, so I asked her to model for me on her slender perfectly manicured fingers. She was now enjoying herself, flattered that someone had noticed her beautiful hands. She slowly rotated her wrist under the light.

Summoning up the spirit of Arthur, I told her I had lied—my wife really had short, stubby fingers, nothing like hers. She smiled and laughed, tossing her blonde hair back, forgetting trinkets and baubles worth more than 200 000 euros strewn across the glass counter. If I had had the skill to palm or switch one of them, this would have been the moment—a split second when she dropped her guard. Of course, I wouldn't have got two paces out the door—hearing the alarm, the gendarme at No. 13 would have calmly shot me. He would have left me lying face down on the red brick cobbles, as a reminder to any other fools. The effect of thinking about stealing was dramatic. I had done nothing and yet the blood was pounding in my temples. It instantly reminded me of my own brief shoplifting career.

That's the thing about hoisting. So many have done it and know the feeling—even if it was just a bag of lollies from the corner store. I have never robbed a bank or cracked a safe, so I can't imagine what that's like; but I have shoplifted jewellery. And so have many of you reading this book. A leading investigative reporter told me he had proof that a famous son of a former Australian prime minister had been caught shoplifting in London in the mid 1960s. I was unable to verify that information but, in the writing of this book, many associates and friends have come forward to confess their crimes.

In 1972 my mother had taken me to the Sydney department store Grace Bros. I was in the market for a very distinctive piece. Mum was exchanging some goods at the fashion accessories counter where she began a lengthy discussion with the assistant, leaving me to my own evil devices. Bored and restless, I became fixated on a ghastly chunky costume ring in a display by the counter—it had swirls of brown, orange and gold. I imagined that, if I got it home, either I would extract the yellow metal and make a fortune selling it at school, or Mum would get it for her birthday. It was set in a velvet block on a revolving stand with dozens of others. It was probably worth about a buck fifty but, to me, it was the Hope Diamond. This was my moment.

Though unschooled, I used the time-honoured principles. Mum was unwittingly pulling the head of the shop assistant while I used the display as a screen between me and the staff, to prevent my actions being seen. I started gently easing the ring from its block, expecting some heavy hand to descend at any moment. When it came free, I closed my eyes and dropped it in the pocket of my corduroy shorts. What a rush! Suddenly I was desperate to get out of there. I cajoled and begged Mum to go home.

She must have known something was up as she drove the getaway car. When I got home, I ran to my bedroom and tried to get at the gold inside the ring. To my disgust, I found it was nothing more than painted plastic—I had stolen a 'fawnie'. Just as I was working out what to do with it, my mother burst in. She instantly knew where the ring had come from, and dragged me by the ear back to the store.

The store manager acted like I had lifted his best diamonds. Perhaps he had been so thoroughly worked over by the likes of Arthur and Alexis that he was going to nip my career in the bud. A life of crime would lead to ruin and damnation, he said gravely. My mother nodded in agreement. Shop stealing was a serious offence, he said; he really should call the police, he added, pointing a finger at me.

I flushed crimson and felt like bawling. My mother had fizzed on me; now I was going to the boys' home. Maybe, like Oliver from the 1968 movie, I would escape and find a Fagin, who would let me join his gang of pickpockets. My options seemed dismal, but then the manager softened. Because I had admitted my guilt, he would let me off with a stern warning—I was from a good family and was attending a decent school, so I had a chance to redeem myself. He warned Mum to keep an eye on me in future. Going shopping with Mum was never the same again.

So here I was 37 years later—the boy with the light fingers again. I decided that, before things got out of hand and a diamond dropped into my pocket, I should move on; but first I asked for a catalogue of FRED's latest range. The sales assistant produced a thick glossy brochure and dropped it into a cardboard bag emblazoned 'FRED Paris'. Hey presto! Skulking suspect had become a potential customer, transformed by means of a paper bag and two bits of string. As I walked across Place Vendôme, I would get the benefit of the doubt.

I tested the idea, striding purposefully across the square and through the revolving doors of the Hotel Ritz. The commissionaire actually looked at my glossy paper bag as he stood aside to welcome me. How easy it was to impress people, I thought, if you ponced about like you owned the place. But only thieves and potentates truly possess the kind of confidence to belong in a place like the Ritz. It had been the second home and inspiration to influential French writers like Simone de Beauvoir, Marcel Proust and Jean Paul Sartre, but this hack couldn't afford a *café au lait* here, let alone the cheapest room. If the Ritz's famous guests had actually been engaged in writing, I felt sure they would have chosen the more modest L'Hôtel Coeur de Lion, as I had. Whatever images one could conceive here would surely be upstaged by the sheer grandeur of the joint.

I walked through its foyer to an avenue of gleaming Italian marble down a heavy brocaded carpet so plush that I could feel my toes sink into it through my shoes. I was flanked by showcases displaying the treasures of Place Vendôme, a rollcall of world famous design—Boucheron, Gianmaria Buccellati, Mikimoto, Alexandre Reza, Chanel, Mauboussin and Chaumet. I was unfamiliar with many of the names, but they tripped off my tongue like deities in a temple of elegance. Dropping my cover, I tried to take a photograph, but a concierge appeared from nowhere, waving a finger. He looked at me apologetically, as if to say I could stay but, really, what business did I have at the Ritz? Ernest Hemingway had advised guests they 'must come here for forgetfulness, for meetings, for discoveries'; but now they came to remind themselves of their wealth, to mingle with their own class, to discover nothing but the price of everything.

As I left the Ritz, the sun was peeping above the eastern parapet of the square, illuminating the centrepiece of Place Vendôme, a 44-metre bronze column celebrating the military brilliance of Emperor Napoleon I. He ordered its construction after his victory over the combined armies of Europe at Austerlitz in December 1805. The column is decorated with 425 bas-relief images sculpted from the bronze of 133 cannons seized from the vanquished enemies. Napoleon, dressed as Caesar, cuts a rather lonely quixotic figure atop the column. Once reviled in France as a proto-fascist, Napoleon is now restored as a symbol of French identity and style, a marker for conspicuous consumption and over-the-top design. Certainly he looks right at home overlooking the splendour of the Place Vendôme.

When Arthur came to rob here in the mid 1970s, the square would have been lined with cars and trucks, but now parking is banned and only a thin stream of traffic flowed through the square. I made for the sunniest corner, where Frederic Boucheron opened the first jewellery house in Place Vendôme in 1893. Legend had it that Boucheron chose the site at No. 26 because the diamonds in the window would sparkle all the brighter in the sunshine.

A tall dark young man named Sofyann, dressed immaculately, approached me before I had got ten feet inside the store. '*Bonjour, monsieur*,' he said with clipped efficiency.

'*Bonjour, monsieur. Ça va?*' I replied, but he knew straight off I was a tourist, albeit one with a FRED bag.

'I am very well, and you, sir?' he replied in English. But he was more interested in my purchases at FRED's. I put the bag behind my back. 'And where are you staying in Paris?' Sofyann asked in a well-worn routine, expecting to hear the name of some fleabag far from Place Vendôme.

He cocked a sculpted eyebrow at my reply: 'The Ritz actually . . . My wife likes it for the history.'

His attitude softened. 'But, monsieur, you must know that Maison de Boucheron was here first—we opened in 1893, five years before the Ritz,' he said with a dismissive wave of his hand. 'And every morning, Bonaparte atop his column casts his shadow on Boucheron first.'

Upstairs, in what is now workshops, had been the residence of Napoleon III's famous mistress, the Italian courtesan Countess de Castiglione. This scandalous relationship had apparently changed the course of European history, helping to deflect French opposition to the unification of the nation states of Italy. 'La Divine Comtesse', as she was known, was described as having 'long, wavy blonde hair, pale skin, a delicate oval face, and eyes which changed colour constantly from green to an extraordinary blue-violet'. But in the way of such creatures, she was vain and difficult to please. As her luminosity waned she shut herself away upstairs at 26 Place Vendôme in a suite of rooms, painted funereal black, where no mirrors were allowed. She spent her last years with the blinds drawn, perhaps so Napoleon I's shadow could not fall upon her. Not even the sumptuous baubles below could tempt her out.

'*Alors*,' said Sofyann, finishing his dramatic spiel, 'what brings you to Boucheron today?'

'A gift for another *femme fatale*,' I said, borrowing the spirit of La Divine Comtesse.

'*Monsieur*,' he said firmly, 'I am sure we have something here that will be suitable.' From under his jacket, he produced a set of keys attached to his belt by a spring-loaded steel cord and began opening showcases behind him. 'Perhaps madame would like our Ava earrings—two round diamonds, 36 smaller stones set in white gold?'

'How much?' I asked.

'Just 24 000 euros!'

I turned my nose up. 'Very nice, but what else have you got?' I asked, looking at my Singapore-bought Bulgari knock-off watch.

This was now a challenge. 'Perhaps a chameleon ring, *monsieur*? Tsavorite garnets; blue, pink and yellow sapphires. For 23 000?'

I shook my head—it was cute, but what other animals did he have?

Soon the table was alive with a jewel-encrusted bestiary of octopi, tortoises, hedgehogs, snakes and frogs.

Nothing moved my spirit, I said. But please go on, I urged.

Perhaps madame would like something from Boucheron's newest range, '*Gaieté* Parisienne', celebrating some of the most infamous *femmes fatales* in French history. For example, the Josephine Collection, inspired by the black American dancer Josephine Baker, who had cavorted half-nude and adorned with flowers on the stage of the Théâtre des Champs Élysées in 1925. The pendant was set with flowers of pink rubies and sapphires in wild erotic sinuous profusion, he said with a straight face. 'Surely such a piece would make madame happy, *n'est-ce pas?*'

'Perhaps for a fortnight,' I deadpanned, patting him on the forearm.

He was taken aback. Leaving half a million euros worth of tom on the table, he dived into another showcase, producing his pièce de résistance: 'The Delilah necklace. This is my favourite of all our designs,' he confided. Sofyann held a shimmering foil of gold mesh fringed with diamonds up to the morning light. He let it fall from hand to hand, and it flowed like golden syrup through his fingers. 'One hundred and sixteen round diamonds, set in 206 grams of yellow gold, each link is hand-crafted and finished upstairs in Boucheron's workshops.'

He let the Delilah necklace drop into my hands. It was surprisingly heavy for something so frivolous and insubstantial. Until now I had resisted the siren song, but now a wicked joy, like sexual desire, swept through me.

'But this is not just a necklace,' said Sofyann.

'I can see that,' I replied and we both laughed.

'Madame can wear it in so many unique ways, to express her individual style. I have found ten so far. So, I will demonstrate,' he said, plucking Delilah from my hands.

'Firstly, as a necklace so simple, so sophisticated,' he said, draping it around his neck. He suddenly looked so gorgeous and feline, I wondered if he was gay. Or whether I was.

'Or as a scarf of gold,' he said, expertly knotting the mesh. He drew the knot to his throat and flipped the ends twice around. 'Or as a choker, *peut-être?*'

He turned away, loosened the knot off and let the gold mesh cascade down his back: '*Alors*, madame would look so sexy in a backless dress with this,' he cooed.

'Or she may wear it as a bracelet in several different ways,' he said, like a boy scout showing off his range of knots.

He finished his little act with a flourish, unwinding the rich mesh with a flick of his wrist. 'And when madame would like to dress down . . .' The Delilah necklace dropped from his wrist and disappeared into his coat pocket. 'Pouf!' he said, patting the pocket. 'One piece, ten styles, all for just 31 960!' he trilled.

This was Boucheron's idea of a 'special' at a time when the world was suffering allegedly the worst economic crisis since the Great Depression. I had to agree that the Delilah necklace was the best antidote I could imagine. I told him to put it aside for me—I would come back with my wife later in the day. He presented me with a fine leather wallet as a present, and tucked a leather-bound catalogue into a Boucheron bag.

With FRED and BOUCHERON swinging by my side, I was unassailable as I covered the fine boutiques in the square one by one—Van Cleef and Arpels, Chaumet, Mauboussin and the rest. Over the next two days I visited all the main shopping districts in Paris, from the Belle Époque splendour of the Boulevard Haussmann, with its department stores like Galeries Lafayette and Printemps, to the antiques of the Marais quarter. Smaller jewellers were even easier to play with than the haughty shopkeepers of Place Vendôme.

I can see how Arthur and the team, 30 years earlier, must have slaughtered these merchants. In a shop off the Boulevard Haussmann I asked to see a tray of two- to three-carat stones for an engagement ring. The fat little jeweller spoke only broken English, but he knew what I meant when I asked for bigger stones, maybe four or five carats? He dived into a strong room to get them, leaving half a dozen smaller two- or three-carat sparklers unguarded on the table. I stole his biro just to show how easy it would have been to hoist his diamonds.

14
Los ladrones extranjeros (foreign thieves)

There is one kind of robber whom the law does not strike at, and who steals what is most precious to men: time.

Napoleon Bonaparte

Cannes 1979

Finally I have time to relax, Alexis thought as she stepped onto the balcony into the blazing Mediterranean sun. It was mid 1979 and for the first time in more than a year there was no plane to catch, no job to rush to, and no Arthur—no gambling, drinking, womanising Arthur—to worry about. She was finished with that lunatic, she thought, as she stretched out on a sun lounge to work on her tan.

They had both loved this beautiful bay on the Côte d'Azur. The south of France had long been a great place to earn, too. Alexis had wanted to make a home here in Cannes, but to Arthur this was just another stop on an endless tour. It was odds-on that he would eventually find her down here, she thought, as she watched the millionaires in their boats go up and down the horseshoe-shaped harbour. But he could beg and plead all he liked—she was staying here. This was the life she had left Australia and her daughter Debbie for. She was done with all that running around now—so many countries, so many jobs that she had sometimes lost track of where she was. Sure, it had been exciting at times, but it ultimately felt like all the colours had run together.

She had only joined him in Europe to make enough money to create a home for themselves. But she quickly realised that Arthur simply couldn't stop. If she allowed it, this would be her life—an endless cycle of hotel rooms and airports, midnight flits and heart-pounding tension. Even when they earned big, there had been no rest.

It would usually begin with a phone call to her in London from Arthur, ordering her to muster the troops. Jump on a plane or a boat or whatever, he would say—just get to Paris, there's a red-hot go here. Within 24 hours, she would watch him hoist another priceless piece. She had never imagined she could tire of diamonds, but now they had lost their lustre. No longer rare and exquisite, the stones seemed nothing more than sparkling cut glass—a means to an end.

After a big job, there was no time to sit back and enjoy the Parisian lifestyle. Once word was out of a big job at Place Vendôme, the Paris police would be looking for '*les étrangers voleurs*' everywhere. Airports were dangerous—there was nowhere to run if they were recognised and the itinerary would give away the next destination. So Arthur and the other men would go off and get cars from somewhere, and a few days in Paris would soon become a couple of weeks in Europe. In five hours they might be into Switzerland; in six they would have reached the diamond centres of Basel or Zurich. The next day they might be in Rome after a scenic drive through the Italian Alps. There was rarely a plan—Arthur would make his mind up and the team would jump in the cars.

The line-up of the team had changed from the old days. Though they were still great mates, Arthur and the Fibber were gradually drifting apart. With the Fibber living in Malta and most of the best troops now back in Australia, Arthur had settled on a new international line-up he could trust. He called them his soldiers and they respected his leadership.

Crucial to the success of the new team was 'Petite Philippe', one of the best head pullers in the business (his nickname was the gang's invention and revealed their faltering familiarity with the French language, given that, strictly speaking, he was *petit*). The more they worked in Europe, the closer Arthur and Petite Philippe became. You needed a local speaker to work successfully in Europe and Petite Philippe was the best in the business. He could also get by in Spanish and Italian, so they had most of the Continent covered. Smooth, charming and debonair, he had stepped out of the pages of *Gentleman's Quarterly* or off a yacht in the harbour at Monte Carlo.

Petite Philippe's family was a disinherited branch of the French nobility. His parents had given him an education and a taste for the finer things of life, but no means to fulfil it. So he had become a gentleman thief, just like those he had seen in the movies. Like John Robie, the cat burglar played by Cary Grant in *To Catch a Thief*, Petite Philippe stole not because he was bad but because he had standards to maintain. In one scene in Hitchcock's classic, Robie is quizzed by an insurance agent from Lloyd's of London as to his motivation. The thief replies: 'Why did I take up stealing? . . . To live better, to own things I couldn't afford, to acquire this good taste which you now enjoy and which I should be very reluctant to give up.' Like the fictional Robie, Petite Philippe bore no grudge against the rich. He—and his gorgeous French wife Karen—merely wanted to live like them. And dodgy credit cards were his passport. With his wallet full of stolen plastic, it was always Petite Philippe's treat. But he was not one of the takers, like Robie or Arthur. His responsibility was to keep an eye and an ear on the staff during a job. If someone became suspicious, he would alert Arthur and the job would be off immediately, no questions asked.

There were still a few Australians on the team, such as 'Bushie', 'Bimbo' and 'the Colonel'; but they too were head pullers, along for the ride mostly. The Colonel was a distinguished white-haired middle-aged gent with a regimental moustache and a patrician bearing. The routine was so well-practised that the head pullers were in no danger of arrest at all.

On these tours, the loot had accumulated so quickly that Alexis' make-up case would be overflowing with it. There were moments of exhilaration and outright silliness, like the time when they stole the tiara from some minor European royal and Arthur decided that, because it was too identifiable, they needed to remove the dozens of stones with which it was studded. So, half-drunk, they had set about prising the diamonds from their settings. This took a fair amount of force and leverage, which meant that soon there were diamonds pinging across the room and into the deep shag pile carpet. Afterwards they had to send for a vacuum cleaner to recover the stray stones.

Through her sunglasses, Alexis looked out at the aquamarine waters of the Bay of Cannes, shimmering and sparkling. She now had plenty of time to reflect on the fantastic journey she had taken since leaving Australia. During that time, she had visited virtually every major capital in Western Europe, seen the best shops and robbed most of them. They had earned more than a million, she and Arthur, and yet there was nothing to show for it, beyond her personal jewellery and a passport full of immigration stamps.

But inevitably this life, or living with Arthur, had begun to take its toll on her. It was the gambling that really ticked her off. She would risk her life and liberty to help Arthur earn, and then he might lose the lot in the casino that night. An entire week's work could go in one spin of the roulette wheel. If she questioned him, his answer was always the same: 'Don't worry, darling, we'll just go out tomorrow and get some more.' He could not understand why she was concerned. To Arthur, Europe was an amusement park where they could take every ride for free—he never thought of the future. Then, when they had been drinking for a while, her anxieties would start to bubble over. Arthur would put up with this, until something inside him snapped and he'd give Alexis a back-hander. It was usually just to shut her up.

He might have gotten away with that with old girlfriends like Paddy Burridge, but Alexis was a different proposition. She would stand toe to toe with Arthur and give him a taste of his own medicine. On more than one occasion he came down to breakfast with a black eye or a split lip. On some nights, when his blood was really up, it was better for Alexis to get away from the trouble she had started for a while. When she got back, he had always cooled down and so wouldn't be expecting any further drama. She would creep up when he was reading the newspaper and deliver a stunning blow with a frying pan or a shoe, whatever came to hand. 'There you are, you miserable bastard—cop that!' she would shout, bringing the frying pan down on his head with a sickening clang. She would have to head for the hills again, but the bullet lodged in his back meant Arthur couldn't put up much of a chase.

Always when she returned—hours, or sometimes days, later—he would be sad and remorseful about how he had treated her. It was all his fault; how could he make it up to her? he would ask. But Alexis would stay silent. She was impervious to Arthur's charm, and that drove him to distraction. After invocations of love and sorrow failed, he would run off to buy her flowers, but she would remain unmoved. He would disappear again, returning hours later with some jewellery—always the finest pieces that he knew she loved—or a fur he had stolen from somewhere. But she would turn her nose up at these offerings. She had loads of jewellery now, and a wardrobe full of designer clothing—he couldn't impress her with that.

This silent treatment would go on for a few days, until he could persuade her to go out on the town. After a few drinks, she would loosen up. Arthur drew people to him—not just crooks, but good people too. A quiet evening would soon turn into a party, with laughter and lively conversation, fine food and wine. In the glow of good fellowship, the resentments seemed to melt away. It had pleased Alexis to mingle like this—she could pretend they were a happy middle-aged businessman and wife on holidays in Europe, not a fractious pair of thieves on a road to nowhere.

But Italy had been the last straw. The team had been in Rome enjoying a long lunch when Petite Philippe suggested there was a boutique nearby where they could buy the girls some new handbags on his dodgy credit cards. It was an easy go—they could be back before their desserts were on the table, he said. And so they had tumbled into the shop, half-drunk and full of joie de vivre. Unfortunately, Petite Philippe had been in the shop the day before and the staff had been suspicious, noting down the name of the card he had used. When he pulled out a different credit card, they quickly locked the shop.

The girls were already out of the store, leaving Arthur and Petite Phil to face the music. The *polizia* were summoned and the drunken thieves were hauled away. It wasn't a serious affair—they were eventually bailed and ordered to return in two years, when the case would finally come up. But for Alexis this was one lark too many. Her dreams seemed more distant than ever—she was certain this would end with them all in a dank jail cell somewhere in Europe. She wanted to control her own destiny—not go down for a handbag because of Arthur's recklessness.

When they returned to London, she packed her things and made for the south of France. In Cannes she had found this apartment overlooking the marina and La Croisette, the city's famous seaside boulevard. The rent on the three-bedroom two-bathroom apartment had been reasonable. This would be La Dolce Vita—at the cost of a few small jobs.

But of course, after three months, Arthur turned up. One of the team had been nicked in Paris and his wife was left stranded with a baby, so Alexis relented and invited her down to stay. Soon the whole team, including Arthur, turned up from London.

At first he made no attempt to woo her back onto the team. This was purely a social visit, he told her. If this was what she wanted, then she would have it. He wanted whatever made her happy. Of course, there were big earning jobs coming up . . . He was going to find enough money to buy a house back home . . . And maybe give this caper up for good . . . But that wouldn't concern her, of course.

Over the next few days, he laid on the charm with a trowel. He really did love her, he told her, half-drunk. He couldn't live without her. She was his soul mate. He adored her, not just because of her skills on the hoist. But they had been quite a team, hadn't they? No-one could ever replace her. She was the best, no matter what anyone else said. Little by little, he was winning her over. No matter how good life on her own seemed to be, the Kangaroo Gang was something to belong to.

At the heart of many thieves there is a person struggling to find fulfilment. No matter how much they steal, no matter how fine their lifestyle, there comes the desolate self-reflection that everything has been for nothing. The only answer is to keep stealing and moving. At least in a team, you belong to something. There is a reason to get up in the morning. Occasionally on sleepless nights, Alexis felt that disorientation.

Arthur kept working on her until her defences dropped. Whatever his faults (and there were many), he did love her in his way. It wasn't lovey-dovey and tender, but this relationship was something to depend on. At the end of the summer, she would be turning 40—maybe Arthur was as gallant a man as she was going to get. He had forgiven and forgotten all their fights—the flying fists and frying pans. It was like none of it had ever happened. The team was back in business.

Arthur had sniffed out a go in Madrid—a jewellery boutique that offered rich pickings. Spain had been a happy hunting ground for the Aussies since the mid 1960s, but it was not a place for novices. If you were collared there, there was no getting off with a fine—it was straight to jail for five years, no questions asked. The whole team assembled in Madrid.

Even the Fibber came along for the lark. He was now living in Malta after surviving his stretch in Cinderella Prison, which had proved a turning point in his life. The Fibber had spent more than a year there and had begun to reassess his career options. In 1979 the Fibber was 58 years of age. He was getting too old to waste more time in the boob, he told friends. Even a virtuoso thief and conman like him had to expect a lagging from time to time. If you couldn't hack that, you were in the wrong business. To finish up with anything and stay out of jail, you had to find a business where you didn't have to front up to earn. But with Arthur running the team, this Spanish jaunt would be a doddle. It would be a few minutes' work, a quick flit and then a nice holiday with the King.

The job went off without a hitch, though, unusually, Arthur had not been the taker this day. To get the keys for the showcase, the taker had to negotiate a low counter. It would have been a tight squeeze for the now portly Arthur. Rather than risk becoming wedged under there, he decided to hand that responsibility to a new offsider on the team. He was young and green, but Arthur could see real talent in him, just as he had in the Kid ten years earlier—this was a good moment to blood him, while the King stood back and appraised his work.

The youngster had done extremely well—they had made off with nearly £100 000 worth of merchandise. But Arthur wasn't taking any chances—he ordered the team to disperse and get out of Madrid as quickly as possible. The Fibber and the rest bade their goodbyes while Arthur, Alexis and the young man made for the airport. Once inside the terminal, they were to pretend they didn't know each other. By now the staff at the jewellery store would have noticed the theft and the Spanish police would be scouring the city. The airport was the most obvious escape route, but if the three of them stayed away from each other, everything would be okay.

Alexis had changed her dress and put on a wig; she felt confident all was sweet for their escape. Tomorrow she would be back relaxing on her balcony at Cannes. She had resolved that she would work with Arthur again, but not as consistently as before. He was okay in small doses, she decided.

Then, out of the corner of her eye, she saw the young taker approaching from across the terminal. Surely he wouldn't come straight up to her? A large group of uniformed police, armed with sub-machine guns, had just strode in. She watched the leader of them give orders to the rest to fan out across the terminal. As a couple of the cops passed her, she heard them talking of *los ladrones extranjeros*—foreign thieves. One mistake here and the trio would be history. And still the young man kept coming, a worried expression on his face. Although he'd been cool on the hoist, he was unravelling now. He anxiously grabbed her sleeve as if he had found his mummy in the shopping mall. 'We're off!' he said, panicking. 'What do we do?'

She pushed him away haughtily, as if he were a beggar or a curio seller, and walked straight into the bathroom, locking herself in a toilet cubicle. Maybe the cops hadn't seen this exchange, she thought; maybe her disguise had helped. Her mind racing, she resolved to wait in the toilet cubicle till she calmed down. Arthur would have a plan—just take it easy, she told herself.

Seconds later, the cubicle door was brutally kicked open and a dozen cops had their machine guns trained on her. They had got the young taker too and Arthur, but not the jewels, which had made their way home with the Fibber.

Later, as the jail cell door slammed shut, Alexis had cause to review the events of the past fortnight: 'Bloody Arthur, this is all his fault,' she sighed.

It wasn't so bad, as jails went. The female inmates were separated from the men in a kind of shared unit arrangement—it was more like living with friends, just that you couldn't get out. Soon she was sweet with the head screw, who would ask Alexis to lock up the rest of them while she headed home. Arthur was also in custody, with the young taker who had brought them undone.

The Spanish police didn't quite know what to do with them. The trio fitted the description of the jewel thieves, but there was no evidence against them. Without the diamonds, there was only suspicion, but no basis to charge them. So the Spanish cops did nothing—Alexis and Arthur were left in limbo, as remand prisoners with no charge. Under Spanish law they could remain locked up at the court's discretion for years to come.

Soon word spread via Interpol that the Spanish had caught the Australian thief who called himself the King. German police from Frankfurt made the journey to interview Arthur—they suspected the gang had hit one of their leading jewellers some time before and, even though they knew they couldn't charge Arthur, they just came to teach him a lesson. The German cops bashed Arthur in his cell, right under the noses of the Spanish screws. Still, it was better than a couple of years in a German jail.

They spent a total of 20 months on remand in Madrid. Alexis' daughter Debbie, now an attractive teenager, came to visit her mother from Australia. She even dated one of the senior warders, posing for pictures outside the jail, but that didn't secure their release. Their lawyers back home organised for a Catholic prison chaplain to travel from Australia to visit them. Neither had been in a church for years, but Arthur calculated this would demonstrate their piety to the authorities in this deeply Catholic country. But it didn't help.

Finally, the Spanish authorities suddenly announced they would be released. It seemed too good to be true, and it was. They were released, but only into the hands of a contingent of Danish police who had travelled down from Copenhagen. They were wanted for a string of robberies in Denmark, including the theft of one large diamond in particular.

Jail in Denmark was more civilised than in Spain. Alexis and Arthur were allowed conjugal visits and frequent visitors. Friends from London brought food and fine grog for the pair, and Arthur's spirits remained high. Once they had cleared this hurdle, he reckoned, they would be back in business. But this time, they would have a stake that would set them up back home. That was the thing about Arthur—his optimism was irrepressible. All the time in jail, he maintained his sartorial standards—his prison greens would always be meticulously pressed with a sharp crease—and he kept his cell immaculate, welcoming visitors as if they were stepping into his suite at the Ritz.

After another year on remand, Arthur and Alexis were offered the chance to make restitution at a discounted value for the items they'd stolen. They could pay up, or face a trial and possibly a lengthy incarceration. They chose the fine and preparations for their deportation from Demark were made. They didn't want to be sent back to Australia, where both of them would face arrest on old theft warrants going back years. So they chose Rome, even though Arthur was wanted there for failing to appear in court on the handbag theft with Petite Philippe. It was one of Arthur's favourite cities, a place where they could quickly build up a stake. From there they planned to return to London, which they hadn't seen in three years.

As the plane touched down at Rome airport in mid 1981, they both felt their luck was turning. But, as they emerged from the plane, waiting at the bottom of the stairs was a posse of Italian police. It seems the

Spanish, the Germans and the Danes had sent some advance warning. 'You will not be entering Italy. You are bad people,' said the smartly dressed detective.

'Here we go again,' thought Alexis. They were marched into the transit lounge, where immigration officials told them they could take a flight home to Australia. A homecoming being out of the question, they refused the offer and were left in the transit lounge to consider their position. For once, Arthur seemed unable to devise a plan—the three years in jail had dulled him a little—so they sat and waited for something to happen.

Hours passed, until finally the immigration officer on duty finished his shift. Alexis was desperate now—they had gone from jail to limbo, and she couldn't work out which was worse. She approached the new immigration officer with their passports. 'Why do you think we are bad people?' she asked sweetly. The officer, who was starting his shift, seemed unaware who these foreigners were. 'The way we're being treated, you would think we were terrorists and murderers,' she said.

'Well, what are you people then?' asked the immigration officer.

'We're just jewel thieves!' she said.

The officer's face softened. 'Well, why didn't you say so?' he replied, stamping their passports with entry visas.

Police who knew these thieves suggested the Delaneys must have bribed the immigration officer, but this appears not to have happened in this instance. After three years in jail, they had little more than the clothes on their backs—after making restitution in Denmark, there was nothing left for bribery. But soon they were checking into the splendid Cavalieri Hilton. Petite Philippe and some of the old team were waiting for them.

They had been hard at work on the Via Condotti, in the shadow of the Coliseum, hoisting a new wardrobe for Arthur and Alexis. The firm was back in business, and tonight they would celebrate their liberty. After three years in jail, the Cavalieri must have been wondrous.

According to its website, the Rome Cavalieri 'has the tranquility of an oasis. Enclosed in fifteen acres of lush Mediterranean parklands, it is a calm retreat . . . an elegant refuge where time slows and hearts quicken'. What a pleasure it must have been for Arthur and Alexis to sink their toes into the deep pile carpet of their room, with its heavy brocaded furniture and original artworks on the walls. On their first night of freedom in three years, they toasted their good luck and looked out over the lights of the Eternal City.

Rome was beautiful, but Alexis was desperately homesick. Her daughter Debbie was growing up without her. It was time to go home, she said; but Arthur would have none of that. He was already making plans to meet the rest of the team in Paris and go on a big spree to make up for lost time. Then he would set up a base in London. There was nothing at home for him but jail. Having slipped into Rome unbeknownst to the Italian police after departing Copenhagen, Arthur believed they had virtually dropped off the radar of international law enforcement. If he went back to Australia, word would spread quickly and his anonymity would be over. New South Wales cops would be lining up to arrest him or to put the bite on him.

But this time Alexis could not be swayed—she was going home and that was it. When she arrived home, some coppers were waiting for her with an old stealing warrant. She got a few months in jail as a welcome-home gift from New South Wales justice.

15
Raffles in Paris (and Bruges)

Happiness in this world, when it comes, comes incidentally. Make it the object of pursuit, and it leads us a wild-goose chase, and is never attained. Follow some other object, and very possibly we may find that we have caught happiness without dreaming of it.

Nathaniel Hawthorne

Arthur went on to Paris with Petite Philippe and the team. More of the old crew were summoned from London to join the party. It was a rousing reunion and Arthur was in rare form. He promised that this time they would lay siege to the great retailers of Europe and none would be spared. The King was back to claim his throne.

Of course, though Arthur would never admit it, he was feeling the strain of living up to his self-styled persona. In recent times 'The World's Raffles' had seen the inside of more low-rent jails than high-class jewellers. He was growing envious of the thieves he had seen go into the drug trade—they were making fortunes with little risk, it seemed. International authorities were as ill-prepared for the drug barons as they had been for the shoplifters in the sixties. At 54 years of age and still on the hoist, there was only more jail to look forward to.

While in jail in Madrid, he had met an East Asian gentleman who had suggested he could hook Arthur up with a syndicate which was importing large-scale shipments of marijuana into various Western countries. Already a number of the young travellers who had acted as foot soldiers for the Kangaroo Gang had become couriers for Australian drug syndicates like Terry Clark's notorious Mr Asia gang. Carrying heroin in suitcases with false bottoms was more risky than pulling heads, but the rewards were greater.

But the Fibber and Arthur wanted nothing to do with hard drugs like heroin—none of Sydney's Euro Milieu did. Heroin was killing kids on the streets in ever-increasing numbers. From 1964 to 1996, heroin deaths rose 46-fold and related crime also soared. However, by way of contrast, Australian society and its crooks adopted an attitude of ambivalence towards dope—some state governments were even pushing for decriminalisation of the use of the drug. This seemed to signal that government might take over the marijuana business, just as it had created a legal monopoly over gaming through state-sanctioned casinos or off-course betting through the totalisator. But in the meantime, men from the Euro Milieu were happy to take care of the business on behalf of the government, meeting the demand that existed. This was a socially acceptable drug, much like tobacco or alcohol. The Fibber would eventually become one of the largest importers of marijuana into Australia.

Ironically it was Arthur who had helped the Fibber into this business, hooking him up with the middle-man he had met in jail. Arthur had expected to be invited into the deal, which included a series of shipments from Pakistan. But the Fibber knew Arthur too well—he feared the King would not be able to keep his mouth shut once the money started rolling in. And the penalties for international drug smuggling were a lot tougher than for hoisting. The places they were working in barely distinguished between hard and soft drugs—if they got pinged in South-East Asia or the Middle East, it could be 'Bye Bye Blackbird' for the Fibber. He couldn't take a chance with Arthur big-noting them all into trouble.

Arthur was unimpressed, but covered it up by publicly declaring his opposition to drugs. 'The World's Raffles' would never become involved in a business as grubby as drugs. Privately he was seething with jealousy, especially when he heard the kind of money the new drug barons were making.

The relationship between Arthur and the Fibber gradually began to wane from this time on. The Fibber was now importing massive shipments of marijuana (between five and ten tonnes a time) dropped by ship along Australia's east coast and ferried to shore in smaller boats. He had been one of the few members of the Kangaroo Gang ever to have saved any money on the hoist and now he was piling it away by the millions. In the late 1970s, his son Barry had moved to Thailand and had followed his father into the new business. But there was a cost for this—Barry died of a heroin overdose in Bangkok just as the Fibber was striking it rich.

Meanwhile, the King's liberty did not last for long. After he'd rejoined the team in Paris, they headed out to a favourite nightclub for a big celebration. But someone had recognised them, or informed on them. During the night a detail of French police descended on the nightclub and arrested them all on a conspiracy charge.

Arthur spent the next year on remand in Paris. When he was released, the Belgian police were waiting for him, and the next year he spent in Bruges prison. Old friends were smirking behind his back. The King was now spending more time in jail than free, and it was his own big mouth that put him there.

But Arthur was undeterred. When he came out, he told people, he would be back in London to eventually claim his prize. It would be the biggest payday any hoister ever had. Just you wait and see.

When Arthur finally finished his long tour of European jails in the mid 1980s, he came home—not to Sydney, but to Surfers Paradise. There were too many cops wanting to put the bite on him in Sydney and life there would have been intolerable. So instead, he and Alexis set themselves up at Surfers, making forays into Sydney and other cities to earn. This worked for a while but, with crooks and their families coming up to spend holidays with them, their new location soon became common knowledge. When they discovered someone had broken into their high-rise flat, they suspected police and immediately made plans to return to England.

The Monarch Hotel commanded the corner of Ferdinand Street and Chalk Farm Road in Camden Town, just a block up from the Crowndale.

These two tall skinny corner pubs had shared the patronage of the Aussies since the sixties. But in 1985, the then owner of the Monarch was hard-up for cash—desperate in fact. When Alexis suggested they could bail him out in return for the management of his pub, he jumped at it. She had the keys to the place the very next day. They had a front-man to manage the place— 'Little Mickey' Horn, who was a Crowndale regular—but Alexis took care of every detail. With new décor and greater emphasis on cleanliness and hygiene, the Monarch was soon pulling in the punters from all over.

Arthur and Alexis still hoisted, popping over to the Continent from time to time, leaving Little Mickey in charge. The Monarch gave them a front if any coppers came snooping but, more than that, Alexis enjoyed running a legitimate business—the publican has always enjoyed a special status in English working-class society. But having a partner like Arthur wasn't especially good for business—the Monarch became the King's court. If any Aussie turned up in town looking for a start, he would come looking for Arthur; and, of course, Arthur's hospitality was endless. As fast as Alexis and Little Mickey could make money selling pints over the bar, Arthur would spend it on French champagne for his new pals.

Alexis' daughter Debbie, now in her early 20s, came over at this time. They rented a stylish flat which backed onto the prestigious Hurlingham Club in Richmond in south-west London. Here the Delaneys blended in well, and with the Monarch running nice and smooth, Alexis could once again look to a life beyond stealing. But her old life had a way of holding on to her.

On many nights in the packed bar of the Monarch thieves mingled with young partygoers. There were still a few of the old shoplifters going around London, but most, like Keith Albert Collingburn, had moved on to other businesses now. Keith, an apprentice when first taken on by Arthur, was now dabbling in drugs, but he still enjoyed the King's company—it brought back nostalgic feelings of earlier times. Collingburn was a regular visitor to the Richmond flat.

One evening in 1986 Collingburn, unaware that he was being followed, visited the Delaneys' home for dinner. He had previously come to notice as a drug trafficker and the police were tracking his movements. It was assumed that, because he had visited Arthur and Alexis, they were somehow mixed up in the drug business also. Now Scotland Yard began following them too.

It's unclear whether they knew they were following the infamous Arthur Delaney or not. At that time he was operating under the alias William Ryan and held a British Visitors passport in that name. Alexis was using her own name but, as she had no form in the United Kingdom for the past decade, it's unlikely Scotland Yard had identified her. The Australian Index, which proved so effective in controlling the Kangaroo Gang, had not been published since 1975. There was no offence in using an alias (even today)—most police were content to lock up a villain, if they could catch him, whatever his name. Certainly, they weren't looking for the Australian master thief and his glamorous accomplice.

However, the pair had not been idle either. Using a small team, they had recently taken a fortune from Cartier on New Bond Street, using time-honoured methods. There were video cameras in the store, new high-tech locks on the showcases and professional security staff keeping an eye on everything; and yet Arthur had still managed to carry out a massacre, cleaning out showcases of watches and jewellery. Cartier had been taken completely by surprise. The theft hadn't been noticed until the team had all safely returned to the Monarch. There were no suspects and no evidence—it was like the work of a magician, some speculated. Yet there was no magic, just a well-worn trick that everyone seemed to have forgotten.

It wasn't long before Arthur noticed unmarked police vehicles parked in the street near their home. He was nervous: he wondered how much they knew about him. Did they know he had a safe deposit box chock-full of cash, passports, international driving permits and jewellery? That was how C11 had brought down Georgie G's operation in 1968. It was time to move the precious tools of his trade. Not realising the police were in tow, the two of them rushed down to the bank and removed the contents of their safe deposit box.

Their mission accomplished, Arthur's mood lightened. But, as they left the bank, neither of them noticed that Alexis had left her Australian passport (with her own name and true identity inside) on the counter. Her mistake was enough to send them down—later that day police swooped on the Richmond flat and arrested them. Charged with passport offences, Alexis got two years' jail while Arthur, under the name of William Ryan, got three years. The days of the Monarch were over. The King's new address would be care of Wormwood Scrubs prison. At least they were even now. Arthur's Madrid fiasco had cost Alexis three years of her life; now her mistake had squared the ledger.

While in remand, the Delaneys had a visit from a very senior officer from Scotland Yard. Alexis remembers it might have been the Chief Commissioner, Sir Kenneth Newman, but I was unable to verify this. It seemed that this officer knew that William Ryan was in fact Arthur William Delaney. He was acquainted with the prisoner's long history, but he had not come to expose Arthur or even to chide him. 'Mr Delaney, I have followed your career for some time,' he said. 'I know you and your wife did the job on Cartier, not to mention a string of other robberies.'

Arthur was unmoved. He was William Ryan, and that was all he would say.

'It matters not,' said the officer with a smile. 'I just wanted to pay you a visit. I am retiring soon, and I just want to know how you did it—how you pulled off the Cartier job. Would you please tell me? This is not a formal interview—there will be no charges. I just want to know.'

The temptation must have been overwhelming for Arthur. Here was one of the world's most senior policemen openly admiring his artistry. Behind the uniform, with all its ribbons and braid, the Chief Commissioner was a fan. Yet Arthur couldn't take the chance. He was already looking at three years—even he knew when to keep his mouth shut.

'Sir, I am pleased and flattered by your visit, but I am afraid I have no idea what you are talking about,' he said, though it must have nearly killed him not to take credit for Cartier.

'Farewell then,' said the officer. 'It's been a challenge and pleasure dealing with you,' he said, closing the cell door behind him.

The party finally came to a crashing halt when Arthur and Alexis got nicked. It was as though the Pied Piper had suddenly disappeared—there was no-one left to play the tune.

Many of the Monarch regulars continued to visit Arthur and Alexis in jail, bringing with them the delicacies the pair had become accustomed to—foie gras, quince paste, fine smallgoods and glacé fruit. Within weeks of getting to Wormwood Scrubs, Arthur had straightened out a few screws and they let him get away with blue murder. As ever, his prison greens were always immaculately pressed—ironed to a knife-edge crease by another inmate. After the hard years he had done in European jails, he told visitors, he was confident he would do this lagging on his ear.

It started as a croak in his voice—a scratchy feeling he couldn't get rid of. It was only when Arthur lost his voice entirely that he finally consulted the prison doctor. The doctor found a cancerous lump in his throat, near his vocal cords. Arthur said this showed his luck was still in—imagine if he hadn't given up smoking four years earlier! Also, on the outside, he never would have gone to the doctor. So getting nicked had saved his life, he concluded with satisfaction.

Surgeons removed the tumour, which had not yet spread. He didn't even have to undergo chemotherapy; but he lost a huge amount of weight. The prodigious pot belly disappeared, and he was left gaunt and painfully thin. But he had lost none of his charm and charisma. Towards the end of his sentence, he was allowed supervised day release and he would turn up at the Crowndale with a screw in tow.

This all went well until Arthur decided that he wanted a little more freedom. So one night, with the screw waiting outside in his car, Arthur absconded from the pub to visit some other friends. The screw was distraught until Arthur's mates slapped a wad of notes in his hand, suggesting a story about some medical emergency would cover Arthur's absence from Wormwood Scrubs. He returned the next day full of apologies.

At the end of his sentence Arthur was to be deported back to Australia, via Singapore. Whether he was William Ryan or Arthur Delaney mattered not to the authorities as long as he got on that plane. Whoever he was, they had seen the last of him. As the sun set over London, police and immigration officials deposited their thin, bedraggled prisoner into the plane. After the door slammed shut and the plane taxied down the runway at Heathrow Airport, their job was done. A short stopover in Singapore and he would be Australia's problem again.

Truth be told, police in Sydney had missed Arthur. He was always good for a quid or two in bribes, and he was also the best story-teller they had ever met. If half of what he said was true, then his had been a unique career. For nearly 30 years, he had kept law enforcement all over the world busy, but now it was over.

Alexis had been deported a year earlier and, upon arrival in Sydney, was immediately arrested on some old warrants. Now, with Arthur winging his weary way home, they would have the box set. They thought of him as no more than a shadow of his former self, a curiosity from another time.

A golden era was over. It was assumed that Arthur, now 62, would join his old mate the Fibber in the marijuana trade. The Fibber and a few of the old Kangaroo alumni had become Australia's largest importers—in deference to their age, the cops had dubbed them 'The Grandfather Mob'. They had brought hash and dope into Australia in truly staggering amounts. There would be more jail ahead for the Fibber before his death in 2003, but by then he could fairly claim to have done better than all his peers. In the 1950s the Melbourne gunnies had mocked him; but they had all finished up with nothing, or dead. The Fibber, on the other hand, was said to have squirrelled away more than $12 million. He had bought all his relatives houses and helped a legion of old mates down on their luck. Yet he had always remained a thief at heart. On Anzac Day every year, with his double-headed coins in his pocket, he would find a two-up game. He couldn't help himself—if there was a mug left walking, the Fibber had to find him. He would con a mug out of $500 and then send him home with a thousand, slipped into the bloke's pocket when he wasn't watching.

But Arthur would land in Sydney with nothing more than the clothes on his back. Old coppers, who had lost track of Arthur in 1981 after his stint in Copenhagen, would be keeping a close eye on him when he arrived home. However, when Arthur's plane from Singapore touched down in Sydney, he was not among the disembarking passengers—he had vanished again. The World's Raffles was not coming home just yet.

Arthur had filed into the lounge at Singapore's Changi Airport with the other transit passengers bound for Australia. There he had greeted an old friend, John 'Bimbo' James. It was no coincidence that Bimbo was in Singapore. He had watched them put Arthur on the plane in London, carefully keeping his distance in case he was recognised. Now he handed Arthur an envelope containing a British passport bearing his photograph in the name of James Duffield. Inside the passport was a business class air ticket on the next flight back to London. By the next evening, Arthur and Bimbo were back in the Crowndale, enjoying a drink with the rest of the team.

But there was little time for celebration—Arthur had work to do.

16
Asprey, By Appointment to The King

In the wee small hours of the morning I plan, in meticulous detail, a
wild, reckless and infinitely satisfying robbery. The details are vital.
I linger over them on my journey to Green Park tube station and
the gentle, civilised stroll through those most civilised of all London
streets that take me at last to Bond Street.

Christopher Long, *London Hotel Magazine*, 1986

Arthur knew Asprey was a red-hot go as soon as he walked in. It was an
instinct—a calculus of angles, light and timing, the human factors of
mood, atmosphere and demeanour. If it all felt right, he just knew it was
on.

New Bond Street was utterly changed from the thieves' paradise Arthur
had encountered when he had pulled his first job here, the Vacheron
Constantin heist in 1962. Yet 28 years later, he was prepared to try to
rob the citadel of British luxury with the same techniques. Asprey and
the rest of the Mayfair retailers had learnt so much about security from

the Aussie massacre of the 1960s. But, despite all this knowledge and the technology developed since then, specifically to thwart him, Arthur would show them a superior thinker could always find a way. No matter how many cameras and inventory systems there were, so long as a staff member still had to open a cabinet with a key, they were vulnerable. And Arthur had that key in the pocket of his hound's-tooth jacket.

Two days earlier, Arthur had launched stage one of the Asprey heist. It was the old routine—the head pullers worked the staff away from the counter of the mezzanine level, where the showcase Arthur wanted was located. Using a block man to cheat the video cameras, he ducked under the counter. The movement was so quick and fluid that the shop jacks might not even have picked it up on their monitors. That is, if the Asprey security detail were *actually* watching at the time. The cameras are a great deterrent to the amateur, but the professional knows that CCTV can tell you everything about how a job went down afterwards, but contributes very little to preventing it.

Behind the counter, Arthur had found the keys. The temptation for many would have been to make a lunge for the prize, having got so close, but not Arthur. He planned to rob Asprey at his convenience with his own key. From his pocket, he withdrew a small bundle of tissue paper, which he quickly unfolded to reveal a damp cake of hotel soap. (As was his custom, he had enjoyed the Dorchester Hotel's Sunday roast the previous week; afterwards he had taken the opportunity to lift this soap memento from their men's privy.) With his thumb he now pressed the key into the soap, making sure he had a clear, precise imprint. You need just enough pressure so the top surface of the key sits flush with the top of the soap; any deeper and the duplicate will be too thick. Arthur, confident his mould was just right, had then called a tactical retreat. An associate with key-cutting skills was then put to work, making the duplicate by pouring molten lead into the soap mould.

On a dry run back to Asprey, the key was tried for size in the showcase. It fitted like a bought one. The second phase was about to begin: waiting for Arthur. The team would be summoned when he was ready. And he couldn't predict when that would be. He returned there once more, taking a long time choosing a set of luggage. Finally, he decided he needed to go and ask his wife. He would be back, he told the elegant and friendly sales assistants. He now felt comfortable with the staff, as they did with him. Where once the thief employed the trick of invisibility, he now needed the skill of blending into the scenery, visible but not a threat.

The King believed he deserved this moment. There was nothing to show for the years of graft around the world, for getting shot in the back and battling cancer. He had spent too long in jail, while his mates made millions from drug trafficking. He had never complained about getting locked up though—he had always taken it in his stride. If he got nicked, so be it; but he sensed that this moment would define Arthur William Delaney. He could almost read the headline in *The Times* before it was written.

But this was not the time for hubris. There was work to do. Two days later Arthur and Petite Philippe were standing in the foyer of the mezzanine level at Asprey, savouring the lull before the take. Everyone was in position, but even now he could call it off. If Arthur's inner voice spoke to him, they would be 'seeing Tommy' (getting out) without delay; but now everything was flowing nicely.

The gang was divided into three teams totalling ten members. The first team of four had, minutes ahead of the rest, entered Asprey and begun to browse on the ground floor, chatting amiably to staff, keeping them close at hand. A second team of four came in and went upstairs to the mezzanine level. Their job was to draw the four floor-walking staff deep into the gallery, leaving the lobby unattended. With the two teams in place, Arthur and Petite Philippe had made their entrance, climbing the staircase past the mezzanine to the first floor. There were video cameras sweeping every square inch of the store, but Arthur and Petite Philippe posed no threat as they stood discussing luggage in the Boat House gallery on the first floor.

And then it was time—that exquisite moment that Arthur had channelled his entire life into. He and Petite Philippe took their time descending the stairs, talking all the way—there could be no change of mood at this critical phase. Arthur paused at the showcases in the mezzanine lobby, as if their glistening treasures had just caught his eye. The cameras would have picked up Arthur motioning Philippe over to the showcase, until the Frenchman was standing just at his shoulder. He wasn't big enough to block Arthur, who was a couple of inches taller, but it was only the taker's hands Philippe needed to conceal. The cabinet had a glass lid, hinged at the top. Arthur needed to open it only a few inches to get his hand inside. The lock was at waist height.

With a final look around the store, Arthur eased his key into the lock, feeling the serrations raising the pins inside the cylinder to the correct height that would allow the key to turn. He heard a faint click as the last of the five pins slotted into place—the showcase was now unlocked. He looked down into the gorgeous deep purple velvet, where the ice-white diamonds and brilliant blue sapphires lay.

As with all of the precious wares on show, this collection had been hand-made in Asprey's workshops, upstairs on the top floor. Everything here was unique, at the very top of the range—the society mavens who bought Asprey jewellery would be horrified if they were to bump into friends wearing exactly the same baubles. Yet the pieces he was looking at recalled the famous wedding gifts the Saudi Crown Prince had given Lady Diana Spencer to celebrate her marriage to Prince Charles in 1981: the centrepiece was a necklace boasting a solid chain of brilliant cut diamonds set in gold with a large detachable sapphire. There were matching earrings and rings, cut in the classic cushion style. Each stone above 0.50 carats came with its own individual gemological report, attesting to its colour, its cut clarity and its carat weight. It was £1.8 million worth, and it would fit right in the palm of Arthur's hand.

Under the halogen downlights, Arthur could see the showcase's glass was spotlessly clean: the merest touch would leave a perfect fingerprint for the jacks. But he was prepared for that and from his coat he drew a thin metal comb, just like he had carried since the 1960s. He slipped it under the glass rim and gently levered it up. He held his breath. Some boutiques had already installed alarms that went off even when you had a key, if you had failed to disarm the system. If that happened, the rest of the head pullers would walk scot-free, but not Arthur and Philippe.

The Frenchman watched Arthur as he inched the glass lid upwards, slowly, painstakingly. There were staff just metres away, cameras swept the floor, but such was his focus and concentration, Arthur could have been perfectly alone. With the lid raised no more than four inches, Arthur's right hand moved like a striking snake. With two lightning movements, he lifted the four pieces—leaving only the slight indentations in the velvet where the treasures (now in his jacket pocket) had been. He lowered the lid back down noiselessly and relocked the cabinet, dropping the key into his pocket.

I recall the thrill that went through me when I stole that fabulously tacky costume ring as a ten-year-old. I can only imagine what it was like to have £1.8 million's worth of booty in your pocket, but I suspect it felt much the same. As they started down the staircase to the ground floor, the head pullers glanced over for their cue from Arthur. But timing was everything—too soon and security would know something was amiss. If the slightest hint of choreography was evident in their exit, security would lock down the store merely on suspicion.

As they came down the stairs, Arthur could see most of the ground floor layout; he could feel the mood and rhythm of every person there. The atmosphere had not changed; there was no panic, no sense of foreboding. They were going to walk right out of there, smiling. He got to the bottom of the stairs before he gave the signal to pull out, a little cough. He and Petite Philippe walked casually towards the front doors.

The sales assistants on the ground floor were now released by the head pullers. They might have assayed a friendly approach to Arthur and Petite Philippe, hoping to interest them in a purchase, or at least a friendly chat. The two men looked like people who would be fun to know, but the staff intuited that they would be back. Right now the pair was consumed in jovial conversation—it would be impolite to interrupt.

The semi-circular doors opened onto New Bond Street, and the clamour of London traffic broke the moment. With a smile, Arthur bade the doorman farewell. As they walked away, he put his hand in his pocket and felt the cold stones he had just stolen. He couldn't help but finish the song he had been humming just ten minutes earlier as they entered Asprey. 'Help yourself . . .' he sang out loud.

It was another quarter of an hour before staff discovered that £1.8 million of stock was missing. By that time, Arthur, Petite Philippe and the rest had casually strolled to their cars and were on their way back to North London. It was nearly a month later that news of the robbery was reported in *The Times*, under the headline 'GANG STEALS £1.8m IN JEWELLERY FROM ROYAL GIFT SHOP ASPREY'S'. Their report began: 'Asprey's, the Bond Street jewellers renowned as the gift shop of the royal family and the rich, has been robbed of jewellery worth an estimated £1.8 million by thieves who unlocked a display case with their own key while staff were kept occupied.'

Asprey's managing director, Tim Cooper, maintained his sangfroid throughout this embarrassing incident. 'If there is anything between ourselves and the police, it is between ourselves and the police,' he told *The Times*. This was no doubt a grievous loss but, compared to the fortunes Asprey ripped from its customers, it was a mere bagatelle.

The effect of the publicity was far more discomforting. Asprey had been knocked over by the old-fashioned distraction method. It was remarkable that Asprey was still such a soft touch, people said. Its MD tried to quell the talk by denying the diamond and sapphire necklace had been stolen, and ordering an identical piece be displayed right in the front window. And the fact that Asprey had attracted a better class of criminal, as *The Times* later noted, must have been some small consolation to Cooper as he went through the insurance process. The opulent diamond necklace in the window by the front door was a reminder that it was business as usual.

A month after the heist, Asprey had reviewed its security arrangements inside the store and said they wouldn't be caught out again. There was therefore no reason to suspect anything when, just after 10 am one morning soon afterwards, a builder's lorry turned right briskly into Bond Street from Grafton Street.

A window washer cleaning the front glass saw it first. The driver swung the lorry hard to the left till it blocked the street, mounting the pavement in front of Piaget watchmakers, directly across from Asprey. The window washer had to leap out of its way. Onlookers thought the lorry was attempting a rough three-point turn.

The staff in Asprey would have heard the lorry's reversing alarm just as the driver gunned the motor and careened back across the street. A girder welded to the back tray smashed with pinpoint accuracy through the window where the necklace was displayed. An Asprey security guard who rushed out to see what had happened was sprayed with ammonia by one of three accomplices on foot. Another reached through the hole in the glass and reefed the necklace off its purple velvet stand. The gang then leapt into a Ford Escort and drove away, leaving the lorry parked in front of Asprey and the pavement strewn with glass.

While Asprey could pretend that Arthur hadn't got them with the first robbery, this was rather too public to deny. Asprey now conceded their vulnerability. In *The Times*, Asprey financial director Naim Attoallah maintained it had been right to display the second necklace. This was a necessary evil in their business. 'We display good pieces of jewellery to the public, because it is expected that we do,' he said. 'The necklace is a nice piece of jewellery and we very much regret its loss.' And that was the last word on the robberies.

Police were unable to establish that the two heists were the work of the same gang, though it seemed the two gangs had at least a passing acquaintance. The modus operandii were very different, they said, but Asprey's reaction to the first job had almost certainly precipitated the second. Someone was watching. Certainly, Arthur took full credit for the entire haul, telling associates he had 'got Asprey's for six million', the sum total of both heists in Australian dollars.

As police searched in vain for them, the team celebrated their success long and hard. Word circulated that Delaney was the mastermind of the Asprey jobs, but the bobbies who had chased him in the 1960s were virtually all retired. One night that summer two detectives met their informers in a club in Hammersmith. It was a warm night, so they left their jackets in the cloakroom. When they went to leave, they discovered the coats, along with everyone else's, had been stolen. The police were extremely unhappy with this and threatened to prosecute the owner of the club if he didn't make restitution. Later the owner invited the cops back and presented them each with a brand new cashmere overcoat. He admitted the coats had come from Arthur Delaney. The King, he said, was very sorry—in a moment of exuberance, one of his team had hoisted them for fun.

Arthur stayed in London a little longer, but Scotland Yard was hot on his trail and he couldn't stay on his toes for too long. He would still visit his old haunts, like the Crowndale, but only after hours, when he would order French champagne and behave as if it was still 1966. He had been triumphant after the Asprey job, but it was bravado. The two hauls combined may have been worth £3 million retail, but the lot raised only about £600 000 from the fences. And that was shared ten ways among the other team members. Arthur would have netted no more than £60 000 for all the risk and effort. And he could blow that away in one decent gambling spree.

When he got back to Australia, he told Alexis very little about Asprey. She might have belted him if, after a job like that, he still couldn't buy her a house. The final departure from London had been as low-key as his arrival in 1962. There wasn't even a farewell to his old friends. One night he was there in the pub in Chalk Farm and the following week he rang from Australia to say he was home in Sydney.

12 December 1992, Bangkok

Even if he felt lousy right now, Arthur could console himself with the thought that finally he was going to make some serious money. After years of watching the others make millions trafficking drugs, it was his turn. He should have been home already, but he was resting under an umbrella in the steamy heat of the hotel pool deck.

The deal had gone smoothly. There had been none of the excitement and tension he had experienced on the hoist—that would presumably come when he counted the money later on. He had gone to Amsterdam to do the deal. In the Tasman Sea, a large-scale consignment of Kashmiri hashish would be off-loaded from a mother ship to smaller vessels for the final leg to Australia's eastern seaboard. The cargo would then be split up and sold through well-established distribution networks. There would be nothing to do but sit back and watch the money roll in.

But when he arrived in Bangkok to change planes, he hadn't felt well. In the past few years, since the cancer, he had regained some weight and the belly was starting to recover its previous dimensions. His general health had been good, but this nausea and dizziness had been enough to extend his stopover. A day by the hotel pool was all he needed to restore him, he told Alexis over the telephone. He told her that he loved her—he would be home tomorrow.

He was doing this for Alexis as much as himself, he had told friends. She had put up with a lot from him. They had been through years of jail together, not to mention his relentless philandering. She had even left her daughter Debbie behind to be with him overseas. And he had never properly married her either. Not that Alexis had been passive. She had been the one woman to stand up to him—she had stood toe to toe with him when he'd tried to hit her, but she had always believed in him. Now he was going repay that faith. He had quietened down a lot since the cancer. He had stayed home and given up the gambling; he wasn't chasing women anymore.

He seemed to be using his brains for the first time in his life. He had been a good provider and had always put the family first; but now that he had given up the cards and the cheap broads, he and Alexis could put together a stake. With a few million in his pocket, he could give her the life that she deserved. This shipment would be the turning point—once it went through everything would change, he had told himself. He was anxious to get home to let her know this.

It was hot and sultry, so he decided to take a dip in the pool. He stood by the edge ready to dive in, but he hesitated for a second. Onlookers watched him stagger, holding his chest. Then he collapsed by the pool, just like he had been shot.

The King was dead before he hit the ground—a massive heart attack had taken him out. There was not even enough money to get him home. His old mates, including the Fibber and some of the surviving Kangaroos, passed around the hat to bring the body of the King home. When he arrived at Sydney Airport, police ordered the simple pine coffin be opened—they just wanted to make sure that it really was the Duke. He was the last of them coming home. At least he had stayed true, they thought, as they closed the box. Authorities never discovered that he too had tried to move into drugs.

So the myth had overtaken the truth. But it was right to say that only Arthur had carried on to the end, just as he had begun. Near the end of his life, Arthur had taken a young kid to buy lollies for his birthday. He had spent $20, filling the kid's arms with treats. But as Arthur went to pay, the kid noticed that Arthur had slipped a packet of marshmallows into his pocket. It was like he had no choice—it was expected of him. He expected it of himself.

He had roamed the world living up to the image that he had created— a King without a castle, a traveller destined never to reach the journey's end. He was the monarch who could never abdicate—because there was no glory in doing that. And that's how the survivors of his Kangaroo Gang would always remember him: the shiny man with the darting blue eyes, forever alive in the moment.

On 9 February 1993, the *Sydney Morning Herald* reported that six weeks earlier 'an intriguing cross-section of Sydney identities turned up at St Jude's Church [Randwick] to farewell former Sydney crime boss Arthur William 'Duke' Delaney'.

Glossary

blag/blagger: a smash and grab team
block: to physically shield a taker in the course of a hoist
boob: jail
bottle firm: pickpocketing team
bottle man: pickpocket
break down: to bribe
bust man: burglar
cockatoo: a lookout
dip: pickpocket
drop off: to desist in an inquiry or endeavour
egg flipper: dipper (pickpocket)
feel a collar: arrest someone
fizz: inform to the police
gunnie: armed robber
hammer: (as in 'on your hammer') in hot pursuit
head puller: a team member who distracts shop assistants during a hoist

hoister: shoplifter

jack: a detective or security guard

King Solomon's Mines: the London Underground (Tube)

kiting: passing stolen or forged cheques

mark: a target to be robbed

minder: a team member who watches out for the whole team during a hoist

monkey: £500 bribe

notchie: the space between a thief's armpit and elbow

push-up man: a head puller for pickpockets

screever: forger

smother: a team member who conceals a taker with his body

taker: the team member who literally hoists the goods

tank man: safecutter

tea-leaf: thief

toecutter: crook who robs other crooks

tom: jewellery

whack up: divide the spoils

Acknowledgements

K*ing of Thieves* draws on the memories of many. It was my privilege to bring them together for the first time in this work. Thanks to the team at Allen & Unwin: publisher Sue Hines for believing in a crime book where hardly anyone gets killed; editors Alexandra Nahlous and Christa Munns, copyeditor Jo Jarrah and lawyer Michael Hall preserved the spirit of the story but made it grammatical and legal. Special thanks to my friend and commissioning publisher Richard Walsh for his tireless support and encouragement.

Thanks also for the cooperation of survivors of the Kangaroo Gang: Alexis, her daughter Debbie, the Kid, Baby Bruce and several others who asked to remain nameless. Special thanks to Arthur Delaney's Sydney mates, the Raven, Little Bird, the late Stan 'the Man' Smith and Greg Freeman. In Melbourne, thanks must go to Brian 'Skull' Murphy, Billy 'the Texan' Longley, Jon Lelleton, Sekai Nzenza, Brian Bourke QC, Phil Dunn QC and Dennis 'Greedy' Smith.

In London, I received sterling support from the Association of Ex-CID

Officers of the Metropolitan Police including Mike Pearce, Brian James, Jimmy Smith, Colin Kinnaird, Richard Strange, Gerry McGowan and Bob Fenton. Andy Woodgate of the National Policing Improvement Agency cut through to swathes of red tape to make available the Australian Index of the *Police Gazette* from 1967 to 1975. Yes, Brian James, it was gold dust for this project. Thank you to the former Australian chief of Interpol Dick Dixon for alerting me to their existence.

This work took me all over Australia and halfway around the world. In the United Kingdom, I owe a debt of hospitality to Wayne and Amanda Bos, Dr Simon Gibbs, Douglas Orr and Cordelia Griffiths, not to mention John, Larry and the Crowndale Crew, including the gracious Molly Gunner. In Paris, M. Ammour, proprietor of the Hotel du Lion d'Or, was the perfect host. In Fochabers, Scotland, Mr and Mrs George Shand were brilliant too.

This book took four years to write, requiring the forbearance of several bosses, including John Lyons and Paul Steindl of the Nine Network's late and lamented *Sunday* program and *A Current Affair*'s Darren Wick and Grant 'Grunter' Williams. Grunter put up with many absences and unconfirmed sightings, and also donated the phrase 'he couldn't knock a pea off a chop'.

Finally, I am very grateful to Noliwe and Jack Shand for keeping me on track and listening wide-eyed to every outlandish story I come up with.